D11171171

THE PSYCHOLOGY OF MUSIC

A SURVEY FOR TEACHER AND MUSICIAN

By

MAX SCHOEN, Ph.D.

PROFESSOR AND HEAD OF DEPARTMENT OF PSYCHOLOGY AND EDUCATION, CARNEGIE INSTITUTE OF TECHNOLOGY

THE RONALD PRESS COMPANY

NEW YORK

PRINTED IN THE UNITED STATES OF AMERICA

PREFACE

IN THIS BOOK I HAVE TRIED to present a survey of those research studies in the psychology of music that I felt had a most direct bearing on musical art, musical artistry, and music education. The book is therefore intended primarily for the musician who may be interested in what experimental psychology has to say about his art and his vocation, whether as performer or teacher. It is my hope, however, that psychologists will find in these pages an adequate and convenient summary of accomplishments in this field of psychological research, and that the more critical-minded in the school music profession might discover in the studies here reported some suggestions for a program and procedure in general musical culture based upon scientifically established principles.

I have appended, in addition to the bibliography of works cited, a selected bibliography to indicate my indebtedness to the numerous investigators whose studies I have consulted in gathering the materials for this book, although their names are not mentioned in the body of the text.

I hereby express my indebtedness to the following publishers and individuals for permission to quote from their works: The Macmillan Company, for the figures from D. C. Miller, *The Science of Musical Sounds.* Longman's, Green and Company, for the quotation from H. Helmholtz, *Sensations of Tone.* Harcourt, Brace and Company, for passages from M. Schoen (ed.), *The Effects of Music.* The editors of The American Journal of Psychology, for the excerpts from the studies by Gilman and Downey. The editors of The Journal of Educational Psychology, for the passages from Jersild and Bienstock. The editor of The Musical Quarterly, for permission to reprint the greater portion of the article by Schoen on "The Basis of Music-Mindedness." Dr. Carl E. Seashore has kindly granted permission for the quotations from *The Iowa*

Studies in the Psychology of Music, and Dr. W. V. Bingham for the paragraphs from his *Studies in Melody.* To Dr. Kate Hevner I am indebted for a survey of her studies in musical expressiveness.

MAX SCHOEN

Pittsburgh, Pa.
June, 1940

CONTENTS

PART I. THE PSYCHOLOGY OF MUSIC

PART I

The Psychology of Music

CHAPTER 1

THE PSYCHOLOGY OF TONE

SOUND IS THE AUDITORY experience the stimulus for which is the vibratory motion of some elastic body. Whenever such an experience is aroused, the hearer designates the sound as being either a noise or a tone. The first step, therefore, in the psychology of tone is to examine the difference between sound as noise and sound as tone.

TONES AND NOISES

If the tones c–e–g–c′–e′–g′–c″ are sounded together, a sound-mass is heard in which the C's stand out. This sound-mass will be called a tone because of the presence in it of one predominant pitch. But in the sound-mass c–d–e–f–g–a–b no one of the constituent sounds is predominant, and the total effect is that of a noise. Tones are thus sounds that have a definite pitch-salient, while noises are sounds without a definite pitch-salient. In other words, a sound to which we are unable to assign a definite pitch—cannot tell whether it is high or low—is a noise. We speak of noises as being sharp, shrill, dull, piercing, soft, harsh, but never as high or low. A few persons often hear tones when most others hear only noises, because their exceptional auditory acuity enables them to detect some one pitch in the mass of sound. Consequently, whether a sound is called a noise or a tone depends as much on who is hearing the sound as it does on the sound itself. For this reason, the only rule that can be laid down regarding the difference between noises and tones is that a sound having pitch is a tone, and a sound without pitch is a noise. Even some sounds produced by musical instruments appear to be more noises than tones. Thus, the lowest tones of the piano or organ, and of other musical instruments having a wide pitch-range, are more dull rumblings than tones, while the highest tones of the violin and piccolo are not so much tones as piercing squeaks.

SIMPLE AND COMPLEX TONES

Graphs obtained from vibrating bodies show that some of them generate simple waves, and others produce waves that are complex. A simple wave is set up by a single vibration, while

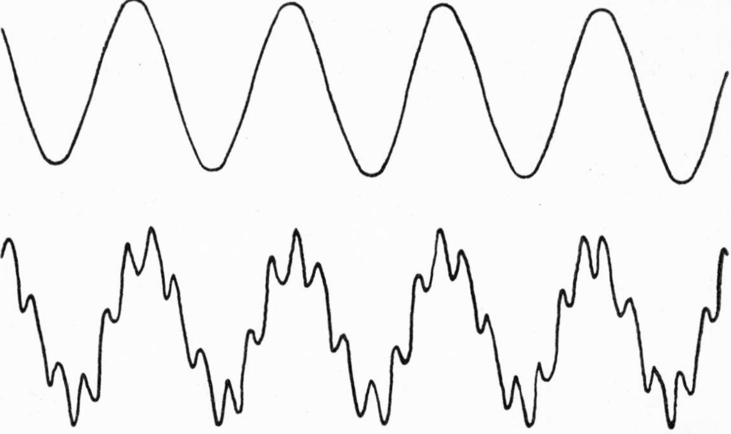

Fig. 1. A Simple and a Compound Wave. (After D. C. Miller, The Science of Musical Sounds, New York, Macmillan, 1916)

a complex wave is produced by a number of simultaneously present vibrations. Almost all elastic bodies, and all musical instruments, produce complex waves. Tones having simple waves are known as simple or pure tones, those having complex waves are called compound or complex tones. Since a compound tone is composed of a number of vibrations it means that the body generating it vibrates not only as a whole, but also in parts or segments. The partial vibrations stand in simple ratio to the vibration of the whole, namely, 1:2:3:4, etc. This means that the body, besides vibrating as a whole, also vibrates in halves, thirds, fourths, etc. A compound tone is then made up of a series of partial tones, also spoken of as harmonics, the pitch of the compound tone being most usually that of the first partial, called the fundamental, the rest being known as the overtones.

WHAT WE HEAR IN TONES

All vibratory motion has the four properties of *frequency, amplitude, form,* and *duration.* Frequency refers to the number of times that the motion occurs per second, amplitude is the extent or range of the motion, form is the composition of the motion, whether simple or complex, and duration means the persistence or lastingness of the motion. Every wave possesses all four properties. It has a certain frequency, a certain amplitude, a certain form, and a certain duration. But any two waves may differ in one or more of these characteristics. And each of the characteristics has a psychological counterpart. A change in any one of them means a change in the kind of tone we hear. This means that a tonal experience is complex, that it is made up of a number of experiences producing a single impression.

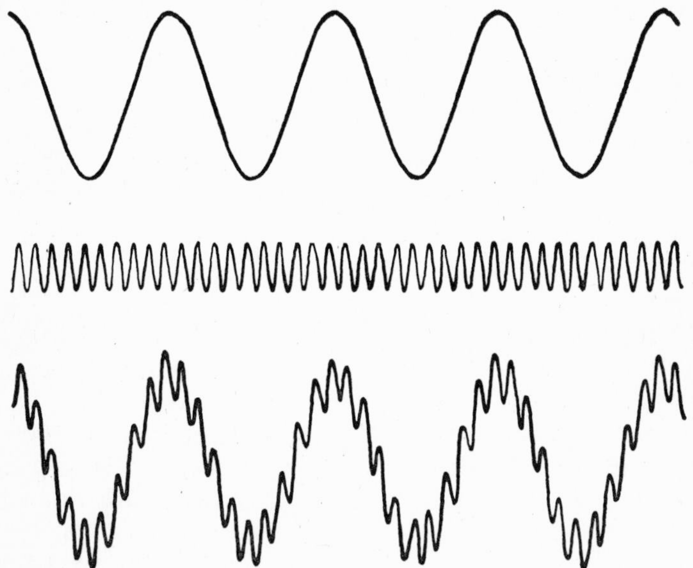

Fig. 2. Waves of Different Frequency, Amplitude, and Form. (After D. C. Miller, The Science of Musical Sounds, N. Y., Macmillan, 1916)

We can isolate these constituent ingredients of the tonal experience, and thus speak of the attributes of a tone. These attributes are pitch, loudness, duration, quality, and extensity.

PITCH

A change in the frequency of a wave will cause a change in the pitch of the tone. If the frequency is increased, the pitch rises. If the frequency is decreased, the pitch drops. Thus pitch is related to the *frequency* of the vibratory motion. Our musical scale is made up of frequencies that bear a definite mathematical relationship to any frequency on which the scale begins, as well as to each other. Thus, supposing the first tone of a major scale has a frequency of 200 cycles per second, the second tone will then have a frequency of 225, or 9/8 of 200, the third 250, or 5/4, the fourth 266.6, or 4/3, the fifth 300, or 3/2, the sixth 333.3, or 5/3, the seventh 375, or 15/8, and the eighth 400, or 2/1. We can thus write the scale as follows:

1, 9/8, 5/4, 4/3, 3/2, 5/3, 15/8, 2

Between tone and tone we have the following relations: Between the first and second tones, 9/8; the second and third, 10/9; the third and fourth, 16/15; the fourth and fifth, 9/8; the fifth and sixth, 10/9; the sixth and seventh, 9/8; the seventh and eighth, 16/15. If we assume, for purposes of illustration, that the scale begins on the tone c, we have:

c.......d.......e........f.......g.......a........b.....c
1 9/8 5/4 4/3 3/2 5/3 15/8 2
9/8 10/9 16/15 9/8 10/9 9/8 16/15

We might raise the question at this point as to why it is that instead of lettering the scale c–d–e–f–g–h–i–j, we letter it so as to have the first and eighth tones designated by the same letter. The reason is that the first and eighth tones, or tones in the frequency ratio of 1:2, are similar in effect. This similarity appears clearly in the fact that if we sound the octave simultaneously it is difficult to say whether we hear one tone or two tones. It is also manifest in the further fact that if we begin a progression on any tone and ascend or descend in regular order, step by step, we reach a tone that invariably reminds us of the first tone we heard, although it differs from it in pitch, and this tone is always the eighth tone from where we started. These two tones are always in the ratio of 1:2, or octaves. There is thus a unique quality to every pitch, a *c-ness, d-ness, e-ness,* etc., which occurs in every tone eight steps above or below itself. This quality is called *octave quality* or *tonality.* The eighth tone is a return to the first tone in quality, the scale thus presenting a series, or circle, within which every tone has a relationship to the two tones of the octave, but never identifies itself with either, because the two tones of the octave are different in pitch. Hence, in giving the scale letter names, or fixed pitch names on the staff, this fact of octave quality is given recognition by assigning the same letter to the octave. The octave quality, or tonality, thus divides the tonal range into orderly units.

The use of the phrase "tonal range" calls attention to another phenomenon of tones, namely, that our ears are not responsive to all the frequencies that exist in nature or that can be produced by human means. We refer to this as the range of hearing for pitch, and to the upper and lower limits of hearing as the upper and lower threshold of the auditory range. It is fairly well established that the lower threshold for pitch is around 20 cycles per second and the upper threshold at approximately 20,000 cycles per second. This means that frequencies above and below these numbers are not heard by the normal average ear as pitch. However, only a section of this pitch range is useful for musical purposes. The important frequency range for music is approximately from 50 to 10,000, and even this range is but rarely used, since tones of frequencies below 150 and above 4,000 begin to sound "noisy."

PITCH DISCRIMINATION

The human ear is limited not only in the frequencies it can hear, so that we have a lower and upper threshold for hearing, but also in the power of hearing pitch differences between tones, giving rise to a threshold of pitch discrimination, or a point at which a difference in pitch becomes just perceptible. This point differs for the lower, middle, and upper regions of the tonal range. Unless the tones in these regions reach a certain frequency difference they give the impression of being the same tone. This indicates that there is no one-to-one relationship between frequency and pitch, in that there can be a change in frequency without a perceptible change in pitch. For tones of medium loudness the increase in frequency for a just perceptible pitch difference is about 1 per cent for the low tonal range, 0.3 per cent for tones of the middle range, and 1 per cent for the high range. There are about 1,500 discriminable pitches in the tonal range. But the number of musically used pitches is considerably smaller, because for musical purposes pitch differences must be larger than the just perceptible difference, due to causes which will be examined later. In the middle region, for instance, the semi-tone is over 20 times as large as the smallest discriminable pitch difference. The piano, which has a large range compared with other instruments, has 84 pitches, the organ, which covers practically the whole musical range of tones, has about 108 pitches.

An interesting psychological problem in auditory phenomena is why we use the terms "high" and "low" to describe differences in pitch, as if tones had spatial position. Adjectives meaning high and low are used almost universally to designate pitch. Why should this be so? Do tones actually possess height and depth, are they actually high and low in space, or are these terms just borrowed from the spatial sense to describe feelings similar to spatial relations that accompany tones?

The most widely held view is that tones do not actually occupy space, do not move up and down, but that spatial terms are used because tones produce secondary effects that have spatial implications. Gurney (33) states that the reason must "be in the fact that since higher sounds are more penetrating and more conspicuous than lower ones, the higher register of the voice has been for long ages employed in all circumstances where an effort has been made to attract attention or to give force and wide reach to the utterance of vocal sound; and has thus become associated with elevation and dilatation of the physical frame, which are not only, in the case of the head and chest, directly connected with an upward strain of the voice, but are on their own account the natural movements, under the same conditions of desire to attract attention or impress a spectator. To this we may add that bass notes have normally a volume and fullness which easily associates itself with the idea of mass and weight; and the connection of weight with sinking and depth is obvious." (33, p. 140) This account is considerably in keeping with that of Stumpf (107), who finds the explanation primarily in the "feeling effect" of tones. Low tones give a feeling of gloom and darkness, while high tones are penetrating and bright. Low tones are massive, broad, heavy, voluminous; high tones are thin, small, light. Passages in low tones are lumbering, labored, and plodding, as compared with the incisiveness, rapidity, limpidness, and lightness of passages in the high register. And thin, small, airy, light suggest something high or off the ground, while heavy, large, dark, massive, impress us as characteristic of something low and on or close to the ground.

The problem was investigated experimentally by Pratt (79), and his conclusions indicate that tones do actually possess a spatial character. He asked observers to locate on a numbered scale running from the floor to the ceiling the position of tones produced by an audiometer. The scale was 2½ meters in height and divided into 14 equal parts. The tones used were the frequencies 256, 512, 1,024, 2,048, and 4,096, or middle C and four of its octaves. The observers were instructed to indicate by one of the numbers on the scale the region from which the tone appeared to come. The results indicate that high tones are heard as being actually higher in space than low ones. Every observer placed the tones in the order, from top to bottom, 4,096, 2,048, 1,024, 512, and 256. It seems, then, a tone of greater frequency is called higher because it is perceived as occupying a higher position in space.

SOME OTHER PHENOMENA OF PITCH

When two tones nearly equal in frequency are sounded together a single tone is heard. But instead of being constant, it pulsates or beats periodically. Such tones are known as beat-tones. The number of beats or pulsations occurring per second depends on the frequency difference between the two tones. If the two tones differ in 1 vibration there will be 1 beat per second, if the difference between them is 2 vibrations there will be 2 beats per second, etc. Up to a certain number of beats per second, somewhere between 6–10, beat-tones are quite pleasant. Beyond this number they get increasingly more unpleasant to the point of pain, until a frequency difference is reached when the beats disappear and two distinctly different tones are heard. The smallest frequency difference where this happens is said to be the minor third.

Beside the phenomenon of beat-tones, there are also what are known as combination tones. These are of two kinds: difference tones and summation tones. The frequency of the difference tone is the difference between the frequencies of the two generating tones. Thus two tones of 100 and 150 cycles, respectively, produce a difference tone of 50 cycles. But they also produce a summation tone of 250, or the sum of the frequencies of the two tones. Both difference and summation tones are heard only under certain conditions. They are also referred to as subjective tones on the ground that their frequencies arise only in the ear, and do not exist outside the ear.

LOUDNESS

Loudness is the magnitude of the sensation produced by a tone, as designated by the terms weak and strong. Differences in loudness result from differences in the intensity or amplitude of the sound wave. But the relationship between intensity and loudness is anything but simple. Because two tones differ in intensity does not mean invariably that the more intense tone will also be heard as a louder tone than the tone having the smaller intensity. The effect may be just the reverse.

THE INTENSITY THRESHOLD FOR HEARING

A tone must possess a certain minimal intensity in order to be heard, and if it attains more than a certain intensity it becomes painful. The intensity at which a tone is just heard is called the threshold of audibility. Now the pitches comprising the tonal range of hearing differ inherently in loudness. High tones are inherently loud, and low tones inherently soft. Experiments on simple tones show that this inherent loudness of tones rises rather sharply from the lower range of pitches to sounds of about 1,200 frequency, thereafter the increase is less rapid, until at about 2,200 frequency it begins to decrease, at first slowly and then quite rapidly, until the upper pitch limit of hearing is reached. A tone having a frequency of 2,200 seems to be about eight times as loud as a tone of frequency 64, when both are produced by the same amount of physical energy, that is, have the same intensity. Hence, low tones must be very intense to be heard, in the middle region a smaller intensity is sufficient, while higher tones require, again, a greater intensity to reach the audible threshold.

TABLE I. NUMBER OF DISCRIMINABLE INTENSITIES AT VARIOUS PITCHES

Frequency	Number of Discriminable Steps
31.25	3
62.5	34
125	94
250	189
500	299
1,000	374
2,000	358
4,000	259
8,000	119
16,000	16

The reason for this difference in the inherent loudness of the tonal series lies in the ear. The ear is not equally sensitive to all the pitches of the auditory range. It is less sensitive to low and very high tones than to tones of the middle range, from 1,000 to 4,000. Therefore, if a tone from the low range and one from the middle range are produced with equal intensity, the tone from the middle range will sound louder than the low tone. It is for this reason that musical instruments are so constructed as regards intensity that tones of different pitch will have approximately the same loudness to the ear. Thus, organ pipe tones for the low pitches are considerably more intense than those of the high pitch range. So are the tones of the piano. An orchestra in the course of rendering a selection varies in the mean power of the sound produced over a range sometimes as wide as 100,000 to 1. The tones of stringed instruments are in general less intense than those of wind instruments, hence the greater number of string instruments in an orchestra as compared with wind instruments. The violin is the weakest in intensity, and the bass drum the strongest. In general, the bass instruments are strongest in intensity, the tenor and alto next, and the soprano the weakest. In the human singing voice the intensity is about constant from the middle range of tones to the higher range. There is a rapid falling off for the low range, until the lowest tone that can be produced well has an intensity of only about 1/30 that of the higher range.

The number of perceptible intensity steps of a tone of constant pitch is largest between 1,000 and 4,000 cycles. Below 30 cycles the number of intensity steps can hardly be determined because hearing and feeling cannot be clearly distinguished.

THE AESTHETICS OF TONAL INTENSITY

Ortmann (71) gives us a searching study of the aesthetic significance of tonal intensity. It has been demonstrated experimentally that the feeling-tone, or pleasantness-unpleasantness, effect for tonal intensities ranges from mild unpleasantness of soft tones through greatest pleasantness for the middle region, to marked unpleasantness for extremely loud tones. Thus, moderate loudness is more pleasant than either extreme softness or extreme loudness. This feeling-tone effect of intensity is the basis, according to Ortmann, for all our more complex reactions to artistic music. It all depends on how readily the ear adjusts itself to the single tone or a simultaneous tonal combination. If the adjustment is made without strain the effect is pleasant, as in a single tone of medium intensity or a simple chord. But when the tonal stimulus calls for a strained adjustment, as in very loud noises or a high degree of discordancy, the effect is unpleasant or even painful.

Now in all artistic music, particularly in chords of modern harmony, the feeling-tone is widely distributed and complex, as each pitch-point stimulates the ear. The complexity and difficulty for the ear grows with the increase in the number of pitch-points or tones. The intensity of a chord is subject to the same law of feeling-tone as the single tone. Hence we cannot divorce the feeling-tone of a chord from its intensity. There is a difference in the feeling effect of the diminished seventh chord when played forte and when sounded pianissimo. In the former case it can signify conflict or a threat, in the latter it becomes the "cry-baby" chord. Thus discord and intensity cannot be dissociated. At equal intensities a major seventh is more discordant than a minor seventh, and likewise a fortissimo major seventh is more discordant than a pianissimo major seventh. A major ninth played forte becomes more discordant than a minor ninth played pianissimo, especially so when the two tones of the major ninth are played at equal intensities while the upper tone of the minor ninth is softer than the lower tone. The following chord, played at the indicated intensities, increases in discordancy from a to d.

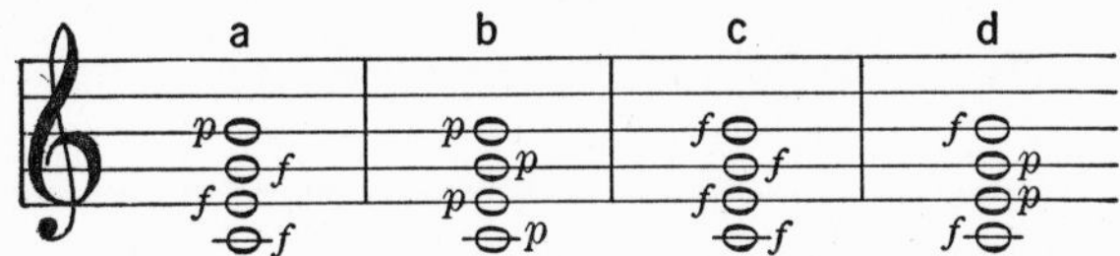

Ortmann cites the familiar chord of Scriabin as an example of the shades of dissonance possible in the same chord by a change in intensity. From b to f there is increase in discordancy without changing the pitch of a single tone.

Ortmann finds the same feeling effect of intensity in chord progressions. For instance, parallel fifths are condemned in practically all books on harmony. Yet, when the intensity of the component tones is sufficiently altered the unpleasant effect is considerably modified. "The auditory value of a progression, therefore, depends, in part at least, upon the various intensities of the tones. A progression can scarcely be called auditorily poor if the intensities of the tones making the poor part of the progression are considerably less than those of simultaneous tones the progression of which is acceptable. A poor progression becomes increasingly 'bad' as the intensity of its tones increases." (71, p. 187)

TONAL QUALITY

Tones from different instruments produce different qualitative effects upon us to such a degree that we are able to recognize the source of the sound, namely, whether it comes from a violin, piano, flute, horn, etc. Quality, then, is that characteristic of a tone that enables us to refer it to a particular source. We designate quality by terms such as thin, full, luscious, smooth, harsh, sweet, and many others. If we compare the waves from different instruments, or different tones from the same instrument, we note that they present a variety of patterns or forms, namely, the wave of a violin tone will present a different pattern, a different wave form, from that of a flute tone, even when the two waves have the same frequency and amplitude. Likewise, two tones from the same source but of different pitch, or two tones of the same pitch but of different intensities, will have different wave forms. A difference in wave form may or may not produce the effect of different quality, but two tones differing in quality always present different wave forms.

The form of a wave is determined by the partial tones of which it is composed. As we have seen in the discussion on simple and compound tones, musical tones are produced by bodies that vibrate in orderly segments or parts, and each segmental vibration produces its own pitch. A tone of a musical

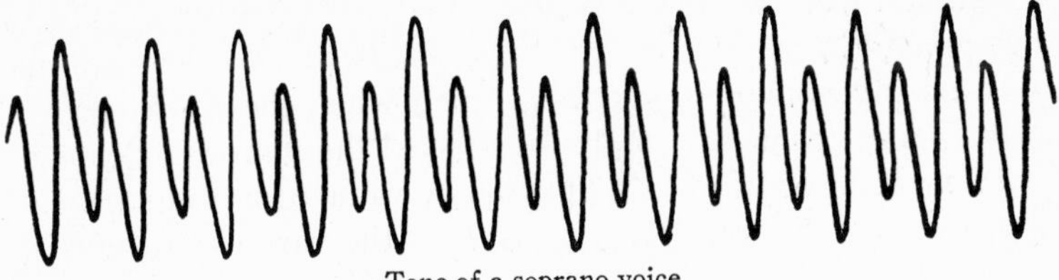

Tone of a soprano voice

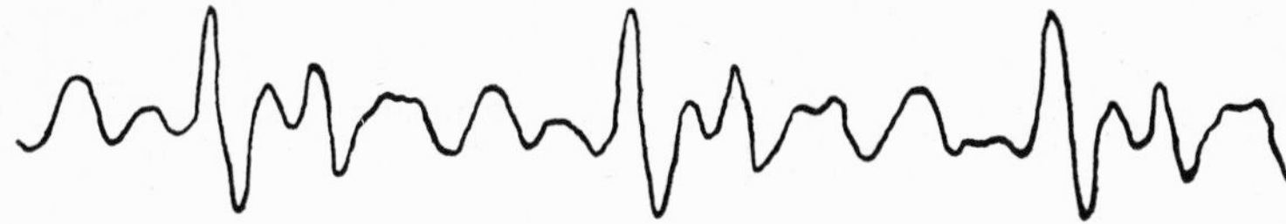

Tone of a bass voice

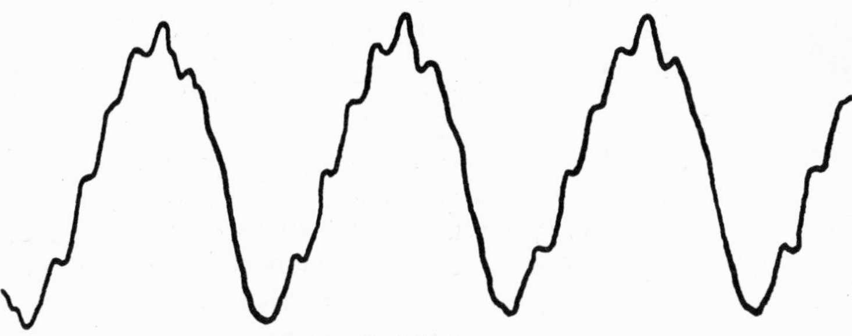

A violin tone

An oboe tone

Fig. 3. Waves of Different Form. (After D. C. Miller, The Science of Musical Sounds, New York, Macmillan, 1916)

instrument, or of the human voice, is thus made up of a complex of pitches, with the pitch of the first partial usually being the outstanding pitch, covering up the other pitches, and therefore giving the complex its pitch. The laws of the relationship between wave form and quality were for the first time thoroughly investigated by Helmholtz (38). He found four general rules showing the dependence of quality on the mode in which a musical tone is compounded. The laws are as follows:

1. Simple Tones, like those of tuning-forks applied to resonance chambers and wide stopped organ pipes, have a very soft, pleasant sound, free from all roughness, but wanting in power, and dull at low pitches.

2. Musical Tones, which are accompanied by a moderately loud series of the lower partial tones, up to about the sixth partial, are more harmonious and musical. Compared with simple tones they are rich and splendid, while they are at the same time perfectly sweet and soft if the higher upper partials are absent. To these belong the musical tones produced by the pianoforte, open organ pipes, the softer piano tones of the human voice and of the French horn. The last-named tones form the transition to musical tones with high upper partials; while the tones of flutes, and of pipes on the flue-stops of organs with a low pressure of wind, approach to simple tones.

3. If only the unevenly numbered partials are present (as in narrow stopped organ pipes, pianoforte strings struck in their middle points, and clarinets), the quality of tone is *hollow,* and, when a large number of such upper partials are present, *nasal.* When the prime tone predominates the quality of tone is *rich;* but when the prime tone is not sufficiently superior in strength to the upper partials, the quality of tone is *poor.* Thus the quality of tone in the wider open organ pipes is richer than that in the narrower; strings struck with pianoforte hammers give tones of a richer quality than when struck by a stick or plucked by the finger; the tones of reed pipes with suitable resonance chambers have a richer quality than those without resonance chambers.

4. When partial tones higher than the sixth or seventh are very distinct, the quality is *cutting* and *rough.* The reason for this will be seen hereafter to lie in the dissonances which they form with one another. The degree of harshness may be very different. When their force is inconsiderable the higher upper partials do not essentially detract from the musical applicability of the compound tones; on the

contrary, they are useful in giving character and expression to the music. The most important musical tones of this description are those of bowed instruments and of most reed pipes, oboe, bassoon, harmonium, and the human voice. The rough braying tones of brass instruments are extremely penetrating and hence are better adapted to give the impression of great power than similar tones of a softer quality. They are consequently little suitable for artistic music when used alone forte, but produce great effect in an orchestra. (38, pp. 118-119)

Since Helmholtz first investigated this tonal phenomenon his rules have been refined by further research. Today we know that tonal quality depends also upon the frequency and the intensity of the tone. We have seen previously that the character of simple tones changes with their pitch, from soft and mild to shrill, from massive and heavy to pointed and thin, and from dark to bright. Now, since the pitches of the upper partials of a musical tone are determined by the pitch of the first or fundamental partial, and since the quality of a tone must be made up of the qualities of its partials, it follows that tonal quality also depends upon the pitch of the musical tone.

Again, as we have seen previously, the ear is not equally sensitive to tones of different pitch. In the auditory pitch range for the human ear there is less sensitivity for the low and very high pitches than for the middle pitches. Since, then, auditory sensitivity depends upon pitch, the partials will differ in inherent intensity in accordance with the pitch of the first partial. And since the relative intensities of the partials influence the quality of the complex tone, we have another reason why the quality of a tone depends upon its pitch.

Finally, the pitch at which a tone is produced by any one source affects the number of its partials, and the number of partials present influences the quality of the tone. Fig. 4 gives three trombone tones of different pitch, obtained by Ortmann (73). From the number of smaller peaks present in each of the waves we see that they differ in the number of partials, or in complexity of composition. As the tone rises in pitch it decreases in the number of partials, and therefore changes in quality. The low tone has more smaller peaks between the peaks that mark the fundamental pitch (indicated by the vertical arrows) than does the medium tone, and the medium tone has more than the high tone.

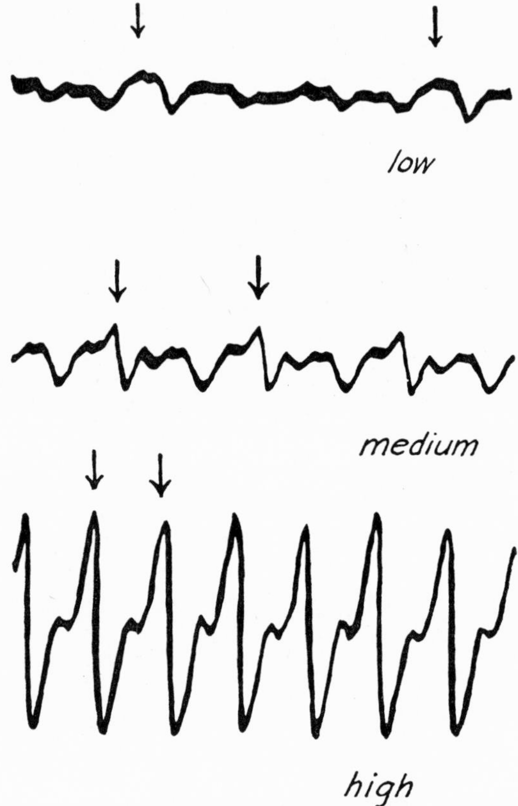

Fig. 4. (After Ortmann)

What holds true for pitch also applies to intensity and duration. A change in the intensity or duration of a tone produces a change in the wave form, and therefore in its quality. In Fig. 5 we have three waves of the tone A (frequency 440) sung by a mezzo-soprano: very soft, (pp), medium loud, (mf), and very loud, (ff). The difference in wave form is very conspicuous. The waves increase in complexity from very soft to very loud.

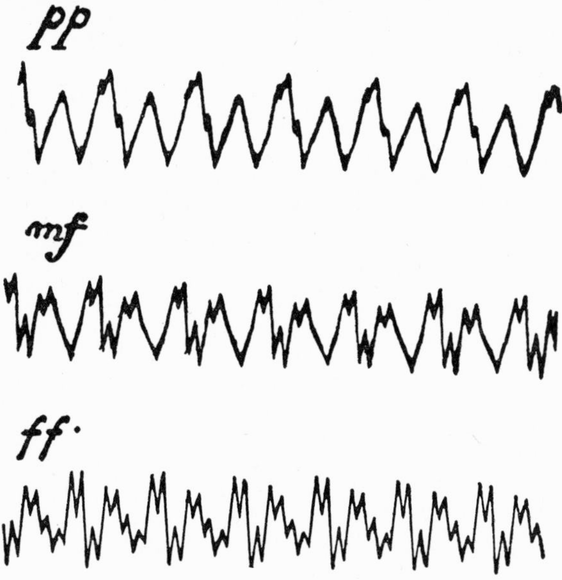

Fig. 5. (After Ortmann)

Fig. 6 shows the effect of duration on wave form. The tone is of a frequency of about 293 and produced by the piano. At the beginning of the tone (a) we have only noise, a half-second later (b) a tone of one quality, and two seconds after

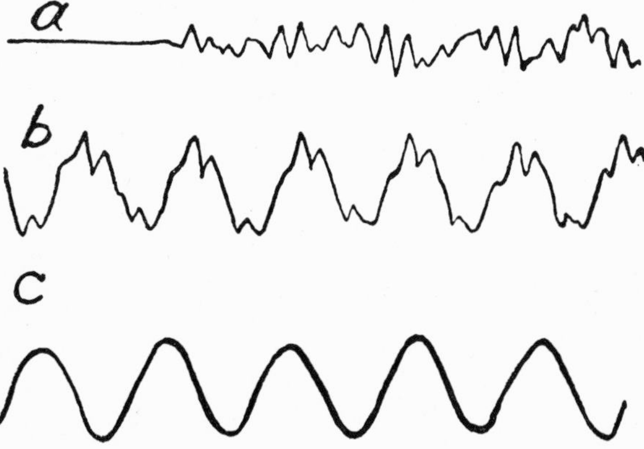

Fig. 6. Piano Tone, D=2937 "mf." (After Ortmann)

the sounding of the tone (c) a different quality again. Thus the initial and final qualities of a tone differ from the quality of the sustained tone. This is particularly the case with tones of the human voice, as we shall see in the chapter on singing.

Pitch, intensity, duration, are then the determining factors of tonal quality, since they determine the wave form. A change in any one of the three can produce a change in the quality of the tone, because it can produce a change in the number and relative intensities of the component partials. Whereas it is true, then, that quality depends upon wave form, it should be added, to complete the picture, that wave form is determined by pitch, intensity, and duration.

DURATION

Duration is an attribute of all sensory experience. It is the basis for time and rhythm, but is quite distinct from both, in that we can experience duration without time, or time without rhythm. But rhythm includes time, and time includes duration.

Duration is simply the consciousness of a "going-onness" or persistence of an experience. Without duration, then, there can be no experience, and the duration must last for a certain period to give rise to the consciousness of presence. It has been estimated that this lasting period for a tonal sensation is a minimum of 1/20 of a second. This means that unless the stimulation has at least that duration there is no tonal experience.

Duration can be present without time. Time is a judgment of the duration, and comes usually after the duration is over. It is the awareness of long or short or longer and shorter. As I am listening to a sustained tone I may or may not be aware of its time, but I am invariably aware of its duration. If I am aware of its time it is an experience entirely separate from my awareness of its duration, namely, it is a pronouncement on the duration, an estimate of how long the duration endured. Thus, time involves the consciousness of before and after, of beginning and ending, while duration involves no more than the experience of presence.

The consciousness of time is more vivid than the consciousness of duration, since the duration is at the background and the time at the foreground. As I listen to a series of tones I am aware primarily of their time, of the difference in their duration, because of a break in the total duration. Duration is the substratum for time.

Similarly, time is the substratum for rhythm. There can be no rhythm in a simple duration. The duration must be broken up into time units, whether of equal or unequal periods, to give rise to rhythm. Rhythm gathers together a number of time units into periodically recurring equal time intervals or time spans. The number of time units within each time interval may vary, but the time interval covered by all the units is the same. The first six measures of "America" contain three rhythmic intervals, each two measures in length. In the first and second there is the same number of time units, namely, six. In the third there are four. But the time interval is the same for the four units as for the six. Psychologically, rhythm in music gives the effect of movement in time, as pitch does of movement in space. Pitch goes up and down, rhythm goes forward. Pitch gives tones a spatial unity, rhythm a temporal unity. Investigations into the nature of the rhythmic experience run into the hundreds. They are devoted primarily to an attempt to determine how the experience arises. Practically all investigations find a motor or muscular factor. Dr. Ruckmick, who has studied these motor accompaniments very thoroughly, gives a good summary statement of the situation when he says that since "rhythm and attention are so intimately related, it would be gratuitous to suppose that motor phenomena which are admittedly very closely allied to primary forms of attention do not also find a place in rhythm. Undoubtedly we tend to group experiences through movements of varying intensities, many of them not overt because they involve infinitely small contractions. All of these, however, go to make up a background in terms of which rhythmical experiences are emphasized. I have shown in published experimental work that these motor phenomena may drop out without bringing the rhythmical experience to an end. That is to say, the rhythm may continue without motor phenomena, but invariably a rhythm is started on its course by some sort of muscular contraction." (84, p. 60)

It is a psychological fact that whenever we are presented with a succession of sensory experiences we at once tend to organize them, bring them together into a unit, or into a number of equal units. As we listen to the ticking of a clock for any length of time we begin to hear groups of sounds rather than single sounds. A number of persons walking together will keep step. As we keep on repeating a number of words they fall into a pattern. All these are rhythmic phenomena. Consciousness is rhythmic, that is, orderly. It is only ordered experience that is meaningful, satisfactory. In chaos there is discomfort. So mind organizes the experiences that come to it in fragments into progressively larger units, each smaller unit becoming integrated into the next larger one. In the realm of tone this tendency results in motifs, then phrases, then sentences, and finally whole movements. Rhythm, then, only performs the same function in music as it does in all other sensory realms, and there is no difference between musical rhythm and any other rhythm.

EXTENSITY

Tones strike us not only as occupying positions of high and low, but also as broad and narrow, or big and small. This phenomenon is also spoken of as volume or volumic effect. It is directly related to pitch. Large bodies spread out more than small bodies, they have more volume, and they also have slower frequency or are low in pitch. Small bodies also have smaller extensity, less volume and greater frequency, or higher pitch. As tones rise in pitch they become narrower, less extensive or voluminous. From being greatly spread out in the low range, they narrow down to a point in the highest range. It seems, then, that frequency of vibration accounts for both pitch and volume. But there is one difference of considerable interest, and perhaps even of significance, between pitch and volume. It is that pitch discrimination and volume discrimination are not equivalent. A just noticeable difference in pitch is not accompanied by a just noticeable difference in volume. For volume discrimination there must be a larger frequency difference than for pitch discrimination. Thus, in experiments with simple tones it has been demonstrated that at a frequency of 275 a rise in pitch of about 6 cycles was necessary before a difference in volume was noticed, an octave higher, 12 cycles, and another octave higher, 24 cycles (83). This would indicate that volume discrimination calls for a geometrical increase in vibrational frequency, the discrimination threshold for volume being about 1/46 of the vibrational frequency. For pitch discrimination in the same tonal region the threshold is a constant increment of about one vibration. Tones lose in volume as they rise in pitch, but the discrimination for the rise in pitch is finer than for the attendant loss of volume. This fact has some bearing upon the possibility of quarter tone music, which we shall discuss later.

There is also a relationship between intensity and volume, since there is a relationship between intensity and pitch. As we have seen, low tones are inherently soft and high tones inherently louder. Therefore, as tones rise in pitch they increase in loudness and decrease in volume.

CHAPTER 2

TONES IN SUCCESSIVE COMBINATION: MELODY

MUSIC DOES NOT CONSIST of any haphazard succession of tones, but of tones that form intervals, and which in turn give rise to larger tonal units that culminate in a melody. The smallest musical unit is thus the musical interval, and the first problem in the study of the psychological structure of melody is an examination of the nature of intervals which can be called musical.

WHAT AN INTERVAL IS

The most obvious definition of an interval would be that it consists of two tones of different pitch. But that is not always so. Two successively presented tones may differ in pitch without forming an interval. For instance, if we begin with any tone and make a gradual transition in pitch up or down, as sliding a finger over a violin string, we do not hear a series of intervals, but a wail. Again, if we raise or lower the pitch of any tone slightly we do not hear an interval but the same tone somewhat modified, namely as sharp or flat. If a singer or player should sing or play off pitch to the extent of forming an interval with the true tone the effect would not be painful but ludicrous. Experimental results show that any one of two tones of an interval can be changed in pitch up to a certain point without changing the interval. All these facts indicate that an interval is more than merely a pitch difference between two tones, although without pitch differences there could be no intervals.

What then is an interval? It is a pitch difference between two tones of sufficient size or distance to produce the effect of two different tones, and not only of a slight pitch modification of the same tone. An interval consists of two definite pitch-points. This raises the question as to the threshold for interval judgment, namely, what is the smallest pitch difference that is recognized as constituting two definite pitch-points. This is not only a question of general interest in psychology, but bears directly upon the possibility of our having quarter tone, or even eighth tone, music, and why it is that the smallest interval in our scale and in our music is the semi-tone. Certainly there can be nothing arbitrary about it, a mere matter of convenience. There must be a psychological reason for it, a reason to be found in the very nature of tonal experience. Our scale was not invented, it evolved. Therefore it must represent the result of a normal and natural tendency.

Pratt (78) reports the results of an investigation on the nature of an interval based upon the phenomenon of interval quality. Every interval has a unique flavor of its own which enables us to recognize it as a fifth, or a fourth, or an octave, no matter what the constituent tones are, just so long as they form that particular interval. Thus, whether the fifth is made up of d–a, or c–g, or e–b, we recognize it as such. It has the quality of "fifthness" wherever found. Now, if the quality of "fifthness" were made up entirely of the sum of the qualities of the constituent tones then there should be a difference between the "fifthness" of c–g and e–b. But such is not the case. An interval is then more than merely two different tones the nature of which can be accounted for either by the difference between them or by their sum. The quality of the interval is not present in each of its tones separately, but emerges from the relationship between the two. It is something new, a form or configuration. As Pratt puts it: "The fifth is made up of the notes c and g; but the peculiar quality of the fifth which distinguishes it from every other musical interval involves more than the separate auditory qualities of c and g in combination. Fifthness, that unique character which every musician recognizes so readily, that musical impression which has something hollow, flat, open, something incomplete and perhaps a bit commonplace about it, can be equated neither to the c nor to the g, nor to the mere togetherness of c and g. No more can the character of the major seventh, with its astringent, gritty, granular, nippy, biting effect, be equated to the sum of the qualities c and b. None of the differentiating qualities of any of the musical intervals correspond to the quality of one of the components plus that of the other." (78, pp. 118-119)

Now, if it were true that any change in pitch is also a change in interval, it would follow that a change in the pitch of one of the tones of an interval would result in a change of interval quality. But such is not the case. The interval quality does not change with any change in pitch. There is a range over which an interval may vary in pitch without losing its distinguishing unique quality. Obviously, then, when we discriminate between two intervals our discrimination is based upon something more than mere pitch change. What is this something?

It has been found experimentally that two intervals must differ from each other in not less than 50 "cents" in order to be uniformly recognized as being different in quality, to be different intervals. A "cent" is a unit of measurement adopted as a convenience to designate 1/1200 of an octave, or 1/100 of a semi-tone. Thus, all fifths are equal to 700 cents, minor sixths, 800 cents, diminished fifths, 600 cents, fourths, 500 cents, major thirds, 400 cents, minor seconds, 100 cents. On that basis, 50 "cents" is 1/4 of a tone. The quarter tone is then the smallest pitch difference between two tones that can be perceived regularly as an interval and not a mere change in the same tone.

But that does not mean that we could have quarter tone music. For artistic purposes the least is not enough. It is but a warning of what to avoid. It therefore seems that the half-step is the smallest safety margin for musical purposes, and that our diatonic scale of 12 half-steps is the normal culmination of a natural musical evolution.

STATIC AND DYNAMIC INTERVALS

When we examine the different intervals of the scale as regards their effect, we find that they divide themselves into two classes: those that are incomplete or dynamic, and tend to move on to a third tone, and those that are complete or static, and tend to rest within themselves. If we arrange the intervals of the diatonic scale in accordance with their dynamic and static tendency we get the following result:

Interval	Letter Name	Numerical Ratio	Class
Octave	c – c′	1:2	Static: remain on c′ or 2
Major second	c – d	8:9	Dynamic: return to c or 8
Major third	c – e	4:5	Dynamic: return to c or 4
Fourth	c – f	3:4	Static: remain on f or 4
Fifth	c – g	2:3	Dynamic: return to c or 2
Major sixth	c – a	3:5	Uncertain
Major seventh	c – b	8:15	Dynamic: return to c or 8

It is noticeable here that all dynamic intervals exert a pull toward 2, or 4, or 8, that is, to 2 or some pure power of 2, while the second tone of the static intervals is 2 or some pure power of 2. This phenomenon is known as the law of the tonic. As the relationships between tones become more complicated mathematically the interval also presents more complex and variable tendencies. All this plays an important rôle in melody, as we shall see later.

INTERVAL DISCRIMINATION

A considerable amount of experimental research work has been devoted to the question of the relative accuracy with which intervals of different sizes are recognized, and how accurately the same interval is judged at different pitch levels.

It has been found that descending intervals are harder to judge than those ascending, even by persons of considerable musical education and practice. It takes a longer time to recognize a descending interval than one that ascends. Watt (120) attributes this to the fact that the tonal series is judged from below upwards. "Rising makes the impression of tonal recession, falling, that of approach. We begin a scale involuntarily from below, not from above, and we end it below again. When a major chord is given successively or simultaneously, we take the lowest, not the highest, tone as tonic; we consider the major, not the minor, third as the first interval. Also, when an interval is mistaken for unison, the tone heard in the majority of cases is the lower of the two." (120, p. 89) Difficult intervals are recognized, according to Watt, by the device of inverting them, or comparing them with familiar intervals, or resolving them, as for instance, the major seventh into the octave, or by remembering the interval as it occurred in some melody.

Maltzew (58) conducted a series of experiments on the relative accuracy of judgment of different intervals. His results show that seconds, thirds, octaves, fifths and fourths are more readily recognized than are minor sevenths, minor sixths, tritones, and major sevenths. He attributes the difference to the frequency with which the different intervals occur in music. Thus, if we count the number of times that each interval occurs in the major and minor scales, ascending and descending, over the range of a twelfth, which is about the largest interval usually found in music, we get the following count:

Interval	Frequency of Occurrence
Major second	32
Fourth	30
Fifth	26
Minor third	24
Octave	20
Major third	17
Major sixth	16
Minor seventh	16
Minor sixth	13
Minor second	12
Tritone	10
Major seventh	8

From the above we see that the intervals that occur most frequently in music are also those recognized with greatest ease and accuracy. The figures also show that smaller intervals are more easily recognized than larger intervals. The octave seems the one exception to this rule. But the octave belongs, by its very nature, among the most familiar of intervals.

Maltzew's results also show that intervals of the higher octaves are less accurately recognized than those of the middle region, as indicated by the fact that persons who named every interval correctly in the middle region made frequent mistakes in the higher region. They interchanged seconds with thirds, sixths with sevenths, thirds with sixths, sevenths with tritones, and fifths or fourths with the octave. The major seventh was confused with the octave, the minor seventh with the major sixth, and the tritone with the fourth and fifth.

The results showed, further, that tones of very high and very low pitches have a negative effect on interval judgment. More errors occurred in the 4th accented octave (g'''') than in the octave below. Intervals accurately judged in the third octave were erroneously judged in the fourth. The easiest and most familiar intervals were confused with the neighboring hardest and least familiar. This occurred most when the upper tone of the interval lay in the region of g''''–d'''''. The upper tone of the interval was judged to be a half-step lower than it was. Thus, the major third was mistaken for a minor third, the fourth for a major third, the fifth for the tritone, the minor sixth for the fifth. Major and minor sevenths and the octave were almost invariably judged to be smaller than they were. This shows that the judgment of the pitch of a tone tends to become increasingly less accurate in the higher regions until it collapses in the fifth accented octaves. A similar distortion of pitch occurred in the lowest tonal region. According to the results of Maltzew, tones below a frequency of 40 cycles appear somewhat sharp, while tones of 3,000 cycles and above are somewhat flat. At about 4,000 cycles, accurate judgment of intervals seems to break down completely.

One of the latest, and perhaps most reliable experiments on interval judgment, is that of Pratt (76) on the comparison of tonal distances. He presented his subjects with four successive tones in which the first two were kept constant throughout the experiments and served as the standard distance in terms of which the comparison intervals were to be judged. He used nine comparison intervals: three from a pitch region about a fifth higher than the standard, three about a fifth higher than the first three, and the last three about the same distance above the second three. The distance between the lowest and the highest tones used was a little over two octaves. The subjects were therefore making comparison judgments on three groups of intervals which were removed from the standard interval by about a fifth, a minor ninth and a twelfth, respectively. The standard interval consisted of the frequencies 204 and 283, having the ratio 1.3889, which is slightly larger than the fourth. Each of the three groups of comparison intervals contained one interval having this ratio. One of the other two comparison intervals was slightly smaller, ratio 1.2871, and one slightly larger, ratio 1.4978. Thus there were three comparison intervals repeated at three different pitch regions to be judged with respect to a standard interval, this standard interval being the lowest. The subjects were told that they would be presented with four successive tones, and they were to compare the distance between the third and fourth tones with respect to the distance between the first and second tones, and express their judgment as to whether the second interval was greater, equal to, or smaller than, the first. The results of this experiment show clearly that an interval increases in apparent size, that is, appears to be larger, with an increase in the vibration frequency of the component tones. In other words, an interval in the vicinity of c‴ is not equal in size to the same interval an octave and a half lower, but appears, on the average, to be about a half-tone larger. The interval begins to assume greater size when its pitch is increased by an octave.

It is interesting, as well as significant, to inquire whether the observer (O) uses the criterion of *distance* or that of *interval quality* as the basis of his judgment of the interval. On this point Pratt has the following to say:

> In any work on tonal distance the question immediately arises as to the degree of coercive power exerted by the musical consciousness in the judgments of O. If two tones, when sounded simultaneously, are taken in a musical setting they possess what has been called interval quality; if perceived under a more strictly psychological attitude (difference in auditory quality between the two components) they possess *distance*. The more usual attitude, except for very non-musical individuals, is the one in which interval quality is uppermost in consciousness. Under this attitude an interval with the ratio 2:3 is always a fifth, and possesses the unique characteristic of "fifthness" no matter

from what part of the scale it may be taken. The experience of the present writer, however, has led him to believe that the influence of interval quality in tonal judgments is not as inescapable as has sometimes been supposed. Except for an occasional O with very considerable musical training, the O in the laboratory who has had some practice in psychological observation finds it not difficult to abstract from the musical aspects of intervals and to concentrate on the difference in auditory quality between the two tones of an interval. An examination of the introspective reports of the O's in the present experiment shows that only one O, C, and he very seldom, was at all bothered by the criterion of interval quality cutting across that of distance. The reports are all strikingly alike in their reference to the same sort of criterion of judgment. Each tone, as presented, was perceived in more or less isolated fashion and was placed in its own right, i.e., without reference to its possible musical relationship to the other tones, at a particular point on an auditory qualitative continuum, whence O could then judge as to the relative amounts of separation between the limiting components of the two pairs of points. Each O had his own way of facilitating these judgments of auditory distances. It was not often that the distances were perceived in purely auditory terms. They were supplemented, rather, by various forms of visual and kinaesthetic schematic imagery which served as a sort of framework or point of reference in terms of which the distances could be estimated. This criterion of judgment would seem to correspond very closely to the *Helligkeitsunterschied* which Abraham and von Hornbostel mention in their work on tonal distance. (76, pp. 84-85)

One thing seems certain about intervals, namely, that they have a quantitative and qualitative aspect. Every interval has both. Quantitatively it has distance; the farther the two tones are from each other in pitch the greater being the distance. Qualitatively every interval has a peculiar character or flavor which is more than the sum of, or the difference in, the qualities of the component tones. But the two are difficult to isolate even by experienced observers. It is possible that interval distance corresponds to the brightness of the single tones, while interval quality corresponds to the musical quality of the single tones. Research shows that brightness is the more primitive characteristic of tones, while tonal quality is present mainly for musical persons. For the unmusical, quality is either lacking or occupies a secondary position. It is most probable that to primitive peoples the actual difference between intervals is a difference of distance, and that the musical qualities of intervals appear only at higher stages of cultural development.

MELODY

A melody is a sequence of tonal intervals. But not any such sequence will form a melody. The secret lies in the word *form.* A form is not a collection of discreet units, but an arrangement that produces the effect of unity, oneness, coherence, or belonging-togetherness. A melody is then a tonal movement in which each tone commands what tone shall follow it, each interval commands the interval to succeed it, and the whole movement pulling to one, and only one, close. What we hear in a melody is not a succession of pitches or intervals, but a continuous development of an idea which must go on to completion or fulfillment. If we were to fix attention upon each tone of a melody as it is presented to us, the melody would vanish.

Why, then, is one sequence of tones a melody while another is not? What is there inherent in a tonal sequence that accounts for melodic form, entirely apart from rhythm and harmony? Can we discover any laws of tonal relationship that account for the melodic relativity of tones? This is a problem that has been extensively discussed and quite thoroughly studied by various investigators.

The reader should bear in mind that the concern here is not with the aesthetic phase of melody. We are not raising the question at present as to why one melody is designated as beautiful or significant and another as ugly or trite. The very fact that we speak of some melodies as trite indicates that a tonal sequence can be a melody without producing an aesthetic effect. Our problem is psychological and not aesthetic. Psychologically, any tonal succession becomes a melody if it gives an impression of being a sequence, and not merely a haphazard collection of tones of different pitch. There are then tonal successions that never constitute a melody, and others that invariably do so.

THE NATURE OF MELODIC FORM

Gurney finds the secret of melodic form in what he calls the ideal motion. Musical form is motion. A melodic form evolves in time, moment after moment, as a continuous advance. In music motion and form are one, a fact which distinguishes musical form from visible form and also from physical motion. "When a melody is familiar to us we realize it by a gradual process of advance along it, while yet the *whole* process is in some real manner present to us at each of the successive instants at which only a minute part of it is actually engaging our ears." (33, p. 165) This process Gurney designates as *ideal motion.* By ideal he does not mean idealization or glorification, but "ideal as yielding a *form,* a unity to which all the parts are necessary in their respective places." (33, p. 165) He describes this process of form-yielding as follows: "The melody, then, may begin by pressing its way through a sweetly yielding resistance to a gradually foreseen climax; whence again fresh expectation is bred, perhaps for another excursion, as it were, round the same center but with a bolder and freer sweep, perhaps, on a fresh differentiation whereof in turn the tendency is surmised and followed; till after a certain number of such involutions and evolutions, and of delicately poised leanings and reluctances and yieldings, the forces so accurately measured just suffice to bring it home, and the sense of potential and coming integration which has underlain all our provisional adjustments of expectation is triumphantly justified." (33, pp. 165-166)

Melody is, then, formed motion arising from the succession of expectations and realizations, of tensions and relaxations, around a central core, all culminating in one final triumph of fulfillment.

Thurstone (109) offers an account of melody in terms of motor or muscular phenomena. Pitch is the motor attribute of hearing, and pitch variation is essentially a consciousness of movement. If we ask a person to sing a tone from the highest pitch of his range we note that the eyebrows are raised, the neck stretched and the head elevated. The attitude is that of climbing. For low tones the attitude is that of descending. Pitch means action. Certain pitch variations "can be perceived as representative of a single unified act, whereas other samples of pitch perambulation are perceived as representative of mere random action. This distinction between a single unified act, and a mere random action in the motor attribute of sound sensation gives us a sufficiently flexible classificatory basis for defining melody. A certain form of pitch excursion may be perceived by one individual as a single unified act whereas to another the same pitch excursion may seem chaotic. The former hears 'a' melody, the latter none. . . . The former is perceived as an act, the latter as action." (109, pp. 2-3)

Thurstone's "simple unified act" is similar to Gurney's "ideal motion." But all that we are told by both Thurstone and Gurney is that unless a tonal succession is perceived as a unity there is no melody. Neither tells us as to why it is that certain successions can be experienced as unities while other successions are never so perceived.

THE FACTORS OF TONAL RELATIONSHIP

We have a number of studies that concern themselves directly with the problem of the nature of tonal relationships in a melody. One of the most exhaustive of these is that by Ortmann (68).

Since melody is motion in the pitch series resulting from a succession of pitch intervals, melodic relativity, for Ortmann, becomes the equivalent of pitch relativity, and his problem was therefore to study the factors that govern the pitch relationship of each tone to all the other tones in a tonal sequence. He found two such factors, the one absolute and the other relative. There are three absolute factors: *first and last tones, highest and lowest tones,* and *tone repetition;* and five relative factors: *interval, pitch direction, pitch proximity, emphasis in tone-groups,* and *interval relationship.*

The first and last tones of a melody are more vivid than any of the other tones, the first tone because of its primacy, and the last because of its recency. These two tones bound the melody in the temporal series. Similarly, the highest and lowest tones of the melody mark its boundaries in the pitch series, which gives them an emphasis above that of the rest of the tones. Tone repetition produces a like effect of accentuated impression because of frequency of stimulation. These three kinds of absolute emphasis are usually all present in any melody.

The relative factors function more often and with greater effect than the absolute factors because music is tonal relationship, a phenomenon of relative pitch, and not of the absolute position of any one tone. In other words, in melody we do not hear single tones, but tones standing in a relationship to each other. Now intervals, like single tones, are associated by contiguity in pitch and in time. The closer that two tones are to each other in pitch the greater is their association by contiguity in pitch, and the closer that two tones are to each other in time the greater is their contiguity in time. The same holds for intervals. A melodic major third is most closely associated with a minor third and with a perfect fourth because the pitch distances are most nearly equal. Likewise, through contiguity in time an interval is most closely associated with the intervals that immediately precede and follow it. "The contrast, for example, between a major second and a fifth is more noticeable, is reacted to as greater, if the two intervals are in immediate succession, than if they are separated by other intervals of thirds and fourths. In the first case association by contiguity in time is at its strongest point. In the latter case it is weakened because its intervals are no longer contiguous in time but are separated by intervals the absolute value of which falls between the two. In one case the transition is abrupt, in the other case it is gradual." (68, p. 10)

Tones are also unified by pitch direction. A succession of tones in which each tone is higher or lower than the preceding tone has a common attribute of ascent in the one case and descent in the other. A change in pitch direction therefore becomes "the prime determinant of melodic tone-groups. A melody ascends, descends, or progresses horizontally. In thus moving, it creates melodic outline. This auditory outline is most uniform when there is no change in pitch direction; it loses uniformity with each change of pitch direction. The amount of disjunctiveness thus produced depends upon the amount and frequency of change in pitch direction; small changes in pitch direction will obviously produce less disjunctiveness than large changes. However, each change of direction, be it great or small, acts as a point of disjunction, separating the melodic groups." (68, pp. 11-12)

Another relative factor in tonal association is pitch proximity. The closer that several tones are to each other in pitch the greater is their belonging-togetherness. They form one family group. And each individual tone-group is affected by the emphasis of pitch-extreme, time-extreme, and repetition, in the same manner that these factors affect the whole melody. That is, the first and last intervals, highest and lowest intervals, and repeated intervals receive an emphasis above that of the other intervals in the melody. Then there is also degree of emphasis in interval relationship, namely, that the same interval will vary in emphasis according to its neighboring intervals. A half-step seems much smaller when preceded by a twelfth than when preceded by a whole-step. It is more noticeable in the former than in the latter case because of the greater contrast. Likewise, the greater the proximity of these tones within themselves, and the less proximate they are to the rest of the tones of the melody, the stronger will be their effect as a group.

All the factors of emphasis just discussed are present together in any tonal succession that has a melodic effect. To these must be added the temporal aspect of melody, because a melody consists of pitch variation in a pitch succession. The movement in space is inseparable from the duration in time, in that the time element influences significantly the factors of the pitch element. Thus, the emphasis received by the first tone of a melody because of its primacy is counteracted by the temporal factor. The longer the melody, the more does the first tone lose in its original emphasis. The last tone, on the other hand, gains in emphasis by virtue of the temporal factor, its recency. Similarly, the emphasis a tone receives when it is the highest or lowest in a pitch-series gradually diminishes as the melody proceeds in time, unless the tone is repeated. Tonal repetition, as a source of emphasis, is also affected by the time factor. The longer the time interval between the repetitions the less is the emphasis, because the recognition decreases in certainty.

We see, then, an interaction and an interdependence between the factor of pitch and that of time. Neither determines alone the psychological status of a tone in a melody. The same tone has a different status with a change in its tonal environment. But association is strongest when both contiguity in pitch and contiguity in time are present in the same group of tones.

Ortmann (67) counted the frequency with which the various intervals occur in 160 songs selected from the works of Schubert, Schumann, Brahms, and Richard Strauss, in order to see whether the melodic relationships he presents actually existed and operated in artistic music. If they did, then small intervals should predominate markedly over wide intervals. He counted approximately 23,000 intervals, and found that in 97 1/2 per cent of the songs unisons or seconds were first in frequency, and thirds in the other 2 1/2 per cent. In 60 per cent of the cases the order of frequency was unison, second, third, fourth; or second, unison, third, fourth. This distribution corroborates in a striking manner his analysis of the factors of tonal relationship.

In another study Ortmann (69) shows that the fundamental conditions of melodic relativity function as determinants of melodic memory. Thus, tonal repetition is a factor in the melodic relationship of tones, and it is also found to be the most easily recognized attribute of melody. The immediate repetition of a tone in a five-tone series was missed only six times in 724, and in 2,064 examples that did not contain direct repetition it was introduced by pupils only four times. In tests on one pitch direction, ascending or descending, the pupils made only 22 errors in 691 examples. An entirely ascending series or an entirely descending series was never reversed. Many errors were made in the size of the steps, but the pitch contour was given correctly, in that ascent remained ascent and descent remained descent. With the introduction of an increasing number of pitch direction changes, the per cent of errors increased. Thus, in examples containing one change of direction it was missed by 1.7 per cent of the pupils, while two changes of pitch direction were missed by 22 per cent, and three changes by 32 per cent. It is interesting to note here that more errors occur for descending than for ascending direction. Again, stepwise progression was found to be much easier than skip-wise progression. Errors were found to be most frequent on the skip parts of a melody. The frequency of errors for skips depended on their size. A second was seldom heard as a third or any other skip, but a third was frequently mistaken for a fourth or fifth. Other wide intervals were heard incorrectly even more frequently. Narrow intervals had a smaller range of error than wide intervals. Thus, errors for thirds varied from seconds to fifths; for fourths from seconds to sevenths; for fifths and sixths from seconds to octaves. There was also a tendency to hear an interval as being smaller than it actually was, rather than larger.

THE NATURE OF MELODIC FINALITY

The phenomenon of finality in a melodic tonal sequence is usually accounted for in terms of tonality or the tonic. By finality is meant the feeling in the tonal succession of a goal-building tendency, a striving of the succession from point to point towards a final close. This, it is said, is due to tonality, namely, that all the parts of the succession relate themselves to a fundamental, central tone that governs the succession, and which occurs as the final tone. This final tone of the succession bears a certain relationship to the beginning tone, the beginning tone implying the end tone, so that all the tones that follow the first tone are pulling towards a particular final tone, and this gives all the tones their tonal belonging-togetherness. A succession can modulate from one tonality to another, but the modulation obeys certain laws, and as the hearer is carried into the new tonality he will reject any tone that does not have a meaning in the newly established framework. In this finality-building process, initiated by the first tone and completed by the last, we find tones of especial pronounced tonality significance, namely, the leading tone and the two dominants, whose task it is to give a final unity to the tonality. In psychological studies this finality effect has been the subject of a good deal of speculation and experimentation in terms of *the law of the pure power of 2.*

Among the first to deal with the question was Theodore Lipps (56), who based a theory upon the common observation that several intervals of our diatonic scale show a marked preference for one of the two tones to be the end tone. Thus, the minor second, or ratio 15:16, tends to remain, to repose, on the upper tone, while the major second (8:9) seeks to return to the first tone. The major third (4:5) pulls back to the first tone, while the minor third (5:6) shows no noticeable trend. But the fourth (3:4) tends decidedly to the second tone for its final tone, and the fifth (2:3) towards the first tone. The minor sixth (5:8) and the minor seventh (9:10) pull slightly upward, the major seventh (8:15) downward, and the major sixth (3:5) in neither direction.

Now it is noticeable that in every one of the intervals in which a pull occurs upward or downward, the pull is toward the tone whose ratio is 2 or a pure power of 2, that is, 4, 8, 16, etc. There is no trend when neither ratio is 2 or a pure power of 2. This fact has given rise to what is known as the law of the pure power of 2. Lipps (56) states this law as follows: When two tones occur together which are related to each other as 2^n: 3, 5, 7, etc. (n representing any power of 2) there exists a natural tendency of the second tone to return to the first, there exists a tendency of the inner movement for the second to come to rest in the first. The second tones "seek" the first tones as their natural basis, their natural gravitational center. This is naturally more the case the smaller the n, n being smallest when it is 0. ($2^0 = 2:2 = 1$.) That is, the most complete state of rest and the final gravitational center of such tones remains always the absolute ground rhythm. Thus, the interval of the fifth has the ground rhythm or ratio 2:3, and the resting point is 2. The ratio 2 exercises a dominating power, the power of a tonic, and a melody is a tonal succession that obtains its unity through the subordination of all of its tones, intervals and larger units, to the tonic. The tonic is the common factor of the manifold of tones, forming them into a unanimity. The manifoldness is a differentiation of this common factor, a variety in unity. The tones gain their belonging-togetherness from this ground rhythm, because all of them have the rhythm in common. Melody is an organization on the basis of such ground rhythms, a system of ground rhythms unified by a single, all-pervading ground rhythm. This basic ground rhythm is the tonic. Rhythm here does not have the usual meaning of recurring periodic acoustic impressions, but as micro-rhythms found in the physical vibrations of the tones.

Bingham (6) sought experimental data on this law of the pure power of 2, and on the general problem of melodic finality. He presented two tones in succession and asked the observer to state whether he could make the second tone a final tone, whether the melody ended. He used the ratios 2:3, 5:6, 3:5, 15:16, 45:64, 4:5, 9:16, 32:45, 8:9, 8:15, 5:8, 3:4. The intervals were presented both ascending and descending. Ten of these ratios are relatively simple, while two of them, the augmented fourth (32:45), and the diminished fifth (45:64), involve pure powers of 2, but the ratios are not simple. These two intervals were included for purposes of comparison.

Bingham's results show that the descending major third (4:5), and the descending perfect fifth (2:3), were felt to produce the effect of finality more often than any of the rest of the two-tone successions. Next in order came the ascending perfect fourth (3:4), the descending major second (8:9), the ascending minor second (15:16), and the ascending minor sixth (5:8). The intervals that most clearly lacked finality were the diminished fifth (45:64), both ascending and descending, and the descending minor second (15:16). Next in order in the lack of finality were the ascending major second, the ascending and descending augmented fourth, minor third, minor seventh and major seventh, and the ascending major third. The percentage of negative judgments of the ascending perfect fifth and the descending perfect fourth was the smallest of any of the intervals judged not to end.

The ascending minor seventh (9:16) and the descending major seventh (8:15) were both judged to lack finality, although both contain a pure power of 2, and although their inversions, the major and minor second, were judged to possess finality and conform to the law of the number 2. From his data Bingham concluded that "in general, it is somewhat harder to accept the second tone of a two-tone sequence as final than it is to judge it to be lacking in finality." (6, p. 28)

What about ascending and descending successions? Do descending intervals as such tend to produce the effect of finality? Meyer conducted an experiment on this problem using three-tone successions. He found that in a succession lacking a tonic effect, 57 per cent of the subjects preferred the lower tone, whichever it happened to be, as an end tone. In the successions in which there was a tonic tone, it was preferred as an end tone in 86 per cent of the judgments when that tone was also the lowest tone of the succession. When it was the middle tone it was preferred as an end tone in 70 per cent of the choices, and when it was the upper tone, in 7 per cent. Obviously, these experiments show that other factors besides the law of the pure power of 2 operate in producing the effect of finality at the close of a melodic sequence of tones. (6, pp. 29-30) To bring some light on this point from his own experiments, Bingham separated the finality effect produced by the falling inflection from the effect which is due to the more definite pitch relations of the tones. For this purpose he arranged his 12 intervals into four groups, namely, (1) a group of simple intervals whose ratios did not contain a pure power of 2: the intervals of the minor third (5:6), and the major sixth (3:5); (2) a group of complex intervals that included the pure power of 2: the augmented fourth (32:45), and diminished fifth (45:64); (3) the intervals in which the 2 tone was the higher; (4) the intervals in which the 2 tone was the lower.

Now, according to the law of the pure power of 2, the intervals of group three should end better on the higher tone and the intervals of group four on the lower. In group three the finality effect due to the 2 ratio is opposed by the rising inflection, while in group four the two forces work together.

Bingham found, in comparing the total judgments for all the intervals in these two groups, that for group three there were 59 affirmative judgments and 47 negative judgments, while for group four there were 82 affirmative judgments and 31 negative judgments. Thus, the affirmative judgments are markedly affected by the falling inflection. But when the descending intervals of group three are compared with the ascending intervals of group four it is found that the preference for the descending intervals as definitely final does not appear. The total results show, however, that some such tendency as is implied by the law does operate, in that, when 2 is the end tone, observers report the two-tone group to end in 55 per cent of the instances, not to end in 31 per cent, and doubtful in 14 per cent. But when 2 is the first tone of the series 55 per cent are reported to be lacking in finality, and only 23 per cent to end.

Bingham sought further data on the problem by arranging another series which contained, in addition to the twelve original intervals, five new intervals, namely, 24:25, 9:10, 27:32, 20:27, 27:40. He used in this experiment seven quite musical observers who were asked to state whether they felt any desire to return to the first tone. He found that "some of the observers reported with certain intervals that they desired to hear the first tone again, whichever way the melodies were played, ascending or descending. Thus was forced into notice what has been called the *law of the Return,* the law that, *other things being equal, it is better to return to any starting point whatsoever than not to return*—a simple fundamental principle of musical form, of art form of any kind, indeed." (6, pp. 33-34) Bingham found, however, that even the facts of elementary melodic relationship and the law of finality of two-tone melodies did not tell the whole story, in that some observers reported persistently that neither tone would serve as an end tone, nor was there a desire to return, but that some third tone was needed to produce a satisfactory ending. From this result he formulated the law that: *"Two melodically 'related' tones tend to establish a tonality,* and the melody is judged to end only when the final tone is one of the members of the tonic triad—preferably the tonic itself." (6, p. 34) Tonality Bingham defines as "a group of mutually related tones, organized about a single tone, the tonic, as the center of relations. Subjectively a tonality is a set of expectations, a group of melodic possibilities within which the course of the successive tones must find its way, or suffer the penalty of not meeting these expectations or demands of the hearer and so of being rejected as no melody. Of these different demands, that for an end on a certain tone is the strongest and most characteristic." (6, pp. 36-37) He suggests that such a tonality, now one and now another, arises in the mind of the hearer of a tonal sequence, or one tonality for one hearer and another for another hearer, thus giving rise to anomalous and contradictory reports for the same interval. For instance, the succession e–f might at one time suggest the tonality of f, and therefore end satisfactorily on the upper tone, while at another time the suggested tonality is e, and f does not serve as an end tone.

Bingham summarizes the results of his investigation as follows:

These studies began with a definition of melody which laid stress upon the feeling of unity. When the separate tones of a series are felt to be related to each other in such a manner that each tone forms part of a coherent whole, the succession of tones, we said, is felt to be a melody, and the melody problem was stated to be the problem of explaining how this feeling of melodic unity arises. An analysis of the psychological elements of melodic structure revealed many and varied sources contributing to the generation of this unity. One group of factors, however, stood out as of unique importance, namely, those due to the relative pitch of the constituent tones; and to the consideration of problems in pitch relationships the scope of the present investigation was limited.

A survey of the efforts that have been made to reduce the facts of melodic "relationship" and of melodic trend to simple mathematical formulation was followed by an account of three sets of experiments upon the phenomena of melodic trend in two-tone groups. These trends, with which the feelings of finality or of lack of finality are closely bound up, were found to be due to (a) preference for the lower tone as such as an end tone (phenomenon of the falling inflection), (b) preference for a return to the first tone as an end tone, (c) preference for the expected ending (if one knows that a given tone is to be the last, its arrival may be sufficient to arouse the feeling of finality quite apart from the operation of any other factors), and finally, (d) preference for an end on one of the tones of the tonic chord—and especially the tonic itself—of the suggested tonality.

This formulation, contrasted with the formulation in terms of "the law of the number 2," has the advantage of covering more of the observed facts and the disadvantage, as some will consider it, of conceding that the phenomenon described is probably not elemental, primitive, but rather a resultant traceable to the laws of habit and the harmonic structure of the music with which the observers were acquainted. According to this view, the laws of consonance are primary, not the laws of melodic "relationship."

This latter view finds confirmation in the instances cited where the feelings of "relationship" and of trend were clearly the outgrowth of habituation, of repetition, of custom, of association, of mere expectation. (6, pp. 41-42)

Farnsworth (20) also investigated the law of the pure power of 2 by constructing tonal successions that did not contain this power. In such successions it is supposed that one ending exhibits as much finality as any other.

He chose the three tones g, e, and b♭, in the key of C, representing the ratios 3, 5, and 7, and presented them so that in one group g was the end tone, in a second group e was the last, and in the third group b♭ was the final tone. His observers were college students to whom the following instructions were given: "You will hear two series of three tones each which you are to compare. Which series sounds more finished, more complete, more at rest?" In two tests the tones were presented with a falling inflection, and in a third test the order was, first the high tone, then the low tone, and the last the middle tone. This was done in order to eliminate the effect of falling inflection. His results show that when the series ending on g (3) is paired with the series ending on e (5) the series ending on g is preferred in the proportion 55:45. The ending preference is thus small. When ending on e is paired with ending on b♭, e is slightly preferred, the proportion being 57:43. When ending on g is paired with ending on b♭, the preference is marked for g, in the proportion 66:34. Compared with ending in e and b♭, g is shown to give more finality than e, and e more so than b♭, in the proportion of 51 per cent for g, 34 per cent for e, and 25 per cent for b♭. When compared with the findings of Meyer for the finality effect of 2, the results of this study give the proportion of 58 per cent for c as an ending, 17 per cent for g, 14 per cent for e and 11 per cent for b♭. Obviously, then, a pure power of 2 is preferred by far over other tones as a final tone.

In another study (21), the same investigator sought to determine whether the preferences for endings that he found showed any constancy, or whether the preference for any one ending over another can be changed. He tested this by using the same series as in the former study, but this time he introduced drill periods which consisted in listening to a prepared series of tone combinations. The purpose of these drills was to see whether they affected the ending preferences as shown by the test results. By this procedure he found that ending preference can be permanently altered by training, that increasing familiarity with a certain ending results in increasing preference for that ending.

Updegraff (111) investigated the same problem by using one series of melodies of four tones, a second series of six tones, and a third series of nine tones. She did this in order to be certain that tonality was present. Specifically, she wanted to determine "whether feeling of finality, admittedly present with a tonic ending, is determined by the mathematical relationships of the vibrations *per se,* or by the tonal consonance to which the individual is accustomed. In other words, is the explanation physical or psychological, and to what extent?" (111, p. 180) Her results indicate that finality, instead of being based on a mathematical relationship, is rather determined, in addition to the influence of the falling inflection, by the suggested tonality of the melody, that is, by the experience of the observer.

From the survey of these studies on melody it is obvious that the melodic experience is affected by numerous factors, some of them inherent in the tonal relationships themselves, others due to experience, training, and cultural milieu. That it is neither one to the exclusion of the other is well indicated by one result of the experiment by Updegraff. She presented to seven American and five Chinese students five melodies of nine tones in the tempered scale and five in the Chinese. The rhythm was alike for both the tempered and Chinese melodies. The results showed that the Chinese students judged 52 per cent of their own melodies final, and 44 per cent of the American melodies, while the Americans judged only 34 per cent of the Chinese melodies final and 64 per cent of their own. It was interesting to note, however, that the Chinese melody judged most final by the Chinese was also the most final Chinese melody to the Americans, and the Chinese and Americans agreed in their choice of the most final American melody. There is something here that is certainly not dependent on experience and training alone. The factors of emphasis in melodic relationship discussed by Ortmann must lie in the tonal material itself. Nor can there be any question about the law of the tonic, the law of cadence, or falling inflection, and the law of return.

CHAPTER 3

TONES IN SIMULTANEOUS COMBINATION: HARMONY

When two or more tones of the scale are sounded simultaneously they make either a consonance or a dissonance. A succession of consonances and dissonances is in itself not harmony, since such a succession does not, as such, constitute a harmonic progression. But a simultaneous tonal combination is, nevertheless, the unit of harmony, as the single tone is the unit of melody. Just, then, as there are laws that operate in melodic tonal successions, so there are laws that function in the making of a series of consonances and dissonances into a harmonic sequence. Our concern here, however, is not with the laws of harmonic progression, but with the phenomenon of consonance itself. What is the nature of the experience of consonance? What accounts for the phenomenon? How do the different intervals of the scale rank in consonance? These are some of the psychological questions that have been investigated, and it is this literature we are to survey.

THE THEORY OF FUSION

The most prominent theory of consonance is that of fusion, but the criterion for fusion is not the same for different investigators.

Stumpf (107), who was among the first to examine consonance psychologically, defines fusion as the experiencing of two elements as one. Two simultaneous tones give the impression of a single tone in different degrees, and the greater the impression of singleness of the two tones the greater is the consonance of the interval. But that does not mean that the two tones are heard as one tone. Fusion is a relation of two such sensations forming not a mere sum but a whole. He holds that the perception of a tonal combination as one tone is characteristic of unmusical persons. Musical persons always perceive such combinations as a complexity, but the complexity produces a unitary impression, and as such it is unanalyzable. The fusion is destroyed in the degree to which the complexity is felt as a multiplicity, the degree to which it fails to produce a unitary experience, the experience of oneness. Singleness of impression and singleness of tone must be recognized as being two different matters. When two stimuli produce the impression of singleness there is nevertheless an awareness that more than one stimulus is present. It is the impression that is one, not that which produces the impression, and the judgment likewise is of the impression and not of the stimulating cause. Such an impression produced by a tonal combination means complete fusion of the given tones. As the fusion decreases the impression becomes more and more analyzable as being not one impression but two or three, etc. Stumpf is therefore concerned with the impression produced by a tonal combination rather than with a judgment as to the number of tones in the combination. The number is always more than one, excepting for unmusical persons. Or rather, when two tones are judged by a person to be one tone, that person, for Stumpf, is unmusical. (105)

Fusion is, then, the approach of the components of a tonal combination to unity. It is a special relation in the sensation which makes the analysis of tones difficult, an unalterable property of sensory material which always remains over when all other obstructions to analysis have been eliminated, and which can be recognized as such only after the analysis is completed and the tones have been clearly recognized as two. Tones which produce this effect of fusion in a higher degree are consonant, while those which show only a low degree of fusion are called dissonant.

On the basis of his investigations Stumpf lays down the following laws of fusion:

1. Fusion depends upon the vibration ratio of the tones. According to vibration ratio the intervals are divisible into five grades of fusion. The first grade, or highest fusion, is that of the octave. Next in degree of fusion is the fifth, then the fourth, then the thirds and sixths. The

other intervals have the lowest grade of fusion, excepting perhaps the seventh which may be somewhat better than the other intervals in this group. He states, furthermore, that there may be a slight difference in degree of fusion between major and minor thirds and major and minor sixths. Watt comments on this ranking of intervals that it is "corroborated not only by the musical practice of all times in which singing in octaves is considered equivalent to unison, but also by the frequent occurrence of continued parallels of fifths and fourths in the music of various peoples. These parallels evidently give some impression of unity." (120, p. 57)

2. The degree of fusion is unaffected by the tonal region of the interval, so long as the vibration ratio is the same. This means that a fifth, for instance, has the same degree of fusion wherever it occurs in the tonal range just so long as its ratio remains that of 2:3.

3. The degree of fusion is independent of the absolute as well as the relative intensity of the component tones. A fifth sounded softly or loudly possesses the same degree of fusion. And provided the two tones remain distinguishable the fusion remains the same whether the tones are sounded with equal intensity or whether the upper tone is louder than the lower tone or vice versa.

4. The addition of a third tone does not change the fusion of the interval. Thus, according to Stumpf, the degree of fusion of the fourth, c-f, for instance, is not affected by the addition to it of the tone a. Nor is the fusion affected by the addition of a fourth tone.

5. Very small deviations of vibration frequencies from the simple ratios of the intervals do not cause a noticeable change in the degree of fusion. Thus, if the frequency of one of the tones of the fifth is slightly changed so that its vibration ratio of 2:3 is modified its degree of fusion remains that of the interval 2:3. But if the deviation is increased its fusion becomes that of its neighboring interval, without passing through any intermediate degrees of fusion. An interval retains its degree of fusion, then, until its vibration ratio is changed sufficiently so that it becomes a different interval, when it assumes the fusion of that interval. How rapidly this transition occurs depends upon the degree of the initial fusion. This law holds for all but the lowest degrees of fusion.

6. An interval has the same degree of fusion whether it is within or beyond the octave. That is, the fifth has the same degree of fusion as the twelfth.

Külpe and Lipps also accept fusion as the criterion of consonance, but both differ from Stumpf in defining it.

For Külpe (52), fusion means the experience of belonging-togetherness rather than an impression of the unitariness of binary combinations. The two tones do not so much produce a single impression as they are felt to blend, to belong together. In Külpe's view, the simultaneous presentation of two tones makes the analysis of the impression easier rather than more difficult, as Stumpf holds. So for Stumpf the criterion of fusion is unanalyzability, for Külpe it is analyzability. In consonance, he holds, the two components become re-united, not as a single impression, but as two impressions that belong together. Külpe's rule is that a tonal fusion occurs when the qualitative varieties of the tones present a unified impression. It is the consciousness of uniformity in variety.

Lipps (55) reverses the relationship between fusion and consonance. Two tones are not consonant because they fuse but they fuse because they are consonant. Consonance is then the criterion for fusion, and not fusion for consonance. He claims that simultaneous impressions tend to fuse, to flow together, into a single content. But for each unifying tendency there is an opposing one, namely, that every single experience tends to remain itself. The fusion is the greater as the variety of stimuli present equal qualities, and weaker as they retain their individual qualities. Similarity of mental excitation can arouse similarity of mental content. For instance, the great similarity in the mental excitations of the two tones of the octave arouses great similarity of mental experience, and the octave therefore is the most fused of intervals because it is the most consonant.

The basis for fusion Lipps finds in the existence of what he calls "micro-psychic" rhythms, or the presence of unconscious rhythmic processes resulting from the simultaneous presentation of tones. When the two rhythms of the sound vibrations are compatible the tones are experienced as fused, and they fail to fuse when the rhythms are incompatible. The micro-psychic rhythms of a tone correspond to its vibration frequency, and consequently the degree of fusion of two tones depends upon their vibration ratio. The frequencies 100 and 200 produce micro-psychic rhythms of 100 and 200 respectively. In these rhythms the more rapid adjusts itself to the less rapid, the two thus coalescing into one pattern of rhythm, in which every second beat of the 200 rhythm coincides with one of the successive beats of the 100 rhythm. The octave therefore gives the highest degree of fusion because its frequencies produce the highest coincidence of micro-psychic rhythms. In the fifth, or ratio 2:3, there is a coincidence of every third beat of the higher frequency with every second beat of the lower, and so on. As the coincidence decreases in the ratios of the intervals their degree of fusion becomes increasingly smaller. This difference in coincidence of the different intervals results in differences in the consonance of the two tones, leading to differences in their degree of fusion.

Faist (19), following the method of Stumpf, sought to verify Stumpf's laws. His investigations confirm, in general, Stumpf's first law regarding the dependence of fusion upon the vibration ratio. But he finds some weaknesses in it, as for instance, that some simpler ratios which should show higher fusion, according to the law, are actually experienced as having lower fusion than some less simple ratios. The tritone is a case in point. Its ratio of 32:45 is more complex than is that of the seventh or second, yet its degree of fusion is found to be greater. Stumpf's second law is also found valid, but only within the limits of the seven octaves used in music. Above and below this range, exceptions to the rule are noticeable. But he disagrees with Stumpf's third law. Fusion, he claims, is not independent of the absolute intensity of the components. It is higher for weaker absolute intensity than for stronger absolute intensity of the same interval. More noticeable still is the dependence of fusion on the relative intensity of the components. If the relative intensity of the components remains the same, fusion is increased when their absolute intensity decreases. The fusion is greater when the higher tone is less intense than the lower. And the fusion significantly decreases when the lower tone is less intense than the higher tone.

Stumpf's fourth law Faist corroborates. But he does not accept the sixth law. His results show that intervals beyond the octave possess throughout lower fusion than the corresponding intervals within the octave. The fusion decreases in a progressive manner with the addition of higher octaves. Faist also finds that the addition of overtones increases the fusion of the higher degrees of fusion and decreases that of the lower degrees of fusion.

The most complete study of consonance thus far on record is that of Kemp (51). Kemp argues that the only possible method to investigate consonance is to consider it as a single collective impression. By specially directing the attention the phenomenon of fusion can be isolated from all other effects of tonal combinations. Fusion is a sensationally experimental event, just like the hearing of an overtone in a clang. It calls for a special act of attention on that one feature. When consonance is considered as a collective impression all the theories of consonance are seen as accompanying features more or less allied with fusion. They become its secondary criteria or landmarks. For instance, one landmark of fusion is the approximation of the tonal combination to numerical unity. Another is incompleteness of analysis of the combination, of whether the analysis is completely impossible, as in Stumpf's view, or is only very difficult, as Külpe maintains. Kemp states that every not entirely unmusical person recognizes even in the case of high degrees of fusion the presence of a multiplicity of impression, and by close attention he may even distinguish the two tones and shift attention from one to the other. But the singleness of impression of the tones nevertheless persists, and this the more so as the degree of fusion is greater. Approximation to numerical unity and incompleteness of analysis are therefore phases of each other, although it is possible to separate them in abstraction. But in practice it is questionable whether such isolation and abstraction are ever carried through.

Kemp enumerates three other phenomena of tonal combinations that are related to consonance in its pure sense, but each of them can be more readily isolated from it than unity of impression and incompleteness of analysis. These are sensory agreeableness, sensory conformity, and harmonic conformity. Sensory agreeableness means the feeling effect of the combination: whether pleasant or unpleasant. Sensory agreeableness and fusion are easily mistaken to be one and the same thing, but they are quite different effects, since the feeling effect of a certain interval may keep on changing with repetition, while its degree of fusion remains the same. Furthermore, a high degree of fusion may be pleasant to one person and unpleasant to another. Sensory conformity refers to the felt relationship of the two tones, whether or not they seem to agree with each other. In pure fusion attention is concentrated upon the collective impression of the total sound. But the experience is quite different when attention is fixed upon the single components and their relation to each other. Some simultaneous tones seek each other, strive towards each other, constitute a friendly relationship. Others clash and strive against each other. Tonal combinations also imply harmonic relationships, namely, that even an isolated combination calls for a resolution into another combination for its completion. And each combination finds its completion more so in some one combination than in any other.

In his own experiments Kemp called upon his observers to make a comparative judgment of the fusion of two tonal combinations. The instructions were: "You will hear two tonal-complexes whose degree of fusion you are to judge. You are to report whether you noticed a difference in the unity or oneness of the two complexes. Pay no attention to the musical content of what you hear, that is, as to what chord you hear or how many tones are present. Only get the general impression. Record your reactions as follows: (1) greater >, (2) equal =, (3) smaller <, (4) doubtful ?. Indicate failure to judge by —. Judge the second complex as compared with the first." The results are shown in the accompanying table.

From the table we see that there is predominant agreement among the observers. Only in a few cases are there deviations from a marked general uniformity of judgment. Furthermore, Kemp's results are in close agreement with the results obtained by other investigators for the ranking of the intervals on the basis of fusion. Octaves, fifths and fourths come first, then come the thirds and sixths, then the sevenths, and finally the seconds.

Table II. Showing Ranking of Fusion by Each Subject

A	B	C	F	D	E
Octave	Octave	Octave	Octave	Octave	Octave
5th	5th	5th	5th	5th	5th
4th	4th	4th	4th	4th	Maj. 3rd
Maj. 3rd	Maj. 3rd	Maj. 3rd	Maj. 3rd	Maj. 6th	4th
Min. 3rd	Min. 3rd	Min. 3rd	Min. 3rd	Min. 3rd	Maj. 6th
Maj. 6th	Min. 6th	Maj. 6th	Maj. 6th	Maj. 3rd	Min. 3rd
Min. 6th	Maj. 6th	Min. 6th	Min. 6th	Min. 6th	Tritone
Tritone	Tritone	Tritone	Tritone	Tritone	Min. 6th
Min. 7th	Maj. 2nd	Maj. 2nd	Maj. 2nd	Maj. 2nd	Min. 7th
Maj. 2nd	Min. 7th	Min. 7th	Min. 7th	Min. 7th	Maj. 2nd
Min. 2nd	Min. 2nd	Min. 2nd	Min. 2nd	Min. 2nd	Min. 2nd
Maj. 7th	Maj. 7th	Maj. 7th	Maj. 7th	Maj. 7th	Maj. 7th

In a further experiment Kemp asked his observers to judge intervals on the basis of agreeableness instead of fusion. They were to indicate which one of two intervals sounded the better, was more pleasant or less unpleasant. The results show that there is actually a difference between fusion and agreeableness, and that it is easy for observers to distinguish between the two. On the basis of agreeableness there is greater deviation among the observers than for fusion. In general, however, it is found that the major third is more pleasant than the minor third, the minor sixth, or the tritone; the major sixth is more pleasant than the minor third, the minor sixth, the fourth, or the tritone; while every interval is preferred to the tritone. The major third is more pleasant than the fourth, the minor sixth is preferred to the minor third, the fifth is better than the fourth and also the minor sixth.

For sensory conformity the sevenths came out poorest, and the fifth and major sixth best, with the major third next, then the minor third, the fourth and the minor sixth.

For harmonic conformity, the fifth and major third ranked highest, next came the minor third and major sixth, next the minor sixth and the fourth, and the tritone the lowest. It is to be understood here that harmonic conformity of isolated intervals is not identical with the resolution tendency of chords within a musical composition. The trend of a musical phrase may give an interval, that in isolation possesses harmonic completeness, an effect of incompleteness calling for resolution.

But, nevertheless, harmonic conformity is primarily a phenomenon of resolution.

TABLE III. SUMMARY TABLE OF CHARACTERISTICS OF TONAL COMBINATIONS FOR GRADE OF FUSION, SENSORY AGREEABLENESS SENSORY CONFORMITY, AND HARMONIC CONFORMITY

Fusion	S. A.	S. C.	H. C.
Fifth	Major third	Fifth	Fifth
	and		and
Fourth	Major sixth	Major third	Major third
		and	
Major third	Fifth	Major sixth	Major sixth
			and
The sixths	Fourth	Fourth	Minor third
	Minor sixth	Minor third	Fourth
and		and	and
Minor third	Minor third	Minor sixth	Minor sixth

Table IV shows that different criteria give different results for the same interval. When intervals are grouped into three classes according to these criteria, with highest grade indicated by I, middle by II, lowest by III, we get these results:

TABLE IV

	Fusion	S. A.	S. C.	H. C.
Fifth	I	I	I	I
Fourth	I	III	III	III
Major third	II	I	I	I
Minor third	III	III	III	I
Major sixth	III	I	I	I
Minor sixth	III	III	III	III

From this table we can see the complex nature of the consonance experience. It is not an elementary phenomenon. It presents mathematical, physical, and psychological phases. For the musical theorist and practitioner consonance is determined by musical values. For the hearer it is determined solely by agreeableness.

On the problem of fusion as a criterion of consonance Kemp concludes that the impression of fusion is modified by many circumstances, and that every change that a degree of fusion suffers is only apparent, namely, that it is only the apprehension of the fusion that changes, not the degree of fusion itself. Fusion, he holds, is a phenomenon to be experienced in its peculiarity only by attentive observation of the mass impression. Nor does he hold with Külpe that a difference in the degree of fusion of two tonal masses is only a difference in degree of difficulty of analysis. The essential point for Kemp is that the two masses are experienced as qualitatively different in their fusion.

Pratt (77) corroborates the findings of Kemp that consonance is a complex impression the components of which can be singled out only by a special act of attention and by careful instruction to the observers. Fusion, or unitariness of impression, is but one of these components. Others, according to Pratt, are smoothness, roughness, complexity or separateness of the components, pleasantness and unpleasantness, volume or fullness, and what he calls horrisonorousness, or vibrant qualitative roughness. Pratt describes each interval with respect to the various factors in the total impression which contribute to its constitution.

The octave is unique among the intervals in that it is the simplest, smoothest, least complex, and most pleasant interval. Those observers, however, who judged the interval musically found the octave about as pleasant as the fourth and fifth, and less pleasant than the sixths and thirds. By some the octave was also found to be more voluminous than the other intervals. The fifth was found to be about equal to the octave in smoothness, but slightly less simple. It was also less complex than any of the other intervals, excepting the octave, and was less pleasant than the octave. In volume it was more prominent than any other interval except the octave. The fourth was on an equal plane with the sixths in smoothness, with the sixths being a little less smooth than the fifths. In complexity only the octave and fifth were judged less complex than the fourth, while in simplicity the fourth was about equal to the fifth and minor sixth. On the basis of musical judgment the fourth was placed above the fifth and octave in pleasantness, but those who judged its pleasantness by smoothness placed it after the octave and fifth. In volume the fourth was like the sixths, which were exceeded in volume only by the fifth and octave. There was also a trace of horrisonorousness in this interval.

The minor sixth, like the fourth, was exceeded in smoothness only by the fifth and octave, but in complexity it stood next to the major sixth and the sevenths. Musically the minor sixth was more pleasant than any of the preceding intervals, but in smoothness it was less pleasant. In voluminousness it was exceeded only by the octave and fifth, while its horrisonorousness was like that of the fourth.

The major sixth was marked by complexity exceeded only by the sevenths, while in smoothness it was like the minor sixth and fourth. Musically only the thirds were more pleasant than the major sixth, while in smoothness it was like the minor sixth and fourth. Its volume was less, while its horrisonorousness was greater than for the preceding intervals.

The major third stood below the preceding intervals in smoothness. Only the minor third and the seconds were rougher. Its complexity was relatively marked, and its simplicity was below that of the octave, fifth, fourth, and sixth. Musically it was the most pleasant of intervals. Its horrisonorousness was very prominent, but it was almost lacking in volume. Next to the major third the minor third was the most pleasant, musically. But on the basis of smoothness it was rather unpleasant. It was prominent in roughness, being exceeded in this respect only by the seconds and major seventh. It was relatively non-complex, but its horrisonorousness was more marked than that for any other interval. The tritone was below the sixths in smoothness, and more complex than the seconds, but not so complex as the sixths and sevenths. Its feeling effect was indifferent, and its horrisonorousness rather well marked. The minor sixth was about as rough as the major third, with its complexity exceeded only by the major seventh. It was generally unpleasant and very voluminous. The major seventh was the roughest of intervals, with the exception of the seconds, as well as the most complex. It was also the most unpleasant of the intervals, and had marked horrisonorousness. The major second was very unpleasant and rough, exceeded only by the minor second, which was the roughest and most unpleasant of all. But it was non-complex, since its component qualities could not be isolated.

It is noticeable from Pratt's results that the thirds and sixths varied more in rank order by the different criteria than did the octave, fifth, and fourth. Even on the criterion of fusion there was considerable agreement on the ranks of the octave, fifth, fourth and seconds, but the position of the sixths, thirds, and sometimes the minor seventh, varied in different experiments. The sixths and thirds, and perhaps also the sevenths, seem to be the most equivocal of the intervals. That is, their position varied more with the attitude of the observer than the positions of the other intervals.

For fusion the rank order for Pratt's results was: octave, fifth, fourth, minor sixth, major sixth, major third, minor third, minor seventh, tritone, major seventh, major second, minor second.

OTHER THEORIES OF CONSONANCE

Helmholtz (38) accounts for consonance on the basis of the beats of the upper partials. Dissonance results when the whole mass of sound of the two musical tones is broken up into pulses of tone so that the joint effect is rough. In some combinations having certain pitch ratios either no beats at all are present, or they are of such small intensity that they produce no unpleasant disturbance of the united sound. These form consonances. The criterion for consonance is thus the relative smoothness of the tonal combination as determined by beats. On this criterion Helmholtz calls the octave, twelfth, and double octave the most perfect consonances, because in these combinations the prime tone of one of the combinations coincides with some partial tone of the other. Next in perfection of consonance belong the fifth and fourth, "because they may be used in all parts of the scale without any important disturbance of harmoniousness." (38, p. 194) Of the two, the fourth is, however, the less perfect consonance. The major sixth and the major third come next as medial consonances. For these intervals the disturbance of the harmoniousness in lower parts of the scale is very noticeable, but in the higher positions it disappears because the beats are too rapid to be noticeable. The minor third, minor sixth and subminor or natural seventh are the imperfect consonances. The other intervals are dissonances.

Helmholtz shows that almost all writers on musical theory have proposed an order of consonance similar to his own as deduced by him from the theory of beats. All put the unison and octave as being the most perfect of all consonances, next the fifth, and then the fourth. Regarding the position of the sixths and thirds there is considerable diversity. The thirds were first included among the consonances by Franco of Cologne towards the end of the twelfth century. His order of intervals was: unison and octave as perfect consonances, fifth and fourth as medial consonances, major and minor thirds as imperfect consonances, major and minor sixths as imperfect dissonances, and minor second, augmented fourth, major and minor sevenths as perfect dissonances. In the thirteenth and fourteenth centuries the sixths began to be included among the consonances by musicians. Two writers of this period, Philip de Vitrey and Jean de Muris, call the unison, octave and fifth the perfect consonances, and the thirds and sixths the imperfect consonances, with de Vitrey calling the major third and sixth more perfect than the minor third and sixth. The fourth is not mentioned.

Brues (8), like Kemp and Pratt, finds that the experience of consonance is the resultant of an interplay of various aspects of the interval, that it is a configuration of a multiplicity of factors, one of which is fusion or unitariness of impression. Others are roughness, richness, brightness, and coherence.

Ogden (66) finds the basis of consonance in the harmonic series of partials. He bases his harmonic theory of consonance on what he considers to be a significant fact, namely, that the consonant intervals are the ones that are most conspicuous among the partials of a tone. Thus, in a tone containing 16 partials the octave occurs 8 times, the fifth and fourth 4 times, the major third and major sixth 3 times, the minor third and minor sixth 2 times. No dissonant interval occurs more than once. Therefore, the interval most frequently occurring in the harmonic series is also the one most frequently heard, and becomes the most consonant, since we are most used to hearing it. Consonance "depends upon a dispositional readiness to perceive as a uniform impression any simultaneous combination of tones embracing intervals that have been frequently encountered as inherited and individual adaptations." (66, p. 144) It is, according to Ogden, "an integration of tones in intervals which in the course of racial experience have occurred together so often that the acts of grouping them, and then setting them aside from the more variable components of the sound-mass, have furnished an important basis for auditory discrimination." (66, p. 148)

A theory very similar to that of Ogden is advanced by Redfield (80). Every musical tone is in reality a chord because it is constituted of a series of partials. Redfield calls this the Chord of Nature. This Chord of Nature contains theoretically every partial in the harmonic series, while the partials are weaker the higher they are in the series. Therefore the lower partials impress themselves more strongly upon the ear than do the upper partials. Some partials are so high that they become inaudible. For this reason, the interval formed by the first and second partials, the octave, would be the most familiar to the ear, and also the first to be used in polyphonic music. Next would come the interval between the second and third partials, or the fifth, and so on. Redfield shows how this is what actually happened in the history of music, namely, that the first concerted singing was in octaves, then came singing in fifths. Singing in octaves and fifths produced parts at an interval of a fourth, so that fifths and fourths entered music together. Next came the major third, which is the fourth interval of the harmonic series. With the introduction of the fifth there came the fourth as its complement within the octave, and the introduction of the major third into the octave and into the fifth brought the minor third as its complement within the fifth, the minor sixth as its complement within the octave, and the major sixth as the complement of the minor third within the octave. "We see, then, that the order in which the intervals are found in the harmonic series agrees at all points with the order in which these intervals were historically accepted by the ear in concerted music. The historical development of harmony up to the present time would appear, then, to have been determined by the relative strength of the partials found in the musical tone." (p. 76)

The question whether consonance is influenced if not determined, by habituation was tested experimentally by Moore (63). He found that the consonance of an interval increased with repetition, so that each interval underwent a development from dissonance to a high degree of consonance, with a corresponding affective value, at each stage of its historical progress. Consonance, then, according to Moore, is a historical or cultural acquisition, in that each interval began its historical journey as a dissonance, underwent a relatively short transition period, and then began its gradual development as a consonance.

Some students hold, furthermore, that the consonance of an interval is inseparable from its musical context, namely, tonic effects, anticipated resolutions, and harmonic associations. The judgment of the listener is affected by the present or implied sequence of the interval, that is, whether or not it calls for a resolution. Consonance is associated with a feeling of rest, dissonance with that of unrest. An interval is dissonant when it arouses a feeling of dissatisfaction, calling for further motion towards something satisfactory. Helmholtz implies this view of consonance-dissonance when he writes that dissonances are used partly as a "means of contrast, to give prominence to the impression made by consonances, and partly means of expression, not merely for peculiar and isolated emotional disturbances, but generally to heighten the impression of musical progress and impetuosity, because when the ear has been distressed by dissonances it longs to return to the calm current of consonances." (38, p. 331)

Heinlein (36) has investigated this aspect of consonance experimentally by using the intervals of the Seashore consonance test. He gave the test to 35 male college students and repeated it after a ten-minute intermission. The students did not know that the second test was a repetition of the first. The purpose of the procedure was to see whether there would occur a change in the judgment for the various intervals, and, if so, whether such changes were due to resolution. If resolution does have its effect upon judgment, then certain types of judgment reversals can be expected to occur. For instance, the major third and the fourth are both consonant intervals. By itself each produces the feeling of repose. But when combined as a progression from major third to fourth we pass harmonically from a dominant position to a tonic position, from tension to repose, so that the fourth becomes the more consonant interval. But when the process is reversed and the succession is that from the fourth to the major third we pass from the subdominant to the tonic, and the fourth is now the interval of tension and the major third becomes the reposeful interval and therefore the more consonant. Heinlein's results show this to be the case. Whether the major third or the fourth is preferred as the more consonant of the two intervals depends on how they succeed each other. The need for resolution seems to determine the consonance-dissonance status of the interval.

The historical aspect of consonance was studied in detail by Guernsey (30) in reference to the dissonance tendencies in modern music. Among the problems attacked in this study were: (1) a comparison of the judgments of all the musical intervals of the tempered scale according to (a) fusion, (b) smoothness, (c) pleasantness-unpleasantness; (2) a comparison of the judgments of musically untrained subjects, those with a moderate amount of musical training, and very highly trained musical performers.

She found that the rankings of the intervals on fusion and smoothness were approximately the same. For fusion the order was, octave, fifth, major sixth, fourth, major third, minor third, minor sixth, minor seventh, diminished fifth, major seventh, major second, minor second. For smoothness it was octave, fourth, fifth, major third, major sixth, minor third, minor seventh, minor sixth, diminished fifth, major seventh, major second, minor second. The ranking by the moderately trained and highly trained was practically the same. The highly trained found it difficult, however, to exclude from their judgments the comparison of the given interval with the mental image of various other intervals or with a previously heard interval. Thus, an organist wrote that, "it is hard to say whether a major seventh is 'smooth' without having an actual context or supplying it with an imaginary one." The untrained had no such difficulty. They were not inclined to analyze each interval nor to confuse the feeling with the sensory element.

The influence of sequence upon a judgment was noticeable. When a unison followed another interval than an octave it was frequently called an octave, and vice versa. An octave preceded by a second or major seventh was much more likely to be heard as one tone than if preceded by a fourth or fifth. When a second followed an octave or a unison it was practically always perceived as two tones, and often as four or five.

For degree of pleasantness there was a striking difference in the ranking of the intervals by the three groups of observers. For the untrained the order was: major sixth, major third, fourth, octave, minor third, minor sixth, minor seventh, diminished fifth, major seventh, major second, minor second. For the moderately trained it was: major third, major sixth, fourth, minor sixth, minor third, fifth, minor seventh, octave, diminished fifth, major second, major seventh, minor second. For the highly trained the ranking was: major sixth, fourth, major third, minor third, minor sixth, minor seventh, diminished fifth, major second, major seventh, fifth, octave, minor second.

The very significant conclusions from this study are best presented in the author's own words.

> It remains the difficult task of the aesthetician, who in this case must be primarily a psychologist, to arbitrate this feud of inconsistency. The solution herewith appended is no panacea, but strictly a mongrel and a compromise, based on the observable facts at hand. It would read as follows: (1) Consonance is an aesthetic description, totally dynamic in nature, and is not a scientifically determinable constant. (2) Its perception is conditioned by (a) natural sensory processes, within very wide limits, and (b) the empirical factors of training, environment, musical context, etc. The lower limit of these sensory processes is represented by the minor second, which appears to be universally unpleasant, even with highly trained subjects, and any smaller intervals potential in quarter-tone and eighth-tone scales which incur a *consciousness* of beats. These beats may not be in themselves unpleasant, but they distract attention from the sound as such and consequently detract from the purity of the tonal experience. They are,

in fact, directly comparable to the pulsations of the lowest tones from pipe organs, which, if unrelieved over a long period of time, become an excessive strain and inhibit the thematic impressions of the music. If the objection be raised that these beats disappear under conditions of monaural clang perception it may be stated in turn that without radically different evolutionary tendencies or the universal indulgence in some sort of intricate aural contrivances, sound and music will continue to be perceived binaurally. In light of present evidence, however, it is possible that, could its beats be somehow filtered out, the interval of a minor second might very well become a consonance. (3) Fusion is apparently a simple sensory process, and on the basis of the Helmholtz theory in particular, may be legitimately classified as perfect, imperfect, and very imperfect. It may be a criterion of smoothness, and vice versa, but not of consonance, unless the real derivation and meaning of consonance is in turn arbitrarily identified with simple sensory summation. Fusion, apparently, would fit Malmberg's definition as a "purely cognitive process," whereas consonance will not. Not only the data from extensive experimentation, but the voluntary negations and involuntary admissions (witness the number of times the investigators speak of dissonance as "unpleasant") would indicate that feeling cannot be outlawed as a major component of consonance. The romantic and even political struggle of the major and minor thirds and sixths toward their present high place in our affection, to say nothing of our frequent song-endings in the plaintive diminished seventh, are indisputable evidence for the contention that what we regard as pleasant we also regard as consonant. This attitude, in turn, is a composite social heritage from our entire racial past, and our entire musical present, and is aesthetically and psychologically legitimate so long as its expression does not transcend obvious physical and physiological limitations.

Musical theory and aesthetic principle, as well as the psychology of music, are hence confronted with difficulty in fundamental terms. If we speak of "dissonant" music, we are really combining antonyms; if we speak of "consonant" music in the traditional, narrow sense of the term, we have left no name for the bulk of composition since Wagner's *Tannhäuser* overture set its first audience hissing. The proper compromise, therefore, would seem for us to revert to linguistic purism, and classify consonance, always historically in terms of its original synonym, *i.e., harmony*. Hull, who is prominent among musical theorists, states definitely that all the text-book laws of harmony must be modified in this respect. If musicians are willing to remold their traditional architectural structure, psychological theories of music must likewise concede expansion of their terms and tenets.

The import of this discussion, applied to practical music, is tolerance. Tolerance ordinarily leads to interest, interest to knowledge, and knowledge to catholicity of taste. This tolerance must at the same time be intelligent enough to recognize that these new harmonic values exist because they have evolved or diverged from known values, and that evolution does not imply discarding the classic for the new, though it may represent a shift in affection. It is not that we fail to understand the simple "consonant" music of Haydn or Palestrina, but that we, as modern listeners, prefer in general the rich complexity and emotional vitality of Tchaikowsky or Rachmaninoff as more in harmony with the complex texture of our civilization. "Ultra" modern composers have merely stretched their affections one degree farther, to include the kaleidoscopic subtlety and diffuse tone color of hitherto forbidden intervals. Judging them by their own standards, which are obviously not the old, inadequate "laws" of consonance, we may conclude that "dissonance" is reduced to consonant relativity, and their music violates neither psychological principles nor aesthetic standards. (30, pp. 202-204)

CONCORDS AND DISCORDS

A consonant chord is a concord, a dissonant chord is a discord. Almost all investigators who studied the phenomenon of consonance in intervals have also something to say about concordance.

According to Helmholtz (38), a concord results when each tone of the chord forms a consonance with each of the other tones. If any two tones of a chord would not form a consonant interval there would be beats, and the chord would be a discord. "Concords of three tones are readily found by taking two consonant intervals to any one fundamental tone as c, and then seeing whether the new third interval between the two new tones, which is thus produced, is also consonant. If this is the case each one of the three tones forms a consonant interval with each one of the other two, and the chord is consonant, or is a concord." (38, p. 211)

When a triad is inverted its harmony depends upon the consonance of its constituent intervals. Thus the triad c–e–g contains a fifth, a major third, and a minor third. The triad e–g–c′ is composed of a fourth, a minor third, and a minor sixth. The triad g–c′–e has for its components a fourth, a major third, and a major sixth. What is the relative concordance of these triads? According to Helmholtz, the fourth is less agreeable than the fifth and the minor thirds and sixths are less agreeable than the major thirds and sixths. Therefore, for intervals in just intonation, thirds and sixths disturb the harmoniousness more than do the fourths, so that the major chords of the sixth and fourth are more harmonious than the chords in the fundamental position, while the latter are more harmonious than the chords of the sixth and third. But the minor chords of the sixth and third are more agreeable than those in the fundamental position, and these are better than the minor chords of the sixth and fourth. All this is true only so long as the chords are isolated. Any modulational connections, as in a concluding cadence, introduce a factor which modifies the effect. Furthermore, since in the lower parts of the scale either major or minor thirds are more disagreeable than sixths, these laws for chords hold only for the middle part of the scale.

The difference between major and minor triads Helmholtz explains in terms of combination tones. We should expect that the major and minor triads would sound equally well because each has a fifth and a major and minor third. But the minor triad is quite decidedly less harmonious than the major triad. This is due to the difference in the combination tones of the two triads. When two intervals are compounded the combination tones can produce beats even though each interval separately has no beats. Now in the major triads some of the combination tones are merely doubles of the tones of the triad in lower octaves while others are extremely weak. But in minor triads some of the combination tones are easily audible and begin to disturb the harmoniousness of the triad, because they do not belong to the harmony. Thus, in the minor triad, c–e♭–g some of the combination tones give the dissonances a♭ b♭ c, which do not belong to the harmony of the triad. Whereas this disturbing action of combination tones of minor triads is not marked enough to make them discords, they nevertheless produce a sensible increase in roughness as compared with the effect of major chords.

Kemp (51) studied the relative fusion of two and three tonal combinations by comparing intervals of high degree of fusion with chords containing intervals of high degree of fusion, intervals of low fusion with chords of low fusion, and intervals of low fusion with chords of high fusion. For instance, he compared c–g with c–e–g or c–e with c–e–g; c–b with c–g–b; c–b with c–e–g. He found that: (1) intervals of high fusion produce an effect of higher fusion than chords of high fusion; (2) intervals of low fusion appear more fused than chords of low fusion, (3) but intervals of very low fusion are less fused than chords of high fusion.

Kemp also compared chords with each other. His results were: (1) Chords, like intervals, produce a unified impression of fusion. Practiced observers can notice the fusion and compare its degrees, but not so easily as that of intervals. The various degrees of fusion of chords approximate each other more so than is the case with intervals. (2) Major triads have higher fusion than minor triads. (3) When the constituent intervals of two triads have equal fusion, the triad in which the lower interval is more fused will also have the higher fusion. (4) The fusion of chords is more dependent on the size of the intervals than is the case with intervals. (5) The degree of the fusion of a chord of low fusion is determined by the lowest degree of fusion in it. (6) An interval gains in degree of fusion when it becomes an ingredient of a chord. This is indicated by the fact that it is very difficult to isolate an interval from within a chord. (7) The agreeableness of an interval is modified when it becomes an ingredient of a chord.

Pear (74) conducted an experimental investigation on some differences between the major and minor chords. His purpose was to obtain some data on two theories. One of them bases the difference on whether the relationship of the tones of the chord is direct or indirect. Tones have a direct relationship when they possess some partials in common, the greater the number of common partials the greater being the direct relationship. They are indirectly related when the tones are referable to a common fundamental tone. The nearer that the common fundamental of the tones is to the fundamentals of each of the tones the greater is their indirect relationship.

Pear proceeded to apply this relationship to the major and minor chords c–e–g and c–e♭–g. The first common overtone of c–e–g is the ninth, namely, g. It lies three octaves and a third above the fundamental of the highest tone. The first common overtone of c–e♭–g is the third overtone of g. It lies a double octave above g. The distances of the common fundamentals of the two chords from c stand in a reverse relation, so that the minor chord shows the greater direct, and the major chord the greater indirect, relationship.

The other theory, advanced by Külpe, holds that the degree of fusion of a chord varies with the position of its constituent degrees of fusion. It decreases when the worse degrees are the lower, and decreases when they are the higher. In the minor chord, the poorer degree of fusion, c–e♭, is the lower, and the better, e♭–g, is the higher. In the major chord the reverse is the case, hence the higher fusion of the major chord.

The purpose of Pear's experiment was to examine these two points of view. He examined the second theory first. "The major chord c–e–g, is built up by combining the intervals c–e and e–g. Keeping the terminal notes, c and g, constant, and inverting the positions in the chord of the major third and minor third, we obtain the minor chord c–e♭–g. If, in the observer's opinion, the major third possesses a higher degree of fusion than the minor third, then . . . if Külpe's assumption is correct, the chord c–e–g will be judged as exhibiting a higher degree of fusion than the chord c–e♭–g. For a similar reason the chord c–g–c′ will be more highly fused than c–f–c, which has been made by inverting the position of the fifth and fourth in c–g–c." (74, p. 59)

To test this assumption Pear selected chords for judgment which were composed of intervals possessing very high and very low degrees of fusion and intervals possessing practically no fusion, that is, chords which never or seldom occur in ordinary music. "By taking a musical or unmusical chord of three tones, and (with the terminal notes constant) inverting the position of the intervals within the chord, we form a pair of chords, in which the relative grades of total fusion can then be determined. Knowing the relative fusion-grades of the upper and lower intervals in the chord, we can examine the influence of the relative position of the constituent intervals upon the total fusion of the chord which is formed by them." (74, p. 60)

Pear draws four conclusions from his data: (1) that the theory that the degree of fusion of a chord decreases when the worst of its constituent degrees of fusion is the lower, and increases when it is the upper, is justified; (2) that a chord in which the wider interval, in the physical sense, occupies the lower position is more fused than a chord in which the larger interval occupies the higher position; (3) that the higher degree of fusion of the major chord over the minor chord is correlated with the fact that the major chord possesses a greater degree of indirect relationship than does the minor chord formed from it; (4) that the theory that the greater the simplicity of the ratios of the frequencies of the constituent tones of a chord the greater is the fusion of the chord is supported by the experimental evidences.

CHAPTER 4

THE VARIETIES OF MUSICAL EFFECTS: IDEATIONAL

THE EFFECT OF MUSIC ON THE human being has ever been a fascinating field for speculation and experimentation. History and literature abound with accounts of wonders worked by music, poets sing of its beneficial results, while several attempts have been made to investigate the matter experimentally. We shall survey this literature from the effects of single tones, through tonal combinations, to composition as a whole.

THE EFFECT OF TONES AND KEYS

We have already seen in a previous connection that tones of different pitch produce a variety of effects in the different sensory fields. Low tones are soft, mild, dull, massive, heavy, sluggish, while high tones are pointed, sharp, cutting, shrill, penetrating, thin, bright. Tones are also described as sweet, sour, smooth, rough, caressing, colorless, full, empty, rich, poor, and numerous other characterizations. Composers utilize low registers to depict situations that are dark, threatening, stormy, gloomy, and the higher registers for opposite effects.

There is a considerable amount of literature, both speculative and experimental, regarding the effects of the different keys.

In the *Politics*, Aristotle states that in "poetry and music there are limitations of manners; and this is evident, for different harmonies differ from each other so much by nature, that those who hear them are differently affected, and are not in the same disposition of mind when one is performed as when another is; the one, for instance, occasions grief and contracts the soul, as the Mixolydian: others soften the mind, and as it were dissolve the heart: others fix it in a firm and settled state, such is the power of the Doric music only; while the Phrygian fills the soul with enthusiasm, as has been well described by those who have written philosophically upon this part of education; for they bring examples of what they advance from the things themselves."

Schumann, on the other hand, denies "that this or that feeling, in order to be correctly expressed in music, must be translated in but one especial key (anger, for example, in C sharp minor), so that we can agree with Zeiter, who declares that any feeling may be expressed in any key. The poet Schubart professed to have found in some keys the characteristic expression of some feelings. Though a great deal of poetic tenderness is to be found in his characterization, though he was the first to signalize the great differences that exist between the major and minor scales, there is too much small description, epithet, and specification in his work . . . though this would be well enough were it all correctly applied. For instance, he calls E minor a girl dressed in white with a rose-coloured breast-knot. In G minor he finds discontent, discomfort, worrying, anxiety about an unsuccessful plan, ill-tempered gnawing at the bit."

Gurney (33) speaks to the same effect: "Particular keys are sometimes credited with definable emotional powers. That certain faint differences exist between them on certain instruments is undeniable, though it is a difference which only exceptional ears detect. The relations between the notes of every key being identical, every series of relations presenting every sort of describable or indescribable character will of course be accepted by the ear in any key, or if it is a series which modulates through a set of several keys, in any set of similarly related keys. But as it must have a highest and a lowest note, it will be important, especially in writing for a particular instrument, to choose such a key that these notes shall not be inconvenient or impossible; and also the mechanical difficulties of an instrument may make certain keys preferable for certain passages. Subject to correction from considerations of this sort, the composer probably generally chooses the key in which the germ of his work first flashes across his mind's eye; and when the music has once been seen and known, written in a certain key, the very look of it becomes so associated with itself that the idea of changing the key may produce a certain shock. But the cases are few indeed where, had the music been first presented to anyone's ears in a key differing by a semi-tone from that in which it actually stands, he would have perceived the slightest necessity for alteration; and as a matter of fact, when a bit of music is thought over, or hummed, or whistled, unless by a person of exceptionally gifted ear, it is naturally far oftener than not in some different key to that in which it has been written and heard. Even the difference most commonly alleged, between C major as bright and strong and D flat as soft and veiled, comes to almost absolutely nothing when a bright piece is played in D flat or a dreamy one in C." (33, p. 318, note)

The most common effect of keys is found to be in the realm of color vision. The diatonic scale has been compared with the seven colors of the color spectrum, and a color scale has been suggested for the scale of C, namely, C – red, D – orange, E – yellow, F – green, G – blue, A – indigo, B – violet.

Katz (50) reports the following rare case of association between keys and colors for a subject he calls Herr S.: F major is dull white; F sharp major is silver white; E flat major, brilliant snow white; D major, yellowish white; B major, gold; B flat major, yellow; A major, dull yellow; E major, bright gray; A flat major, dark gray; G major, black; C major, deep black; C minor, dark green; F sharp minor, brilliant green (grass green); F minor, dull green; E flat minor, whitish green; E minor, gray green; A minor, brown with green; B minor, dark red; C sharp major, rose red; B flat minor, brownish red; D minor, chocolate brown; C sharp minor, red brown; G sharp minor, brown; G minor, brown with orange.

Another person reported to the same investigator that G major was somewhat green; A major, rose; E major, red; F major, intense yellow; D minor, pale gray; C major, bright white; A minor, deep blue-violet.

The most recent, and probably the most thorough, study of color-music is reported by Karwaski and Odbert (49). These investigators found no direct relationship between color and music which held for more than a small number of individual subjects. But in spite of this variability, certain general relationships of photism to special aspects of music were found to recur constantly. Thus, increase in brightness tends to accompany rise in pitch or quickening of tempo. Graceful lines accompany smooth music, while jagged lines accompany staccato passages or syncopations. For some subjects, position and direction in the visual field vary with pitch, while for others the background color varies with the first notes or with the key of the selection. The area of the photisms sometimes expands with an increase in the volume of the music. Colors may fit the mood of the music, or its pleasantness, or the timbre of the instrument. Karwaski and Odbert conclude that colored hearing is a complex phenomenon in which several factors contribute in very different degrees to the experience of different individuals. And whereas some one factor like strong visual imagery, or cultural influences, or suggestions, may be dominant in some individuals and another in others, none of them appear to operate in any pure and simple fashion.

A most detailed account of the effects of the different tonalities is given by Power (75). For him, C major expresses feeling in a pure, certain and decisive manner, and also innocence, powerful resolve, manly earnestness, and deep religious feeling. G major expresses sincerity of faith, quiet love, calm meditation, simple grace, pastoral life, and certain humor and brightness. G minor is sometimes sad, but sometimes it is expressive of quiet and sedate joy, and occasionally it rises to a romantic elevation. A major is full of confidence and hope, radiant with love, and redolent of simple, genuine cheerfulness. It excels all the other keys in portraying sincerity of feeling. A minor is expressive of tender, womanly feeling and sentiments of devotion mingled with pious resignation. B major expresses, in fortissimo, boldness and pride, in pianissimo, purity and the most perfect clearness. B minor is a melancholy key, and tells of quiet expectation and patient hope. Nervous persons are said to be affected by that key sooner than by any other. F sharp major sounds brilliant and exceedingly clear, while as G flat major it expresses softness coupled with richness. F sharp minor is dark, mysterious, spectral, and full of passion. A flat major is full of feeling, and replete with a dreamy depression. F major is full of peace and joy, but also expresses effectively a light, passing regret, a mournful, but not a deeply sorrowful feeling. It is, moreover, available for the expression of religious sentiment. F minor is especially full of melancholy, at times rising into passion.

THE EFFECTS OF INTERVALS AND MOTIFS

In Robert Browning's "A Toccata of Galuppi's" there is a description of the effects of several intervals.

> What? Those lesser thirds so plaintive, sixths diminished, sigh on sigh,
> Told them something? Those suspensions, those solutions —'Must we die?'
> Those commiserating sevenths—'Life might last! we can but try!'
>
> 'Were you happy?'—'Yes.'—'And are you still as happy?' —'Yes. And you?'
> —'Then, more kisses!'—'Did I stop them, when a million seemed so few?'
> Hark! the dominant's persistence, till it must be answered to!

In a study on the aesthetic appreciation of musical intervals among school children and adults, Valentine (112) found that the major third is most frequently mentioned as being melodious, sad, and soothing. The minor third is soothing, mournful, solemn, refined, dreamy. For the seconds, the major is described as sad or plaintive twice as often as the minor. The octave is indifferent, tame, dull, thin, skinny, but also bold, bright, stormy, cheerful, restful. Marked individual differences are found for the major and minor sixths, but there is a distinct tendency for the intervals to be felt as sad or solemn. The fourth and fifth are indifferent, ordinary, unimpressive.

Edmonds and Smith (18) report that the terms used by their subjects in describing the qualitative effects of the major intervals of the diatonic scale are primarily those relating to taste and touch. The octave is smooth, like smooth ice cream or smooth molasses, and also smooth like polished glass; the seventh is astringent, like the feel of a green persimmon, or harsh, like fine sandpaper. The sixth is luscious, like a juicy, succulent fruit; the fifth is dilute, like a clear soup, also coarse, like tweed suiting; the fourth is rich, like whipped cream or like ripe cantaloupe, and also harsh, like crushed paper or crash; the third is mellow, like a ripe but not juicy fruit; the second is gritty, like corn flakes, or pebbly, like pebbles in the fingers. The most common description which was given of the fifth was hollow.

The most comprehensive and detailed study on the expressive value of intervals is that by Huber (45). He asked twelve subjects, most of them musical, to listen passively to a given interval, ask themselves what the interval "said," and report the result. The same interval "said" different things to different hearers, but all the effects produced could be gathered into five classes:

1. The character effect—in which a human mood or trait is ascribed to the interval, like colorless, dull, fiery, earnest, secretive.

2. The informing effect—in which the motif issues a call, warning or plea, as an outcry of grief, a yearning, crying question, a fiery declaration, a reproach.

3. The movement or happening effect—like withdrawing fretfully, a desire to hide, climbing up, vigorously stepping forward, pleasant feeling of gliding, painful climbing.

4. Perceptual imagery effect—"I saw a man in military uniform lying on the shore of the sea, dead or wounded"; "Happy people frolicking on the green meadow"; "Small girls gently dancing in a garden"; "See a man in a cowl blowing a horn"; "Picture of an approaching storm, one hears the first thunder"; "The easy, sure movements of a bird rising from the ground."

5. The atmospheric effect—"Had the feeling as if the interval belonged to a story about knighthood of the middle ages, taking place on the sea. I saw a knight standing on a rock looking over the sea. It is darksome and the sea is restless"; "Mood of a shepherd idyl; peace and midday heat"; "The atmosphere of a simple folk song or hymn."

Huber also classifies the kind of meaning conveyed by an interval into sensory, emotional, and ideational. In the sensory field, auditory content, as loud-soft, dull-shrill, quiet, sonorous, occurred 118 times; tactual content, as dull, pointed, soft, hard, sharp, cutting, pressing, heavy, penetrating, 22 times; spatial content, as full, empty, voluminous, broad, thick thin, 13 times; visual content, as bright, dark, light, sunny, dusk, silvery, 113 times; and color, 60 times.

The varieties of emotional content are all of the nature of moods; namely, joyful, solemn, sad, sorrowful, melancholy, happy, satisfied, exciting, reposeful, bitter. Ascending intervals are more often conducive to positive feeling content than descending intervals. The same is true of consonant intervals versus dissonant intervals.

The ideational content is either that of calls and signals, or asking and answering questions. The frequency with which the various intervals are mentioned to possess a signal or call content is: octave–6, major seventh–2, minor seventh–2, major sixth–9, minor sixth–7, fifth–12, tritone–3, fourth–4, major third–5, minor third–4, major second–0, minor second–0, prime–6. The intervals also differ in the type of question raised. The interval d♭–d is an uncertain question, a–b a weeping question, e–f an indifferent question, a♭–b♭ asks "where to" earnestly, f–b "what will happen," c♯–g astonished question.

Huber concludes that the definiteness of meaning of an interval depends upon the degree to which it is felt to constitute a unitary impression. Consonances are therefore more definite in meaning than dissonances. And since three-tone successions are more difficult to grasp as unitary impressions than two-tone successions, the former are more indefinite in meaning than the latter. This would imply that a musical melody has less definite meaning as a whole than have its single intervals.

In two studies (102, 103) Sterzinger concerned himself with the rhythmic and aesthetic characteristics of the intervals of the major scale. The first investigation showed that intervals produce a rhythmical impression, but that they differ in the degree of rhythmical definiteness. Further, there is a definite relationship between definiteness of rhythm and the pleasantness of the interval. In the second study he sought for a more definite description of the rhythmic and aesthetic characteristics of intervals and the reasons for the relationship between the two.

Sterzinger finds ten factors that determine the rhythmic definiteness of intervals, derived from the reports of subjects regarding the relative definiteness of impression produced upon them by two successively presented tones. They are, size of interval, direction, dynamic impression, volume, trend toward a goal tone, finality, harmony, pleasantness, novelty, and clarity. Thus, of the two intervals c–d, c–e, the second is reported as more definite than the first because the second tone of the second interval is higher and brighter. Of c–b, c–d, the second is more pronounced, has a stronger beat, is more dynamic. Of c–b, c–g, the first interval has more dynamic energy, pulls toward a more definite goal. Of c–e, c–f, the second is more pronounced because more final. Of c–a, c–c′, the first is more definite because its second tone is more novel and fresh.

A comparison of the rhythmic definiteness of the intervals shows that the major second is not very definite because both tones are too much alike. The major third is similar in this respect to the major second. It has no special rhythmic character and is tiresome. The fourth is reported by most subjects to possess the greatest rhythmical definiteness, because it has fullness, body, consonance and finality. The fifth is indifferent because it does not have any goal. The major sixth is described by musical subjects as the interval of spirituality. It has fullness, is rhythmical, and carries meaning. The strong dissonance of the major seventh influences its rhythmical character in different ways for different subjects. For some the dissonance gives the interval a marked rhythmic effect, but for the musical the effect is the reverse. The rhythmical character of the octave is influenced by its consonance and finality. Its rhythmic effect depends upon which of these two features strikes the hearer. As a whole, its rhythmic character is lower than that of the sixth, whereas, due to its pleasantness and its finality, it is preferred to the seventh.

The reasons for the aesthetic preference of intervals are many. Unity of impression, or harmoniousness of the two tones, is mentioned most often, particularly so by the less musical. Next comes sensory pleasantness. The finality of the interval is also very influential. Other influential factors are mildness of the interval, fullness, size, clarity, freshness or uniqueness, direction, and rhythmic definiteness. Some of these factors operate together. For instance, small intervals are fuller than larger ones, but clarity and freshness, increase with size.

Aesthetically, the major second is at times described as dark, warm, quiet, pleasant; at other times as simple, tonal, sober. The major third is comfortable, pleasant, warm, and compared with the second, it is lively and bright. The fourth is harmonious, unitary, final, positive, definite, energetic, and contains numerous musical possibilities. The fifth is pleasant, clear, smooth, but also empty, expressionless, hard, thin. The sixth is fresh, lively, bright, lovable, soft, clear, but it is also described as a combination of hardness and lovingness. The seventh is ugly, empty, hard, but is also found by some to be pure, clear, lively, and interesting. The octave is, for some, pleasant, pure, final, fresh, bright, and clear; for others it is hard, thin, and too large.

Sterzinger offers the following general conclusions from his studies: (1) The degree of definiteness of musical intervals is determined by their fullness or volume and by tonal distance. (2) Consonance decreases the effect of an interval. (3) Volume operates quantitatively and tonal distance operates by accent. (4) There are three types of subjects: those who prefer intervals of greater volume, those who prefer intervals of greater distance, those who prefer intervals of medium distance. The tendency is, in general, towards the last type. (5) The character of intervals is determined by the higher of the component tones, the distance between the tones, and the consonance of the tones.

THE EFFECTS OF MUSICAL COMPOSITIONS

The first experimental approach to the problem of musical expressiveness was made by Gilman (29) in several studies. In one study he compared his own reactions to a Beethoven composition with those of twenty listeners. To him the music conveyed the impression of intense labor amid deep gloom, repeatedly directed toward a single achievement without progress. He found, however, that none of the other listeners agreed with him. Nearly half of the listeners did report the music to be more or less tinged with depressed emotion, as melancholy, disheartening, sad, restless, yearning, regretful, weird, but several felt it to be neutral and others serene and buoyant. None found it to be intensely energetic, some reporting mild energy and others as involving no activity at all. Similar differences appeared among the listeners regarding the other alleged meanings of the composition.

Gilman's comment on these results is that the selection "expresses simply recurrent activity without progress, whether grave or gay, intense or mild, purposive or purposeless—all being indeterminate. The determinations of those points in the above formula as well as in the judgments obtained are, it is indicated, mythical creations, which in my mind have grown up around the piece in the course of long acquaintance with it, and which in the listeners' minds have been evoked by the first impact of the music." But if recurrent activity is all that the music expresses "it is a question whether it should be said to have any expressiveness at all, for it may be claimed that this much is *in* the music itself. It is recurrently active, and at least in the fifth bar from the end (beyond which its figure may be said simply to die away) comes round again to exactly the texture of tone that constitutes its opening bar."

Gilman further examined the alleged expressive content of several musical pieces as given by Gurney. Thus, according to Gurney, the melody from "La Favorita," *O, mio Fernando,* expresses weakness and flaccidity; a melody from "Der Freischutz" expresses serenity, permanence, and strength, the opening of the "Sonata Pastorale" conveys the idea of resistless movement. Gilman found that there was anything but agreement among his listeners on the effects of these selections, and no agreement at all with Gurney's characterizations of them.

Gilman also tried out the effect of Chopin's "Ballad in F

Major, No. 2," on his listeners. The instructions were: "The following music has been said to tell a certain story. What dramatic suggestion do you find in it?" The story referred to is that of Rubinstein who wrote of this "Ballad": "Is it possible that the interpreter should not feel the necessity of representing to his hearers: a wild flower caught by a gust of wind, a caressing of the flower by the wind, the resistance of the flower, the stormy struggles of the wind, the entreaty of the flower, which at last lies broken?" But Gilman found that his listeners reported a wide variety of meanings for the music. Following are some samples:

1. Two happy lovers are sailing over smooth seas, the ship is attacked by pirates, who are beaten off. A fierce storm arises, the ship bearing the two lovers is destroyed, and after the storm the sun shines again upon the sea somewhat calmed.

2. The piece naturally suggested a *murder*. It opens with a picture of the assassin creeping *slowly* along and you hear the shrieks of his intended victim when he is brought face to face with his slayer. Here the music, now *shrill,* now *deep* and *low,* seems to mingle cries and groans as the deed is committed and the man finally dies. The assassin slowly crawls off again and the lighter tones that are introduced seem to be the ordinary events of life passing on about him, producing much the same effect as the knocking on the gate in Macbeth. At the end the murderer is by himself and the last notes suggest regret entirely unavailing over what has happened. It ends with wild remorse.

3. The thumping and haste of the latter one-third or one-half were nothing to me but *intolerably disagreeable* noise, quite meaningless. The first uniform segment of the piece was delicious noise, of which the only dramatic suggestion was the passage through life of a rather rich-mindedly sober and patient sort of a man, with one leg shorter than the other. His inner gravity and modesty seemed connected with his lameness. At one point he tumbles off the bank into the water and then, *bang!* is caught in the whirlpool rapids for a long time, until he gets out rather wet; after which nonsense and noise, but for the short gleam of sanity at the very end, which is sweet but irrelevant.

4. Extremely beautiful, especially at first. Early part suggested monastic life, as it should have been, in the middle ages. Then war sweeps over the country and demolishes the monastery. An effort is made to reconstruct the old life (whether it is a tale regarding an individual

or a group I do not know), but the attempt is not finally successful. The life then becomes confused, mingles with the crude movements of cruel times, and ends in physical or moral battle. At the last moment occurs a recollection of earlier peace.

In another study Gilman asked several persons to give any image strikingly suggested to them by the course of Beethoven's "Pianoforte Prelude in F Minor." To Gilman its character was that of "an unending contest with an opposition that bars every advance." But none of his hearers agreed with him. To each one of 15 listeners the music conveyed a different meaning. Among the effects were: the swaying of treetops in a moderate wind, with weird songs sung beneath the trees; the passing of a funeral train; an organist seated at the organ in church; the plunge of a torrent in the woods; a hymn of thankfulness; chime of church bells; a great strife against something; a workman making something by strokes; a life toiling on through disappointment and struggle until at last peace comes; the opening voluntary in church.

Downey (12) tried out several compositions on a number of persons with results similar to those of Gilman. For Chopin's "Funeral March from the Sonata Op. 35," there were the following results:

1. First sensation, that it was one of Mrs. Candle's curtain lectures, interspersed with soliloquies over her own hard lot. Later concluded it represented a tired father walking the floor at midnight with a cross, crying baby, and alternately singing Watts' "Cradle Hymn" and scolding the baby.

2. Funeral of a soldier.

3. I was affected as I would have been had I read a strong, spirited poem. In fact, the first distinct impression was of some sweet poem of Scott; not military, but peaceful.

4. Grief, mourning, swelling to a climax. Reaction. Hope, faith, doubt alternate.

5. A country scene. Old orchard, tremendous trees, blossom-fragrant air. A breeze stirs the boughs. Rain begins to fall, first in large drops, then in rhythmic sheets, driven by gusts of wind. Thunder is followed by increased downpour. The sun breaks through the clouds.

Sun-shower; the reverberations of the summer-shower roll across the distant hills.

6. Funeral procession of Abraham Lincoln.

7. Sadness. An unsuccessful but constantly renewed attempt to throw off the burden of sorrow. A life of possibly more than usual melancholy with ray of hope and happiness brought in unwelcomely; or the hope of something unexpected coming without recognition. A slight recognition of the ideal without overcoming the natural or acquired melancholy.

8. Either a storm at sea, or a battle.

9. My thoughts were of the composer. At the beginning it suggested a storm at sea, then, at times, music on the water, or in the distance. The interpretation does not interest me so much as the harmony of tones.

10. A death and the heavy sorrowing of friends, a sorrow too deep for tears, which soon finds relief in tears. This changes to a feeling of loneliness and resignation which is beautiful. It is the covering of a sorrowful heart with a smile. The repetition of the first part is the rekindling of the sorrow which finally brings the person to an extremely morbid state.

11. Saw a moon-lighted garden surrounding an ancient castle. A band of monks were marching to their church in the distance, where the organ was softly playing. A mother was pleading with her son not to join them. After much pleading on her part, and grumbling answers on his, he still insists on his own way.

12. My impression was of passing a church and of hearing the organ; then of passing into the woods, and hearing a storm; then of walking by the side of a stream which at first seemed but a brook, but which grew in size, yet ever sang a sweet song, sad at times, the stream flowing on and on, and emptying into a river just where the trees met.

13. A calm, clear, sunny afternoon with pleasing landscape. A traveler is lying on the greensward and reveling in the quiet scene. But soon clouds roll up, and thunder, dark, growling at first, then angry. There comes a shower, after which reappears the peaceful, sunny scene. Night falls. A few angry peals of thunder, a few flashes of lightning come, and rain threatens, but does not fall.

14. The first part of the selection brought to my mind a funeral train. I believe I could quite see the picture.

15. A wail of a lost spirit.

16. Sadness. Death. It called to my mind memories of a dear friend who died years ago.

17. A double picture. Something deep and solemn and ominous, like the distant roar of a rising sea. Then a group of women talking, sometimes singing, but always listening. Occasionally the sea drowned the sound of their voices, then is quiet again. In the end there is a flood of lightning and a louder roar, then silence.

18. Well known Chopin's Funeral March. To me it represents the funeral of a soldier. First and third the march to and from a cathedral. The trio between represents the singing in cathedral and the organ-strains which accompany the burial service.

19. Deep, hopeless sorrow for someone lost. A prayer for help. The answer to the prayer. Hope and courage given.

Weld (121) used a descriptive selection, Voelker's "Hunt in the Black Forest," in order to obtain data on the question as to what extent a musical composition may be employed as a vehicle for communication and expression. The problem as stated by Weld was whether the composer or conductor can hope to convey a definite idea to the auditor, such as a story or a description of an incident. According to the publisher the music portrays the following: the break of day; birds singing in the forest; the voice of chanticleer; the huntsman's horn; the village chimes; the assembling of the hunters; the hunters galloping away; the horns sounding the halt; at the forest blacksmith's shop; the smith at work; the hunters' departure; the hounds scenting the game; the dogs in full cry; the game run to earth; cheers; finale. The listeners were asked to report their experiences without knowing the name of the selection.

Below are excerpts from several reports:

1. At the outset I concluded that it was a "barn-yard" selection; then I paid no attention to it although I heard the sounds throughout. I wondered how they make the dog bark. Toward the end, I began to analyze; and from there on I rather enjoyed it.

2. I was puzzled to know what it was all about at first; I thought it was the opening chorus of "Woodland" (a popular musical comedy). I had a visual image of a stage with the sun coming up; Chanticleer and

the birds coming together in chorus; there was much movement and streams of light quivered when the sun came up. Then I went to the circus; this occurred when I decided that it was not "Woodland." I saw a saw-dust ring. When the anvil sounded, I saw some object flying around the ring; at the stroke of the anvil this object was in the fovea. It was like swinging a chestnut around on a string; the entire circle you see, but at one place it seems to be more clear; and this place seems to give the impetus for continuing the movement.

3. In the fore-period, I was conscious of intense anticipation. When I heard the cuckoo, it aroused a visual image of a cuckoo clock and a cuckoo whistle; also of a bugle. The minor music aroused an image of Indians; a cheap stage; Indians stealing about the stage; a sensational mock-murder; a fierce grin as if they enjoyed it. Then a moving picture image of Indians. Something sounded familiar; much excitement; the Indians entered again in a row, but instead of coming through the wings they entered from an incline so that I could see first the head, then the shoulders; they had the same fierce grinning expression on their faces; they shook hands in time to the music; lifted their knees high and stamped. A feeling of amusement such as I have had in a badly played melodrama.

4. In the fore-period, I held my breath for a long time. I saw the gypsy scene in "Carmen." It was dawn; when the bird calls came, I thought of a comic opera called "Woodland," in which the actors were all birds. I recalled one of the duets, "Between a Cold Bottle and a Hot Bird"; then thought of Rostand's "Chanticleer" and wondered if it were like "Woodland." I then went back to "Carmen," where the stage fills up from the cigarette factory. I had all sorts of motor sensations in my hands, feet, legs, everywhere. There was a queer racket in one place like rolling a hollow box; this took me to an amusement park, on the Coney Island order, where I saw all the shows, etc., particularly "Shoot the Chutes." Then the dogs came in, and I went to the circus; there were three rings—trained dogs, horseback riders, etc.—a complete mix-up until the end, with tendencies to move throughout. I saw clowns in all sorts of costumes and it was they who did the shouting at the end (cheers of huntsmen in finale); I also saw riding-masters whipping their horses. The dogs made me think of the blood-hounds chasing Eliza in *Uncle Tom's Cabin*. In my opera picture, no one spoke or sang—people just moved about on the stage.

5. The music came gradually and there was more visual imagery than usual. Near the beginning of the selection there were a number of

whistled notes (probably suggested by the twittering of the birds). I saw the mouth of the person who was whistling. I heard the tramping of horses, and had a visual image of horses trotting toward me. I felt the increasing tenseness; then as my visual picture disappeared, it seemed to get smaller and smaller,—this because the music became less clear. The noise and din which represented a battle brought some excitement; and I also felt excitement when the horses came trotting up. The images of the battle were more like a picture; the armies were standing, but individuals were moving; near the end one detachment of the army was falling back.

It is obvious from the literature we have surveyed that the power of music to depict objects, situations or ideas is, as Gurney maintained long before there were any experimental data on the subject, extremely indefinite. No matter how specific a pictorial or dramatic program the composer may have in mind to present through his music, the listener will never get that program from the music itself. There is no doubt but that music lends itself in great measure to pictorial and dramatic presentation and interpretation. But music, per se, cannot paint a picture or tell a story. If the hearer is told what the music is supposed to depict he will imagine the incidents and fit them into the music. Or, if he is given a title it will suggest to him a train of imagery which he will read into the composition. And if he is given neither title nor program his fancy might take him on a mental journey, the direction of which will depend on his mood, his mental set, his physical condition, his past experience, and numerous other subjective factors, for which the music serves as a stimulus, but all of which lie outside of the music itself. Gurney is undoubtedly correct in his contention that even "when a composer lovingly or humorously connects some musical product with the outward occurrence or the inward vision which, acting through hidden channels, may have stimulated his fancy," there is really no inherent connection between that particular occurrence or vision and the character of the music. He cites the case of Schumann who tells "how a composer had been haunted, while writing, by the image of a butterfly floating down a brook on a leaf, with the result that his composition was characterized by a kindred simplicity and tenderness." On this Gurney comments that very likely it was, "but Schumann would not have denied that in the range of Music hundreds of equally simple and tender compositions might be found, written by writers who, as it happens, had *not* any such particular vision floating before their eyes. . . ." (33, p. 351)

Experimental results certainly point clearly to the conclusion that verbal ideas do not determine the substance of musical effects for the composer, nor does the music have much to do with the sort of ideas a listener finds in it. The ideas are not given him by the music. He puts them into the music. Any other stimulus could have had the same or a similar effect.

CHAPTER 5

THE VARIETIES OF MUSICAL EFFECTS: AFFECTIVE

Of the power of music over the emotions, to stir, soothe and inspire, the poets have sung for ages, while the literature of essay, drama, and fiction is replete with stories, testimonials, and eulogies of its influence over the passions of man. Thus Pope sings:

> By music, minds an equal temper know,
> Nor swell too high, nor sink too low;
> If in the breast tumultuous joys arise,
> Music her soft assuasive voice applies;
> Or, when the soul is pressed with cares
> Exalts her in enliv'ning airs.

More deliberate and studied comments on the effects of music on human feeling are not wanting. Thus Hanslick (35) although repudiating the connection between music as an art and music as emotion, writes:

> Far be it from us to underrate the deep emotions which music awakens from their slumber, or the feelings of joy or sadness which our minds dreamily experience. It is one of the most precious and inestimable secrets of nature, that an art should have the power of evoking feelings entirely free from worldly associations, and kindled, as it were, by the spark divine. It is only the unscientific proceeding of deducing *aesthetic principles* from such facts against which we protest. Music may, undoubtedly, awaken feelings of great joy or intense sorrow; but might not the same or a still greater effect be produced by the news that we have won the first prize in the lottery, or by the dangerous illness of a friend? So long as we refuse to include lottery tickets among the symphonies, or medical bulletins among the overtures, we must refrain from treating the emotions as an aesthetic monopoly of music in general or a certain piece of music in particular. Everything depends upon the *specific* "modus operandi" by *means of which* music evokes such feelings. (35, pp. 26-27)

Hanslick states furthermore that "Music operates on our emotional faculty with greater intenseness and rapidity than the product of any other art. A few chords may give rise to a frame of mind which a poem can induce only by a lengthy exposition, or a picture by prolonged contemplation, despite the fact that the arts to which the latter belongs boast the advantage over music of having at their service the whole range of ideas on which we know our feelings of joy or sorrow to depend. The action of sound is not only more sudden, but also more powerful and direct. The other arts persuade us, but music takes us by surprise. This, its characteristic sway over our feelings, is most vividly realized when we are in a state of unusual exaltation or depression." (35, pp. 107-108)

Likewise Gurney, while maintaining that a tune is no more constituted beautiful by an expression of mournfulness or of capriciousness than a face is, states that, "Under fortunate conditions the vaguer emotions induced by Music may rise to extraordinary power, as when some mighty polyphony, in its resistless blending of tumult and order, calls up deep indefinable associations of the mightier stream of lives and fates. Still, whatever their value may be, such effects are obviously very indirect, quasi-accidental, and subjective; they are not the composer's message; they cannot be presented to the inward ear when the orchestra has vanished, and though combinable with perception of form they can never replace it." (33, p. 307)

Again he writes:

In this connection it is well worth noting that at every stage which comes under our observation, Music seems capable of stirring up the strongest excitement that a being who musically typifies that stage can experience. This enjoyment to the utmost of the best that can be got is exemplified equally in the case of singing-birds, and of the gibbon, moved with rapture at his own performance of the chromatic scale, and of the savage repeating over for hours his few monotonous strains and maddened by the rhythmic beat of the drum, and of the ancient Greek spellbound by performances for the like of which we should probably tell a street-performer to pass on, and of a circle of Arabs sobbing and laughing by turns in ecstasies of passion at the sound of their native melodies, and of the English child to whom some simple tune of Mozart's reveals the unguessed springs of musical feeling, or of the adult in his loftiest communings with the most inspired utterances of Beethoven. And it is all-important to observe that these emotional experiences are essentially connected, throughout the whole long course of development, with the distinctly *melodic* principle, with the presentation of a succession of single sound-units; such series being exemplified in the percussive drummings of the spider and in the song of the gibbon, as well as in the distinguishable lines of tune indispensable to the emotional character of modern composition. (33, p. 315)

The experimental literature on the feeling effects of music deals with its influence on moods, the feeling value of melody, harmony, pitch, tempo, and major and minor modes, the physiological phenomena in musical stimulation, and its value as medicine.

MOOD EFFECTS

An extensive study on the mood effects of music was carried out during the years 1920 and 1923 at the Carnegie Institute of Technology under the direction of W. V. Bingham. The study (91, 92) was based on data obtained from 20,000 persons who had reported the effects produced upon their moods by a variety of 290 phonograph records of vocal and instrumental musical compositions. The data were collected from all over the United States, from persons under various conditions of time and place, and of varied musical training, experience, age and interests. The conclusion from these 20,000 responses may be stated briefly as follows: That a musical composition not only produces a mood change in the listener, but that it also induces a markedly uniform mood in a large majority of the members of an audience.

To test the validity of this conclusion, a more limited and also a more intensive study was made of the effect of music on moods and other questions dealing with the same general problem. Thus, for practical purposes we want to know not only whether a musical composition produces a mood change in the listener, but, what is of greater significance, whether the induced mood is also enjoyed, and to what degree this enjoyment might depend on such factors as the type of mood induced, familiarity of the listener with the selection, and his judgment of the quality of the selection.

The results showed that a mood change was produced in every instance in every listener, or that an existing mood was intensified when it conformed with the mood of the music. The consistency of the mood effects, that is, the tendency of the same composition to produce the same or a similar mood in every listener, was very marked. The degree of enjoyment derived from the musical composition was in direct proportion to the intensity of the mood effect produced, provided this effect was not due to the conditions of the performance, such as poor intonation or faulty interpretation. Familiarity played a more important rôle in the degree of enjoyment derived from the music for the somewhat musical than for the very musical. In other words, the less musical the person, the more was his enjoyment conditioned upon the degree of familiarity with the selection.

In the matter of the degree of enjoyment, listeners divided themselves into three groups: those whose enjoyment was both slight and rare, those whose enjoyment was both frequent and intense, and those whose enjoyment was rare but intense. Into the first class fall the non-musical, into the second class the somewhat musical, while the third class consisted of the most musical. The non-musical, then, as was but to be expected, enjoys music but rarely, and then but slightly, while the very musical, whose taste is discriminating and into whose musical judgment there enter many complex and complicating factors, particularly those relating to interpretation, likewise meets rarely with enjoyment, but when present it is intense. The very musical find themselves, then, in most cases, at one of two extremes: they either experience intense pleasure or very little. The somewhat musical, on the other hand, whose attitude toward music is uncritical, but who are nevertheless attracted to music, find great enjoyment most often. No greater amount of enjoyment was derived from one type of mood than from another type, unless the mood was due to a dislike of the specific type of music or to a poor performance. But when the mood-change was from joyful to serious, the enjoyment seemed to be slightly less than when the change was from serious to joyful, provided the hearer was not hampered either by a knowledge of the critical estimate of the music to which he was listening or by faulty interpretation. The evaluation of the quality of the musical composition was in direct proportion to the intensity of the enjoyment.

What are the feelings most frequently excited by music, and is music equally effective in arousing all kinds of feeling? The data show that rest, sadness, joy, love, longing, and reverence appear most frequently as the effects produced. It is noteworthy that specific emotions such as anger, fear, jealousy, and envy were conspicuously absent from all records. This is entirely in keeping with the general impression prevailing among those most sensitive to the art that the emotions do not enter into the realm of aesthetics, but that the aesthetic effect is of the nature of a general condition of a mood. This conclusion is corroborated by the fact that vocal music has a tendency to arouse well-defined emotional effects far more often than instrumental music, the probability being that the specific emotional effect is due in the main to the words. Even such effects as love, longing, reverence, and devotion result primarily from vocal music, while such general effects as rest, restlessness, and peace are mentioned most often in connection with instrumental music.

Further evidence on the uniformity and consistency of the feeling effects of music is found in experiments by Hevner. (41, 42, 44) In order to obtain reliable data, Hevner's first step was to devise a method which would measure the meaning suggested by the music in objective and quantitative terms, so that the listener could express himself quickly, fully and exactly, and the experimenter could tabulate and classify the results with precision. For this purpose a check list of adjectives was provided for each listener who was urged to check every word which seemed to describe the music, as few or as many as he liked. These adjectives were grouped together and arranged around a circle as shown on the following page.

Hevner studied hundreds of compositions by this method. Several typical examples follow:

The *Scherzo* from Mendelssohn's "Midsummer Night's

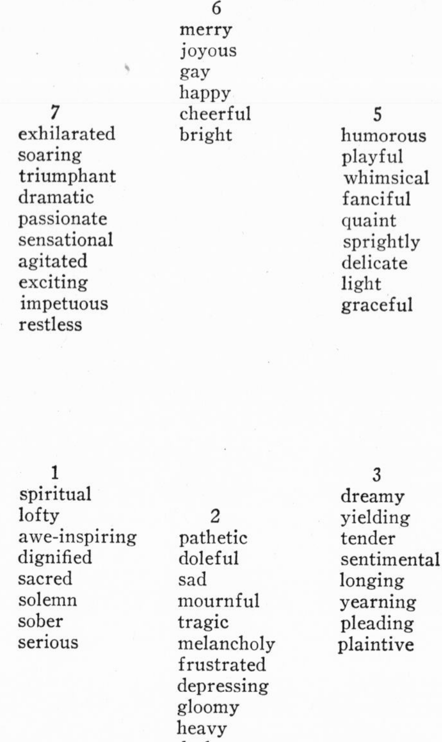

Dream" music was played to 50 college students who checked their responses on the adjective circle, and the experimenter added together the votes for all adjectives in each group. The votes were as follows: group one (dignified), 6; group two (sad), 11; group three (dreamy), 2; group four (calm), 12; group five (playful), 118; group six (happy), 89; group seven (exciting-impetuous), 190; group eight (vigorous), 50. The audience therefore found this piece to be above all exciting and impetuous, happy and gay, somewhat playful and graceful, and to a lesser extent vigorous and dramatic. It is not at all solemn, sad, plaintive or serene. On the whole, the mood effect was quite concentrated, and the audience had no difficulty in discerning the mood which it was the composer's intention to convey.

Another composition heard by this same group, a Liszt-Busoni arrangement for the piano of the "Paganini Etude in E Major," showed a similar pattern. The composition is characterized by emphatic rhythms and rapid tripping arpeggios. For this composition there were only 386 checks altogether as against a total of 477 for the Mendelssohn music, showing that the *Etude* did not have as strong mood suggestiveness as the *Scherzo*. But it resembled the *Scherzo* in that it lacked entirely the feeling-tone of sadness, dignity, tenderness, and serenity, and suggested rather playfulness, gayety, excitement, and vigor. The actual number of votes for each group were: one, 1; two, 5; three, 10; four, 13; five, 142; six, 70; seven, 105; eight, 40.

Quite different in mood was the Tschaikowsky "Symphony No. 6, in B Minor," second part of first movement, which showed 101, 63, 87, and 64 votes on the first four groups, respectively. The subjects recognized that this music was dignified, sad, plaintive, and lyrical. There were no votes for the playful and gay groups.

Another composition, a Debussy piano solo, "Reflections on the Water," was of especial interest because of the apparent uncertainty of the listeners, and the discrepancies which appeared in the data. The adjectives checked were scattered among the eight groups with the greatest number on two groups in diametrical opposition to each other, viz., dreamy-sentimental and exciting-impetuous. Hevner offers two reasons which might account for these differences in interpretation. The first is the nature of the subject with which the composer is dealing. Reflections on the water are likely to be at one time clear, still and distinct, and at another time distorted, restless, fitful and changing; and the composer may have intended several different interpretations to be possible from his music. The second reason, which is important for many other compositions as well as this particular one of Debussy, is the presence of several well-defined sections in the musical structure, sometimes quite different from one another. In order to separate the various parts of the composition and trace the source of the checks for the different adjective groups, the experiments described above were repeated with new groups of subjects and with slightly different instructions. The new subjects began to check their adjectives as soon as the suggestiveness of the music became apparent, by placing the number "1" before each choice. At a given signal from the experimenter which coincided with the beginning of a new section of the music, the subjects indicated their choices by the numeral "2" and for the third section they changed to the numeral "3". Tabulations were made for the three different sections. For the first section, beginning with group one, the figures were: 7, 24, 83, 170, 53, 2, 1, 1. For the second section: 22, 16, 25, 26, 105, 31, 150, 25, with the figures for the third section following very closely those of the first. The listeners therefore perceived the character of this piece with extraordinary clearness, the first part as dreamy-sentimental, serene, and somewhat playful, and the middle section in sharp contrast, as very playful and extremely restless, exciting, and agitated.

In all of these experiments the subjects, college students, had been given many different kinds of tests in order that the experimenter might study the effects of intelligence, musical talent, training, and the like, on their ability to perceive the meaning of the music. In one group of listeners, numbering 205, the students were given the Minnesota College Ability (Intelligence) test, all the Seashore tests for musical talent, and a rating scale for their musical training. The experimenter singled out the papers of the 25 students with the highest intelligence rating and those with the lowest rating and tabulated the interpretations of the two groups separately. But there was no observable difference in the two groups. Both interpreted the music in the same way, and to the same extent. Likewise there was no apparent difference when the best 25 students on the Seashore tests were contrasted with the lowest 25 students on the same test. When the 25 students with the greatest and least amount of musical training and background were segregated, two very interesting groups were found. The average student in the top group had had courses in music theory, private lessons on the piano for two years, voice for four years and cello for a like period. He had played in orchestras four years and sung for six years in choirs, had three musicians in his family, could read music and supply missing parts, and attended concerts regularly. The student who represented the average for the group with the least training had never had any private lessons, did not play a musical instrument, had no musicians in his family, and never attended operas or concerts. He could read music a little for singing, had sung two years in a high school chorus, and had a piano and radio in his home. Nevertheless, the two groups showed very little difference in their abilities to perceive the meaning in the music. The well-trained individual differentiates perhaps more sharply, but it is difficult to detect any appreciable difference in their records.

THE EFFECTS OF MAJOR AND MINOR

It is generally assumed that there is an inherent difference between the major and minor modes in music which accounts for the difference in the effects each produces on the listener. The major is alleged to be happy, bright, exciting, dynamic; the minor, sad, darksome, reposeful, dreamy, sorrowful. We have already seen in the discussion on consonance some alleged grounds for the differentiation between major and minor chords. Helmholtz (38), for instance, attributes the melancholy effect of the minor chord to the presence of a slight degree of dissonance as compared with the consonance of the major. This theory Gurney rejects on the ground that "the same degree of dissonance as exists in the *minor* triad may be made to supervene on a *major* triad, by adding to it a certain extremely faint amount of discordant elements: it would seem then that this major triad thus slightly dimmed or confused ought to sound melancholy; but it does not in the least." (33, p. 271) Gurney himself suggests that the difference lies in the character of the "*characteristic notes* of the minor scale as compared with the corresponding ones of the major. . . ." (33, p. 272) These characteristic notes are the semi-tones. Both major and minor scales have a semi-tone between leading-tone and key-tone, which "conveys to the ear so decided an expectation that the motion will rise, that its fulfillment is accepted as a satisfactory close." (33, p. 273) But the position of the other tones differs for major and minor. "If we ascend the scale of C and strike

E natural, its nearness to F gives the motion a similar tendency to rise; hence the E seems able to supply the strength for the rise, to have got far enough from the D to be sure of its grounds, to have its own balance and the power of making an independent spring, which naturally gives an impression of *confidence.* If, on the other hand, we strike E flat, the sound keeps close to the D and seems dependent on it and willing to sink back to it; if we still advance to the F we seem to press our way through the reluctant E flat, not to be sped onwards as by the E natural; and this dependence and reluctance to advance give an impression of diffidence, a character which at any rate seems more naturally suggestive of pathos than uncertainty and obscurity were." (33, p. 273) The same is true of FGA as compared with FGA♭ in the second half of the scale. The reluctance of A♭ to proceed is even greater than that of E "inasmuch as the instinct to use the B natural as the seventh degree of the scale, in view of the approaching keynote, is so strong that, if the A flat is used as the sixth degree, the motion has to make the long and difficult step of a tone and a half." (33, p. 273)

Gurney holds that "the fact of this *melodic* pathos is indisputable." (33, p. 274) But how will this account for the pathetic character of the minor triad? Gurney recognizes this difficulty when he admits that in hearing the minor triad "we certainly have no distinct feeling of running melodically up and down the notes it comprises." (33, p. 275) But he claims that, nevertheless, the motion of a potential passing from one note to another must "lie at the root of the perception of distance as a relation which they present," and that "some faint perception of distance or interval we found reason to suspect was practically always present in the impression of a chord." (33, p. 275) Hence, "the faint suggestion might suffice to recall by association the feeling with which the relations of the notes in actual melodic progression have been so constantly and vividly connected." (33, p. 275)

Gurney's explanation, as well as that of Helmholtz, is based on the assumption that affective differences between major and minor do exist. The experimental investigations concern themselves entirely with these alleged differences. Two early experiments on this problem give contradictory results. Valentine (112) found that major intervals were described as sad or plaintive twice as often as minor intervals, while the major triad was called sad as often as the minor triad. Danzfusz (37), on the other hand, reports that the predominant response to the minor triad was that of melancholy and sadness, while the major triad was mostly described as clear, strong, joyful, and bright.

The two most detailed studies we have up to the present on the effects of the major and minor modes are those of Heinlein and Hevner.

Heinlein (37) experimented with chords. He used 30 persons whom he classified as trained and untrained. His purpose was to ascertain the extent to which the joyful-melancholy dimension of feeling functions in trained and untrained subjects' verbal feeling responses to major and minor chords when presented under the same and different intensity conditions. He used 48 chords, all in the tonic position. The subjects were asked to indicate the feeling effect of the chord by selecting a word from a printed list. The list of terms consisted of the usual feeling effects associated with major and minor.

Heinlein found that in the case of 25 of his 30 subjects the percentage of minor responses made to major chords was greater than that of major responses to minor chords. For the musically trained the average per cent of minor responses to major chords was smaller than for the untrained, while of major responses to minor chords the average per cent for the musical was much smaller than for the unmusical. But a change in the intensity of a chord had a marked effect in modifying its feeling-tone. Soft chords were predominantly soothing, whether major or minor. Thus, according to Heinlein, it is not so much a question of what a chord is by nature of its tonal structure, as it is a question of how it is presented. A loud chord is rarely soothing; a soft chord is frequently soothing. But to state that a minor chord is not soothing is certainly not justified, for the greatest number of soothing responses was obtained from minor chords when played softly. But the contention that the major chord is always soothing is not borne out. Either loud major or loud minor chords are seldom reacted to as soothing. Loud major chords evoked major responses more often than soft major chords, and soft major chords evoked minor responses more often than loud major chords. Loud minor chords evoked major responses more often than soft minor chords.

Pitch was also a factor in the type of response. For either a major or a minor chord, the chords in an upper pitch register were reacted to by a greater percentage of major responses as compared with the chords in the lower pitch region, and chords of either mode in the lower register caused a greater number of minor responses than did chords of either mode in the upper pitch register.

Heinlein concludes in general that there is no fixity of feeling-tone intrinsic to a given chordal combination. The joyful-melancholy difference between major and minor is rather due to training to react in this specific manner. "The assumption long entertained by theorists in regard to the supposed intrinsic characters of the modes must be dismissed. It has been shown that reaction to harmonic configuration is variable for both trained and untrained subjects. The mode in which a composition is written has little relation to the type of feeling which the composition may arouse. Minor compositions may be reacted to by both trained and untrained subjects as bright, happy, cheerful, joyful, and exuberant, whereas major compositions may be reacted to as gloomy, plaintive, melancholy, and mournful. Any fixity of feeling-tone in relation to a given mode is dependent upon training to react in a specific manner to a purely intellectual discrimination. Mood fluctuations and general temperamental differences provide for variations in interpretation." (37, p. 140)

Hevner (43) reports the results of an experiment similar to that of Heinlein. Her purpose was to determine whether the historically affirmed characteristics of the two modes are apparent to listeners, and if so, to what extent the recognition of these characteristics is dependent upon training in music, or intelligence, and on musical talent. Hevner criticizes Heinlein on the grounds that chords cannot be regarded as music. Composers who speak of the minor as melancholy or plaintive refer to a musical composition as a whole. She therefore used ten short musical compositions with one version of each in the major mode and one in the minor. These ten compositions were played to 205 persons who checked from a printed word list all the adjectives which seemed to them to describe the particular selection.

The results of the responses to the major and minor version of the ten compositions confirmed the historically affirmed effects of the two modes. For the minor mode the melancholy-mournful-gloomy-depressing quality stood out as of greatest importance, and then the plaintive-yearning-longing quality. It had also quite clearly a mysterious-mystical-weird-restless-dramatic effect, and a vague-dark-dreamy-hushed-sentimental aspect. For the major mode the greatest importance was given to such adjectives as happy, sprightly, cheerful, joyous, gay, and bright, and the next group included playful, graceful, and even quaint and fanciful. Training seems to be a more important factor than either musical ability or intelligence in discrimination between major and minor; but Hevner claims that neither lack of training nor musical status or intelligence can obliterate the ability to discriminate the accepted effects of the two modes.

THE EFFECTS OF THE STRUCTURAL ELEMENTS OF MUSIC

Another problem investigated by Hevner (41, 44) in a series of studies was the consistency of the effects of the elements of musical structure, namely, tempo, pitch, rhythm, harmony, and melody. Her procedure was the same as the one used in the study on modality. For each element studied two versions of a composition were prepared in which every factor was held constant except the one to be investigated. The subjects checked adjectives from a printed list to indicate the effect.

The only important difficulty in carrying out such studies lay in the preparation of the two versions of the music for experimental use. In the case of the pitch element this was fairly easy. Thirteen compositions were found which should sound pleasant and musical when transposed one octave either above or below their original position. Dealing with the factor of tempo was also a fairly simple matter. Two contrasting rates of speed had to be chosen so that the music would sound as pleasing as possible at both rates, and so that the pianist should have good control and facility at the fast rate. The speed of the first version was sometimes twice that of the slow, e.g., 72 and 152 quarter notes per minute. Other contrasts were 80 and 102, 80 and 112, 63 and 104.

In the case of melody, rhythm, and harmony, it was necessary to limit the experiment to but one of many possible aspects. The difficulties and complications encountered in rewriting the music excluded any but the most simple and obvious changes. In rhythm, the two patterns studied were a firm beat with a full chord on every beat, as in a chorale or hymn tune, and a much more smooth and flowing motion in which the supporting chords were broken up and spread evenly throughout the measure. A part of the accompanying harmony occurred not only on each beat but on every half beat, with the result that the motion of the flowing version was more continuous and less definitely accented than the firm version.

The particular aspect of melody that was chosen for study was the rising and falling of the melodic line. In preparing the experimental material Hevner chose a number of short compositions representing a variety of melodic lines. In the Op. 13 of Beethoven, for example, there is a long and vigorous rise in melody through two octaves. In the Mendelssohn, Op. 19, the melody opens with three slow climbing phrases. In the Schumann, Op. 15, No. 5, the melody is strongly descending in character, a short descending motif carried down through four octaves. In other compositions, the original melody had only a slight rise or fall, and in others a circular or pendular motion. In each of the compositions the original melody was inverted. The inversion was done as exactly as possible; the skips were of the same size and location, but in the opposite direction from those of the original melody. In trying out the compositions for this part of the experiment, many compositions had to be discarded as unsuitable, either because the inversion did not sound pleasant and musical, or because the harmony for the new melody could not be made to follow that of the original, or because the relation of the melody to the keynote could not be kept parallel in both the original and the inversion.

In studying the rôle of the harmonic structure of the music, a change was made from the simple consonant harmonies resolved in a very smooth and satisfying manner to complex dissonant harmonies more harsh and rough and not always reaching a satisfactory resolution. Nine compositions were treated in this way, and an attempt was made also to study various other more subtle changes in harmony. These latter experiments, however, were without success. The results were fluctuating and inconsistent, showing either that the listeners were not able to discern and interpret these more subtle changes, or that the changes in harmony involved other factors in the musical pattern which complicated and disrupted its effectiveness.

In counting the checks for the listeners, the adjectives in one group were always totalled and treated as representative of one affective state or feeling-tone. For example, the total votes in group one (dignified-solemn) for compositions with firm rhythm was 282, and for those with flowing rhythm, 59. It is apparent therefore that a firm rhythm in contrast to flowing rhythm is much more dignified, spiritual, lofty, etc. For group two, the total votes were respectively 114 and 68, indicating that the firm rhythm is more likely to seem sad, although the difference is not nearly so marked as in the first case. In group three, the totals were 88 and 186, giving a decided advantage to the flowing rhythms for the expression of tenderness and sentiment. In group four (calm-quiet) there was practically no difference, 190 and 216. In group five (playful-graceful) flowing rhythms had the advantage, 178 to 276, and likewise in group six (happy-gay), 123 to 241. Group seven, like group four, offered no appreciable majority to either, 272 to 246. Completing the circle with group eight (vigorous, etc.) the advantage went, as in group one, to the firm rhythms, 239 to 73. Reviewing these data we notice that the factor of rhythm is of greatest importance in two sections of the adjective circle directly opposed to each other, the firm rhythms being vigorous, dignified and solemn, and the flowing rhythms light, happy and playful. In respect to two other contrasting groups, calm versus excitement, neither rhythm is at all effective. In other words, this axis of the adjective circle is not expressed in rhythmic terms.

The most important elements for expressing the various moods were found to be as follows: For excitement the most important element is tempo, which must be swift. Complex harmonies also contribute much to this feeling, as well as lower pitch and descending melodic patterns. But modality is not important, and neither a firm nor a flowing rhythm carries any advantage. Some other factor in rhythm, dotted figures or uneven rhythms, might prove to be very effective, but such rhythmic variations have not yet been investigated by this method. Reading each of the vertical columns in turn, we may note the usefulness of the six elements for the mood effects. Dignity was indicated to these audiences by slow tempos, firm rhythms, and lower pitches, with some help from the major mode, simple harmonies and ascending melodies. Dreamy sentimental moods follow from the minor mode, slow tempo, and flowing rhythm, with simple harmonies and the higher pitches preferred. For the two related moods of happiness and playful grace, the same elements are required, although the proportions are different. Sheer happiness, unmixed with delicacy or humor, demands a faster tempo, simpler harmonies, more flowing rhythms, and not so high a pitch.

A comparison of the relative weight of the various factors in producing a given affective state shows the very small part played by melody in expressing musical meanings. It is possible that the differences in the expressiveness often claimed for certain melodies is to be attributed to the rhythm, tempo, etc., rather than to the pitch pattern of the successive tones. On the whole, tempo seems to be of the greatest importance, although it is very ineffective in achieving delicate-graceful or vigorous-majestic effects. Modality is tremendously effective in the dimensions of sadness, playfulness, happiness, and brightness, but quite useless in the dimension of vigor, excitement, calm, and dignity.

Experimental support for an orderly system of expressiveness in music also comes from Gundlach (31, 32) in his analysis of the reports of 112 listeners to 40 musical phrases. He found that speed was by far the most important factor in distinguishing the pieces, that rhythm was second in importance, and the range of the melodic line seemed least significant. Another factor, the tone quality of the instrument, he shows also to be very significant,—the brasses triumphant and grotesque, never melancholy, tranquil, delicate or sentimental; the woodwinds mournful, awkward, uneasy, never brilliant or glad.

PHYSIOLOGICAL AND MEDICINAL EFFECTS OF MUSIC

In general literature one finds numerous accounts of the power of music over the physiological processes. David is reported to have allayed the melancholy of Saul, and the celebrated male soprano Farinelli is said to have saved Philip of Spain from despondency. Galen valued music as a medical bath for ailing parts of the body, while Gallius prescribed soft music as a cure for epilepsy and sciatic gout. Pythagoras is reputed to have wrought miraculous cures by the aid of music. Henry Beacham wrote in his *The Compleat Gentleman* in 1634 that "the exercise of Musicke is a great lengthner of the life, by stirring and reviving the Spirits, holding a secret sympathy with them; besides the exercise of singing openeth the breast and pipes: it is an enemy to melancholy and dejection of the mind, which *St. Chrysostome* truly calleth, *The Divels Bath.* Yea, a curer of some diseases: in *Apuglia,* in *Italy,* and thereabouts, it is most certaine, that those who are stung with the *Tarantula,* are cured onely by Musicke. Beside the aforesaid benefit of singing, it is a most ready helpe for a bad pronunciation, and distinct speaking, which I have heard confirmed by many great Divines: yea, in my selfe have knowne many Children to have bin holpen of their stammering in speech, onely by it."

Robert Burton, the author of *The Anatomy of Melancholy,* writes eloquently of music as a cure for that affliction:

> Many and sundry are the means which philosophers and physicians have prescribed to exhilarate a sorrowful heart, to divert those fixed and intent cares and meditations, which in this malady so much offend; but in my judgment none so present, none so powerful, none so apposite

as a cup of strong drink, mirth, music, and merry company. . . . Many other properties Cassiodorus, *epist. 4* reckons up of this our divine music, not only to expel the greatest griefs, but "it doth extenuate fears and furies, appeaseth cruelty, abateth heaviness, and to such as are watchful it causeth quiet rest; it takes away spleen and hatred," be it instrumental, vocal, with strings, wind *quae a spiritu, sine manuum dexteritate gubernetur* (such as are played with the breath, without any action of the hands), etc.; it cures all irksomeness and heaviness of the soul. Labouring men that sing to their work, can tell as much, and so can soldiers when they go to fight, whom terror of death cannot so much affright as the sound of trumpet, drum, fife, and such like music animates; *metus enim mortis,* as Censorinus informeth us, *musica depellitur* (for the fear of death can be banished by music). "It makes a child quiet," the nurse's song; and many times the sound of a trumpet on a sudden, bells ringing, a carman's whistle, a boy singing some ballad tune early in the street, alters, revives, recreates a restless patient that cannot sleep in the night, etc. In a word, it is so powerful a thing that it ravisheth the soul, *regina sensuum,* the queen of the senses, by sweet pleasure (which is a happy cure), and corporal tunes pacify our incorporeal soul; *sine ore loquens, dominatum in animum exercet* (speaking without a mouth, it exercises domination over the soul), and carries it beyond itself, helps, elevates, extends it.

We have several accounts from individuals of what music did for their ailments, and also reports from practitioners of musical therapeutics.

George Sand wrote to Meyerbeer:

Two years ago I went into the country in the middle of winter and passed there the two saddest months of my life. I suffered from dreadful depression and during the attacks almost lost my reason; I seemed possessed by furies, demons, serpents. When the crisis, as happens in the process of all diseases, began to wear off I had an infallible means for hastening the course and thus, in a few moments, arriving at a blissful state of repose. I had my nephew take a seat at the piano. At a signal which he understood he played my favorite music, that song by Alice at the foot of the Cross—such a perfect and charming picture of the condition of my feelings, the passing off of my distress and my returning hope. How can I ever bless you, my dear master, who healed me so much more skillfully than a physician would, for you did it without causing suffering and without demanding any pecuniary remuneration.

Berlioz gives the following account of some of his musical experiences:

Nothing in the world could give an exact idea of the effect to one who has never experienced it. My whole being seems to vibrate, at first it is a delightful pleasure, in which reason does not appear to participate at all. The emotions, increasing in direct ratio with the force or grandeur of the composer's ideas, produce, little by little, a strange agitation on the circulation of the blood; my pulse beats violently; tears which usually give evidence of the crisis of a paroxysm, indicate only a progressive stage and greater agitation and excitement to follow. When the crisis is really reached there occur spasmodic contractions of the muscles, a trembling in all the limbs, a total numbness of feet and hands, a partial paralysis of the nerves of vision and hearing.

Retard of Geneva is reported to have successfully employed music to soothe and tranquilize the dreams of persons who had taken ether or chloroform for a surgical operation. The music is begun as soon as the patient is being affected by the anesthetic and is continued until the patient awakes. This treatment is supposed not only to prevent the hysterical effects sometimes occurring, but also to prevent nausea or illness on recovery.

Corning (9) claims that musical stimulation during sleep of persons suffering from neurasthenia frequently results in marked abatement of symptoms. "Persons who suffer habitually from mental and physical atony in the mornings, who are capable of little or no exertion before noon-day and whose complaint is that they derive little or no good from sleep, no matter how prolonged, often experience a decided revival of vigour if subjected to the vibrations of a phonograph during sleep. Natural depression, when not dependent upon some obvious physical disorder, is frequently relieved in this way. All this goes to show, beyond a doubt, that we are here confronted with the material effects of musical vibrations."

Vescelius (114) goes so far as to prescribe music for specific disturbances:

For fever, high pulse, hysteria, arrest the attention. Play softly and rhythmically to bring the pulse and respiration to normal. Tests with instruments prove that music will do this. Do not change too abruptly from one key to another; modulate and pause and let the musical impression be absorbed. Select songs that depict green fields and pastures new, the cool running brook, the flight of birds, the blue sky, the sea.

Deafness is helped by long, free, open tones. Syncopation and jerky music should be used sparingly.

Fear is dissipated by music awakening in the listener the consciousness of the all-enveloping Good. A high nervous tension is relieved and nerves are relaxed under the spell of a composition that swings the body into normal rhythmic movement. Sluggish conditions of body and mind are eliminated by the rhythmic waltz, polka, or mazurka—music affecting the motor system. Insomnia is cured by the slumber-song, nocturne, or the spiritual song that assures one of Divine protection. A baby listens to a lullaby for the first time with wide open eyes. As the song grows familiar, he yields to the rhythm repeated over and over again. (114, p. 384)

The question of the physiological effects of music has attracted the attention of some investigators, and we have some experimental data on the problem.

The pioneer investigator in this field was Dogiel (11) who found that music influences blood circulation, blood pressure, increases the heart beat and accelerates respiration. Féré (24) and Tarchanoff (108), and also Scripture (94), found that isolated tones, scales, motifs, and simple tonal sequences have an energizing effect upon the muscles, while Binet and Courtier (5) obtained interesting results on pulse and respiration with consonant and dissonant chords, major and minor intervals, changes in intensity, and so on. All produce changes of pulse and respiration, dissonant chords, major chords, and chords in rapid succession producing acceleration, while perfect consonances, significant changes in tonal intensity, the approach of the finale, and pleasantness, cause a retardation in pulse beat. A study on respiration by Foster and Gamble (26) showed that respiration while listening to music is no different from what happens in mental application in general as to rate and amplitude, but in musical attention it is less regular.

In his study on musical enjoyment Weld (121) included experiments on organic phenomena present during musical attention. He found disturbances of blood supply which he feels are due more to variation in the function of attention than to the music as such. The respiration is irregular both in rate and amplitude, and varies directly with the intensity of the experienced emotion. The rate of respiration is above normal. Muscular reactions of strain and relaxation, the concomitants of feeling, are, according to Weld, of great importance in the appreciation of music.

Washco (119) studied the effects of a large variety of musical compositions upon organic processes. His results indicate that the raising or lowering of pulse rate and blood pressure depends upon the kind of music used. The more definite the melodic or rhythmic elements in a musical composition, the more certain and effective are the physiological responses.

Experimentally the most significant contribution thus far made on the physiological concomitants of musical experiences is that by Hyde (46). The object of the investigation was to determine the physiological effects of different kinds of musical selections upon the cardio-vascular systems in individuals fond of music, those indifferent or not sensitive to music, and also the effects of vocal music and different kinds of musical instruments upon listeners of different nationality, endowment, and training, and upon varying conditions.

The observers included fifteen men and women, four of whom were Indian students, all adults. Five of the male observers were fond of, and sensitive to, music, two did not seem to be able to distinguish one tone from another. Of the eight women, two were not sensitive to music, one was hysterical, another was a teacher of music, one had a defective cardiac valve, and the others were fond of music. The effects measured were the pulse rate, systolic and diastolic blood pressure, and relative velocity of the blood flow. These items were secured from one to five minutes before the music programme and from one to fifteen minutes after the music ceased.

The subjects were classified into two groups. In one were those who possessed love for and had training in music, and in the other those who did not care for music and had no musical training. The musical selections used were phonographic records of Tschaikowsky's "Symphony Pathetique," the *Toreador*

Song from "Carmen," and "The National Emblem" march by Sousa.

The results of this investigation warrant the conclusion that people are unfavorably affected psychologically and physiologically by compositions that are characterized by tragic, mournful tones, and favorably by gay, rhythmical melodies. Individual differences in native endowment and training are accompanied by individual differences in stimuli and physiological reactions to certain compositions of music. The types of music that stimulate the pulse pressure and rate and electromotive force of the heart muscle probably also excite the tonicity of the skeletal muscles and secretions, and decrease fatigue.

Hyde feels that vocal and instrumental music may be selected that will excite the psychological and concomitantly cardiovascular reactions, the effects of which might inhibit irritability, act as a narcotic, or excite optimism, and be employed practically as an adjunct to scientifically organized labor.

THE SOURCES OF MUSICAL ENJOYMENT

What is the nature of musical enjoyment, and to what extent do the various elements in a musical composition, such as rhythm, melody, harmony, and timbre, as well as the ideational and emotional effects, contribute to the total amount of pleasure? On this problem a number of studies are available with more or less significant and valid results.

Weld (121), who was the first investigator to have obtained data on this question, concluded that the enjoyment of music is a complex act involving at least six components. There is, in the first place, a pleasurable emotion arising from the timbre and tonal nuances of the instruments. This varies from individual to individual, due to a preference on the part of a person for some one instrument or combination of instruments. A second component is the pleasure derived from the rhythm of the music. This motor factor is always present in listening to music, whether as actually keeping time or as motor imagery. Then, third, there are pleasurable associations arising from the person's past experience. A fourth source of enjoyment is derived from the listener's play of imagery, consisting either in an unfolding of a story or drama, or in an anticipation of the line of development of the music itself, or in self-projection into the chorus and orchestra as a participator in the performance. Fifth is a pleasurable mood, and sixth is the intellectual activity of following the musical structure as it is being unfolded. Weld claims that of these components visual imagery contributes least, and motor reactions most, to the enjoyment of all auditors, excepting in the case of those persons whose enjoyment is of the purely intellectual sort. Emotional enjoyment has for its basis motor reaction, while intellectual enjoyment is a function of auditory imagery and the intellectual processes based thereon.

Gatewood (28) arrived at similar conclusions from an experimental study on the nature of musical enjoyment. She mentions four factors operating together in the total pleasurable impression. The first factor is the physical or sensory effect of rhythm, melody, harmony, and timbre. This she calls the *presented* content. The second factor is associational and imaginal, and is the *represented* content. The third factor is ideational, in which the listener engages either in some line of thought stimulated by the music, or is engaged in following the structural unfolding of the composition. The fourth factor is emotional, or enjoyment derived from any kind of affective experience aroused by the music.

Gatewood's study was mainly concerned with this fourth factor. Her purpose was to analyze the feeling effects of music and to determine their bearing upon the pleasure or displeasure experienced by the listener. Data were sought on the kind of feeling or feelings aroused by certain music, on the relation each of the various feelings experienced bore to the total musical response, and whether the individual's feelings could be objectively estimated.

For the purpose of this study, Gatewood used 589 selections, mostly of standard character, which she played for her listeners in sets of 20 numbers to a program. Each listener was asked to record his judgment on each selection on the following points: the degree of familiarity, whether pleasant or unpleasant, whether interesting or boring; mental effect produced such as memory, imagination, fancy, logical thought; the emotional effect produced, such as sadness, joy, reverence; the predominant factor in the particular composition, whether rhythm, melody, harmony, timbre; and an estimate of the technique of the artist.

From the data gathered from this quite extensive investigation Gatewood concluded that there was a direct relationship between the degree of enjoyment and the intensity of the emotional effect, or in other words, that marked emotional effect accompanies marked musical enjoyment. The other factors, singly or in combination, may contribute to the total effect, but emotional excitation and musical pleasure are quite inseparable. Furthermore, the greater the variety of emotional effects experienced by the listener the greater is the pleasure found in the music.

Another interesting point studied by Gatewood was the relation of each emotional effect to the general effect of pleasantness or enjoyment. She wanted to know, for instance, to what extent the presence of a feeling of rest contributed to the musical pleasure, whether selections which give a feeling of rest also produce a feeling of pleasantness. On this point she found that for all her listeners the effect of dignity ranked lowest in pleasantness, so that its presence or absence did not in itself affect the attitude towards a musical selection. The highest correlation between enjoyment and effect produced was found to be for amusement. In this connection Gatewood states that: "There is reason to suppose that a selection which is highly amusing would be greatly enjoyed; and indeed this was found to be true in certain instances not included in this study. The difficulty here is that too few selections proved to be *very* amusing. Many people would find some of those same selections highly amusing and would enjoy them correspondingly. So far as our results indicate, the feeling of amusement plays only a small role in the total experience of musical enjoyment, but the extent to which musical enjoyment is related to the feeling of amusement when present is very marked." (28, p. 89)

Gatewood summarizes her conclusions on the relation between emotional effect and enjoyment as follows:

1. Other things being equal, those selections which show high emotional effect are most enjoyed.

2. Those selections which show several emotional effects are more enjoyable than those which show one or none, other things being equal.

3. Those selections the sum of whose emotional effects is great show greater musical pleasure.

4. One cannot predict the kind of emotional quality from the score on pleasantness, for the simple reason that any emotional quality may be accompanied by marked musical pleasure. However, certain emotional effects are more often derived from highly enjoyed musical selections than are others, the relative correlation varying with individuals. For each of these observers, amusement is the least important factor in musical enjoyment.

5. There are marked individual differences in relative order, but the relationship of pleasure and emotional reaction for each of the nine emotional qualities is very evident. There is a decided similarity between individuals in the *relative* proportions of musical enjoyment associated with each emotional effect. (28, p. 90)

Another study by Gatewood dealt with a comparison of the four elements of music, namely, rhythm, melody, harmony, and timbre, with the fundamental sources of musical enjoyment and with the reported effect of the music on the listener. In this investigation data were gathered from the reactions of thirty-five listeners to ten musical compositions. The observers were instructed to listen carefully to each selection, then at the close of each number to report, first, which one of the four elements was most prominent; second, the effect produced by the selection, namely, feeling of movement, simple satisfaction or enjoyment, images aroused, associations aroused, or an interest either in the composition, interpretation, or in the technique of the artist; third, the emotional effect of the music, whether sad, serious, gay, etc. The results indicated that marked rhythm was the chief factor in arousing the feeling of happiness and the feeling of excitement and stir, while melody and timbre produced the effect of seriousness and rest. Harmony was correlated with the feeling of sensuous satisfaction and with ideational effect.

A similar study to that of Gatewood was made by Washburn and Dickinson (118). The object of the study was to note how frequently rhythm, melody, design, harmony, and tone color were mentioned as contributing to the enjoyment of instrumental music, to observe the relation of pleasantness to the exciting and quieting effects of music, and to classify the emotions produced by instrumental music. Each listener was instructed to supply the following data: the degree of pleasantness experienced from the composition, the sources from which the pleasure was derived, whether from rhythm, melody, design, harmony, or tone color, the effect of the selection, whether exciting, quieting, or neutral, and any other emotional effect not included under the heads of pleasantness, excitement, and quieting.

The results from this study indicated that melody predominated as the most noticeable source of pleasure, with rhythm coming next, followed in order by harmony, design, and tone color. These results simply indicate the relative degree of attention that these elements attracted, rather than the amount each contributed to pleasure. Thus harmony and tone color attracted less attention than melody and rhythm, but it is by no means certain that they contributed less to enjoyment.

It was further found that markedly exciting or markedly quieting compositions were more agreeable than compositions that were neither exciting nor quieting to the majority of listeners. Furthermore, a tendency existed for the pleasantness to be greater the greater the number of sources to which that pleasantness was referred. The emotional states of happiness, gaiety, calm, sadness, and their equivalents were mentioned from 20 to 200 times as often as any others.

Washburn (117) and two collaborators made a further study on the effect of immediate repetition on the pleasantness or unpleasantness of music. Groups of listeners heard a section of a composition five times in succession. Eight compositions were presented in this manner. The sections were always the first part of the compositions, and covered a complete musical theme. The music was chosen by an expert from four types of orchestral selections, namely, severely classical, serious popular classical, easy popular classical, and popular.

On a basis of the data obtained from this study the investigators concluded that, in the case of popular music, repetition tends more strongly to lower than to raise the pleasantness derived from a composition, whereas, for more serious music, five immediate repetitions have a somewhat greater tendency to raise than to lower the pleasantness of the selection. Very popular music reaches the maximum pleasure at an early performance in contrast to seriously classical compositions in which the greatest amount of pleasure is derived from a late performance. The conditions which decrease pleasantness through repetition are thus more operative for extremely popular music, while those which increase it are more operative for seriously classical music. Furthermore, musical listeners have a tendency to lose pleasure on repetition sooner than the unmusical ones, with the exception of the seriously classical compositions.

An interesting study of a practical nature to the concert artist was made by Downey and Knapp (13) on the effects on a musical program of familiarity and of sequence of selections. The experiment was conducted with a class of college students who listened to a musical program of nine compositions grouped into national feeling, poetic thought, program music, and formal construction. The program was given on the phonograph and the compositions were so arranged that the first number of each of the four groups was the more subtle or involved example of the form it represented, while the second number was the most obvious example that could be found. The audience of 33 persons, all of average or less than average musical ability, listened to this program at weekly intervals for five weeks, and were asked to make three reports: first, on the degree of pleasantness or unpleasantness of the selection heard, and second and third, on the vividness and quality of imagery aroused.

The experimenters found that repetition increased the pleasantness of these musical selections, the gain, however, being greatest for the more subtle or aesthetic compositions. This points to the probability that compositions of the greatest artistic value would come to be strongly preferred over the less artistic even by non-musical persons if such music were heard often enough to become familiar.

CHAPTER 6

THE TYPES OF MUSICAL EXPERIENCE

THAT INDIVIDUALS DIFFER TO A significant degree in what music means to them and in what they get out of it, is apparent to even the most casual observer. Even among the best and most cultivated minds in matters of art and literature wide variations are found, as from Dr. Johnson who found music to be "the costliest of rackets" to Carlyle to whom it was a kind of "inarticulate, unfathomable speech which leads us to the edge of the infinite, and lets us for a moment gaze into that." In psychological literature several attempts have been made to introduce some order into this chaos by discovering underlying similarities in the apparent diversities which might be used as a basis for classifying listeners into a number of characteristic types.

The sources from which evidences for the existence of varieties of musical experiences can be drawn are threefold, namely, empirical or experiential, theoretical or speculative, and experimental or scientific. By empirical is meant casual accounts of responses to music to be found in various literary sources; by theoretical evidences is meant more or less studied enumerations of types of reactions to music, the basis for these types being the opinion of the particular writer; experimental evidences consist of scientifically planned laboratory procedures in the attempt to discover individual differences to various types of stimuli.

EVIDENCES FROM EMPIRICAL LITERATURE

In "A Chapter on Ears" in his Essays of Elia, the genial Charles Lamb gives the following account of his musical experiences:

> I even think that, *sentimentally,* I am disposed to harmony. But *organically* I am incapable of a tune. I have been practicing "God

Save the King" all my life; whistling and humming it over to myself in solitary corners; and am not yet arrived, they tell me, within many quavers of it. Yet hath the loyalty of Elia never been impeached.

It is hard to stand alone in an age like this, (constituted to the quick and critical perception of all harmonious combinations, I verily believe, beyond all preceding ages, since Jubal stumbled upon the gamut) to remain, as it were, singly unimpressible to the magic influences of an art, which is said to have such an especial stroke at soothing, elevating, and refining the passions. Yet, rather than break the candid current of my confessions, I must avow to you, that I have received a great deal more pain than pleasure from this so cried-up faculty.

I am constitutionally susceptible to noises. A carpenter's hammer, in a warm summer noon, will fret me into more than midsummer madness. But those unconnected, unset sounds are nothing to the measured malice of music. The ear is passive to those single strokes; willingly enduring stripes while it hath no task to con. To music it cannot be passive. It will strive—mine at least will—'spite of its inaptitude, to thread the maze; like an unskilled eye painfully poring upon hieroglyphics. I have sat through an Italian Opera, till, for sheer pain, and inexplicable anguish, I have rushed out into the noisiest places of the crowded streets, to solace myself with sounds, which I was not obliged to follow, and get rid of the distracting torment of endless, fruitless, barren attention! I take refuge in the unpretending assemblance of honest common-life sounds; and the purgatory of the Enraged Musician becomes my paradise.

I have sat at an Oratorio (that profanation of the purposes of the cheerful playhouse) watching the faces of the auditory in the pit (what a contrast to Hogarth's Laughing Audience) immovable, or affecting some faint emotion, until (as some have said, that our occupations in the next world will be but a shadow of what delighted us in this) I have imagined myself in some cold Theatre in Hades where some of the forms of the earthly one should be kept up, with none of the enjoyment; or like that

Party in a parlor
All silent, and all DAMNED.

Above all those insufferable concertos, and pieces of music, as they are so called, do plague and imbitter my apprehension. Words are something; but to be exposed to an endless battery of mere sounds; to be long adying; to lie stretched upon a rack of roses; to keep up languor by unintermitted effort; to pile honey upon sugar, and sugar upon honey, to an interminable tedious sweetness; to fill up sound with feeling, and strain ideas to keep pace with it; to gaze on empty frames, and be forced to make the pictures for yourself; to read a book, *all stops,* and be obliged to supply the verbal matter; to invent some extempore tragedies to answer to the vague gestures of an inexplicable rambling mind,—these are faint shadows of what I have undergone from a series of the ablest executed pieces of this empty *instrumental music.*

That the case of Charles Lamb's sufferings is not an isolated one, but no doubt represents a group which finds music of a particular type nothing short of torture, if not an abomination, is shown by the following comments of Mark Twain:

I have attended opera, whenever I could not help it, for fourteen years now; I am sure I know of no agony comparable to the listening of an unfamiliar opera. I am enchanted with the airs of "Trovatore" and other old operas which the hand-organ and the music-box have made entirely familiar to my ear. I am carried away with delighted enthusiasm when they are sung at the opera. But oh, how far between they are! And what long, and heartbreaking and headaching "between-times" of that sort of intense but incoherent noise which always reminds me of the time the orphan asylum burned down.

Huge crowd out tonight to hear the band play the "Fremersberg"! I suppose it is very low-grade music—I know it must be low-grade—because it so delighted me, it so warmed me, moved me, stirred me, uplifted me, enraptured me, that at times I could have cried, and at others split my throat with shouting. The great crowd was another evidence that it was low-grade music, for only the few are educated up to a point where high-class music gives pleasure. I have never heard enough classic music to be able to enjoy it, and the simple truth is I detest it. Not mildly, but with all my heart.

What a poor lot we human beings are anyway! If base music gives me wings, why should I want any other? But I do. I want to like the higher music because the higher and better like it. But you see I want to like it without taking the necessary trouble, and giving the thing the necessary amount of time and attention. The natural suggestion is to get into that upper tier, that dress-circle, by a lie—we will *pretend* we like it. This lie, this pretense, gives to opera what support it has in America.

In complete contrast to the types of attitude illustrated in the above passages, we have the view of Robert Browning who speaks the following words through the mouth of his character Abt Vogler:

All through my keys that gave their sounds to a wish of
  my soul,
All through my soul that praised as its wish flowed visibly
  forth,
All through music and me! For think, had I painted the
  whole,
Why, there it had stood, to see, nor the process so wonder-
  worth:
Had I written the same, made verse-still, effect proceeds from
  cause,
Ye know why the forms are fair, ye hear how the tale is told;
It is all triumphant art, but art in obedience to laws,
Painter and poet are proud in the artist-list enrolled:—

But here is the finger of God, a flash of the will that can,
Existent behind all laws that made them and, lo, they are!
And I know not if, save in this, such gift be allowed to man,
That out of three sounds he frame, not a fourth sound, but
  a star.
Consider it well: each tone in our scale in itself is naught;
It is every where in the world—loud, soft, and all is said:
Give it to me to use! I mix it with two in my thought;
And, there! Ye have heard and seen: consider and bow the
  head.

These two types of musical reaction represent the extremes of the scale of musical experiences. Between these two there are gradations and shadings of which we find evidences in the theoretical literature.

EVIDENCES FROM THEORETICAL LITERATURE

Probably the most outstanding contribution of a theoretical nature as yet made to an analysis of attitudes towards music is found in Gurney (33).

Gurney defines and distinguishes two ways of hearing and enjoying music, which "though they shade into one another, and may each of them in various degrees be realized by a single individual in listening to a single composition, are for all that in their typical state radically different. They may be called the definite and indefinite way." (33, p. 304) These two ways of hearing and enjoying music "connect themselves most clearly and conveniently with perception and non-perception of form; the *definite* character of Music involving the perception of individual melodic and harmonic combinations, and the *indefinite* character involving merely the perception of successions of agreeably-toned and harmonious sound." (33, pp. 305-306)

There are various reasons, Gurney states, why "the pleasure arising from any series or combination of sounds which conveys no distinct musical meaning should be lower and less than that attainable through more definite apprehension. . . . First, there is the evidence of the majority of those who at all enjoy listening to Music, and who have experienced at different times both sorts of pleasure. Next, we have the right to identify the higher pleasure with the more specialized, that which is appreciated by the more developed and differentiated sense; and which of course belongs to the distinct exercise of the musical faculty, as opposed to the nearly universal nervous susceptibility to the effect of rich and powerful sound. Next, while the impression of mere beauty of sound-colour is exceptionally sensuous and passive, not admitting of any of the indirect aesthetic effects given (as we have seen) by the material of Architecture, nor of the associations of space and freedom which a painter's most formless hues may gain from the blue sky and the other coloured spaces of nature, the apprehension of musical motives, on the other hand, constitutes a specially active kind of self-realization. And lastly, there is the point already sufficiently insisted on, the power of, in some measure at least, permanently possessing forms which have once become familiar, in contrast to the utter transience of all formless sound-effects." (33, p. 307)

Gurney insists that "a 'musical ear,' in the sense of an ear which distinctly grasps, recognizes, and remembers music" is no criterion of the value of the art to any individual. "While it is natural to consider as unmusical those persons in whom a 'musical ear' is lacking or is only imperfectly developed, and who therefore cannot at all reproduce or perhaps recognize melodies, such persons can often derive extreme pleasure of a vague kind from fine sound, more especially when it rushes through the ear in large masses. They will be apt to find their own meanings in music, which merely shows that the sound has a stimulating or a soothing effect on their nerves, and acts as a congenial background for their subjective trains of thought and emotion." (33, p. 306)

A more systematic theoretical classification of types of listeners is contained in a study by Ortmann (72). Ortmann's classification is genetic, in that he traces the gradual transition of elementary forms of response to the more highly developed and complex forms of musical reaction.

The most rudimentary form of response Ortmann calls the *sensorial* type which has for its basis the raw sensory material of music, namely, to what is given in the auditory stimulus itself, as a single tone, or an unanalyzed chord. This sensorial type of response, Ortmann holds, is typical of children, untrained adults, untalented pupils, and is the predominant factor in popular music. On the mental side, it is characterized by non-voluntary and spontaneous attention.

A more highly developed form of response Ortmann characterizes as the *perceptual* type, which he describes as the interpretation of the sensorial effect. This response is concerned with progressions, sequences, motif, phrase, form, outline, contrast, ascent, descent, movement; in other words, a response to tonal relationships. "The sensorial response represents a single impression upon consciousness. In the perceptual the effect of each separate stimulus is determined by its environment. What has preceded the present stimulus leaves its influence upon it. A tone now becomes a part of a melody, a chord becomes a part of a tonality, and a phrase becomes part of a form." (72, pp. 52-53) On the mental side, the perceptual response involves active or voluntary attention. "Since perception is a conscious process demanding for its proper operation both analysis and synthesis, it is accompanied by active or voluntary attention. It means a response to the stimulus different from the nature of the stimulus itself. This added increment is the result of sustained concentration or mental work." (72, p. 58) This form of response, according to Ortmann, is typical of the musician, the student, and the talented layman. It is also an index of persons of musical talent. "Perceptual response in all but a very primitive form, is largely absent from the response forms of the untalented person. This type of response is preeminently that of the talented person. Between these extremes we have the moderate presence of perceptual response among normal subjects. A subject of normal musical ability can, through training, develop a not insignificant degree of perceptual power." (72, pp. 62-63)

A still higher form is the *imaginal* type which results from the play of imagery. "Perceptual response was essentially presentative, imaginal response is re-presentative. . . . Concepts such as tonality, anticipated chordal resolutions, response to a melody *in harmony,* and the like, are results of an imaginal process in its reproductive form." (72, p. 66) The imaginal response is characteristic essentially of trained musicians and superiorly talented laymen who had frequent association with auditory stimuli.

Ortmann draws the following conclusions from his study:

1. Reaction to music is a form of reaction in general, and obeys the same laws. Definite types of reaction exist only so far as they exist in other sense-departments.

2. The relatively constant element in reaction-types to music is the psychological level at which they occur, for example: sensation, perception, imagination. The variable element is the individual, who changes in the mode of reaction with a change in the stimulus, and also with a change in attitude.

3. Reaction to music is, psychologically, the result of a development, rather than of a given state.

4. The determinant of reaction to music is native capacity plus experience and training. Training has a strong effect on reactions to music.

5. Training or experience increases our enjoyment of music. Any device tending to increase familiarity with artistic music is psychologically desirable. (72, pp. 75-76)

EVIDENCES FROM EXPERIMENTAL LITERATURE

Of the few experimental studies made up to date to determine types of listeners, those by Myers (65) on individual differences in listening to music, and by Lee (54) on the varieties of musical experience are the most outstanding and noteworthy.

The classification made by Myers is based on the results of introspective reports of 15 persons while listening to six musical compositions. These 15 persons consisted of 9 men and 6 women who varied considerably in their musicalness, 2 of them being highly gifted professional musicians, 3 fairly accomplished musicians, 5 of extremely artistic temperament, though not performers, 2 of average degree of musical taste, and 3 relatively unmusical.

The music, which was performed on the phonograph, consisted of the following selections: Beethoven's "Overture to Egmont" (Op. 84), Tschaikowsky's *Valse des Fleurs* from his "Casse Noisette Suite" (Op. 714) and his "Italian Capriccio" (Op. 45), Mendelssohn's "Overture to the Hebrides (Fingal's Cave)" (Op. 26), the first of Grieg's "Symphonic Dances" (Op. 64), and Kreisler's setting and rendition of Couperin's "Aubade Provencale." All but the last of these selections were orchestral performances.

From the introspective reports of the subjects of their impressions Myers deduces four types of listeners to music, which, although not mutually exclusive, are sufficiently distinct to permit of classification. These four types are as follows:

1. *The intra-subjective type,* to whom the musical material appeals for the sensory, emotional or conative experience which it arouses. That is, the attention is held by the sensory effects, or the flow of feeling, or the experience of self-activity induced by the music. The following are some typical reports from subjects belonging to this type: "A restful feeling throughout . . . like one of going down stream while swimming . . . I wanted to throw myself back and be carried along." "That was lovely. . . . Something lifting, raising you inside. Like what one gets in church." "I imagine I am going to die, as though life were just ebbing out." "A great feeling of happiness; followed by expansion inside, leading to great excitement inside and breathlessness

for a moment." "I cannot get anything out of it but depression. A delightful feeling of welcoming the end. . . . I had feelings of sorrow and dissatisfaction with everything. They gained on me. All the time I was trying to get the better of those feelings, but they wouldn't leave me."

2. *The associative type,* for whom the main appeal of the music lies in the associations which it suggests. The following are typical reports from this type of listener: "I was in the Queen's Hall, a fair girl in a pink dress was playing and another girl was accompanying her. The violinist had a sad look about her. I felt she had had a sorrow in her life." "It started with a stage full of people;—a tremendous lot of movement about it and brightness. The people were all in costumes. Then a singer came on from a house on the right side of the stage, telling a pathetic love story. Then I lost the solo part, the stage became dark, and all the people left, except, I believe, the singer who remained in some quiet corner."

3. *The objective type,* to whom the music appeals for its use or value considered as an object, or, in other words, the listener who assumes a critical, analytical attitude towards music. Some typical responses from this type of listener follow: "I noticed the second horn was too loud. . . . When the second tune came in with the cellos, it didn't stand out enough." "I noticed by what simple means in these modern days he gets his effects. . . . I noticed also . . . how he gathered up his climax by syncopation." "As always in Beethoven, one must notice the tremendous . . . contrasts, especially dynamic contrasts. His crescendos always give me pleasure. Beethoven makes scale passages so much more interesting than, say, Liszt." "As usual, the violinist uses too much *vibrato*. . . . The sweep up the strings made me feel quite sick." "I now nearly always view music from the critical standpoint. I conduct; I compose. I always want to know how the conductor is getting effects if it is a *new* work, and what will be his rendering if it is an old one. . . . I never think of 'programme' unless it is suggested to me. . . . To me music is never sad or joyful. I only get aesthetic impression."

4. *The character type,* to whom the music appeals for its character personified as a subject, or in other words, the listener who characterizes the music in such terms as morbid, joyful, dainty, mystic, reckless, playful, etc. Thus, several subjects reported: "Very beautiful, but very mournful and sad; a drawing out of the agony." "I tried to be light hearted, but was all the time very sad." "The piece sounded cheerful

in certain parts." "It is also intentionally sad." "It was quite upsetting; it made me feel sad." "There was a note of sadness among the dancers in parts, a sort of regretfulness." "The music seemed as if it were joking with me; it made me want to smile."

Myers draws some far-reaching conclusions from his study concerning the attitude of the trained musician to music, the place of associations in the musical response, and the relative aesthetic values of the different types of musical responses. He finds that the objective attitude towards music, in which the musical material is considered in reference to the listener's standard, occurs most frequently among those technically trained in music, who tend to adopt a critical attitude and are interested in the material of their art. This type of listener has a tendency to suppress all personal feelings, activities, associations, and characterizations that the music might evoke, in favor of the critical, analytical standpoint. As to the place of associations or imagery in the musical response, Myers claims that the grossly unmusical get no associations from music because it arouses no emotion in them, while the professional musician tends to inhibit associations by his critical, objective attitude. The most highly musical also tend to repress associations because they listen to music for its own meaning and beauty. Four out of the five most artistic of Myers' subjects, with little or no technical knowledge of music, heard music as a pattern, color, or expanse instead of associations. Myers' further comments on this point are worth quoting in full:

When the average person listens to music, then, associations are enjoyed for their own sake, adding enormously to the total aesthetic appreciations obtainable. The associations may be in themselves beautiful: they invite the listener to share in the beauty of a story and in the emotions of the persons created in his imagination. Among the more highly musical I find that associations are more particularly apt to intrude when the music is felt to be "stagey," unreal, meretricious, or vulgar. Thus M. reports associations as the music "began to get more barbaric" and as he "lost interest in the music." He observes, however, "the middle of the second movement (which he enjoyed) switched me off my imagery, and I returned to the pure consideration of the music." (65, pp. 22-23)

In order that associations may be enjoyed for their beauty, either the music must be wholly neglected, and the story, the imagery, the wealth of colour enjoyed as if it were a work of art—which is seldom possible,—or the associations must blend or fuse in their general meaning (on which their beauty depends) with that of the music. Otherwise they can have no *aesthetic* value, but are merely affectively toned with pleasure or displeasure, or at most excite in the listener feelings of joy or distress, according to their cognitive or emotional content. In the following report from one of the listeners we see the distinction between unfused associations and associations of actively aesthetic value which fuse with that of music.

"I object to these suggestions, for I find that the music . . . is not listened to for itself." But, he continues, "when the suggestions and the music absolutely blend, there is the completest and greatest enjoyment, greater than when there is music alone. They won't blend here, because the dramatic scene will go on quite well, independently of the music." (65, pp. 23-24)

Lee's (54) study on the varieties of musical experience is more limited in its scope, in that the experimenter had specifically mentioned two possible types of attitudes towards music, and then asked the subjects to classify themselves into one or the other of the two groups.

Lee believes that an inquiry into what music does to the mind of the hearer, or more correctly, of what the mind of the hearer does in response to the music which he hears is an answer to the question of what music is. She therefore asked her subjects to respond to the following question: "When music interests you, has it got for you a meaning which seems beyond itself; or does it remain just music?"

She reports that "half of the subjects interrogated did precisely answer that undoubtedly music had a meaning beyond itself, many adding that if it had not it would constitute only sensual enjoyment, and be unworthy of their consideration, some of them moreover indignantly taking in this sense my words about music remaining just music. That for these persons music did not remain just music, but became the bearer of messages, was further made certain by pages and pages, often of unexpectedly explicit or eloquent writing which admitted to describe the nature of that message, to describe the things it dealt with and the more or less transcendental spheres whence that message of music seemed to come." (54, p. 751)

The other half of her correspondents "either explicitly denied or disregarded the existence of such a message; insisted that music had not necessarily any meaning beyond itself, and far from taking the words 'remains just music' as derogatory to the art or to themselves, they answered either in the selfsame words or by some paraphrase, that when they cared for music it remained just music. And in the same way that the believers in *meaning as message* often gave details about the contents of that message, so, on the other hand, the subjects denying the existence of a message frequently made it quite clear that for them the meaning of music was in the music itself, adding that when really interested in music they could think of nothing but the music." (54, p. 751)

The nature of the message or the meaning found in music by the first group of listeners was principally visual or emotional, abstract or personal. "But fragmentary, fluctuating, and elusive as it was often described as being, and only in rare cases defining itself as a coherent series of pictures, a dramatic sequence or intelligible story, the message was nevertheless always a message, inasmuch as it appeared to be an addition made to the hearer's previous thoughts by the hearing of that music; and an addition due to that music and ceasing with its cessation." (54, p. 752)

The other half of the listeners did not deny the existence of a meaning or a message in music, but nevertheless claimed that "whenever they found music completely satisfying, any other meaning, anything like visual images or emotional suggestions, was excluded or reduced to utter unimportance. Indeed this class answered by a great majority that so far as emotion was concerned, music awakened in them an emotion *sui generis,* occasionally shot with human joy or sadness, or on the whole analogous to the exaltation and tenderness and sense of sublimity awakened by the beautiful in other arts or in nature, but not to be compared with the feeling resulting from the vicissitudes of real life. It was nearly always persons answering in this sense who explicitly acquiesced in the fact that music could remain, in no derogatory sense but quite the reverse, just music." (54, pp. 752-753)

Lee finally concludes that there are two quite distinct types of responses to music, namely, *listening* to music, and *hearing* music. The listener to music pays active attention to every detail of the composition and performance, "taking in all the relations, of sequences and combinations of sounds as regards pitch, intervals, modulations, rhythms, and intensities, holding them in memory and coordinating them in a series of complex wholes. . . ." (54, p. 755) It is these audible shapes themselves that constitute the meaning of the music to this class of listeners. The hearer of music, on the other hand, being incapable of actively following the musical form as such, excepting momentarily and in spots, compensates for his comparative poverty on the musical side with extra-musical thoughts, memories, associations, suggestions, visual images and emotional states, which ebb and flow about and around the rare moments of musical perception.

CHAPTER 7

THE AESTHETIC EXPERIENCE IN MUSIC

In the preceding chapter we have seen that individuals differ significantly in what music means to them and in what they get out of it. The classification of these differences into types of musical responses at once raises the question as to their relative aesthetic values, whether any one type can be said to constitute the musical response more so than any one or all of the other types, and the basis of the differences, whether they are due primarily to some factors of native endowment or arise mainly as a result of training and experience. On this problem we have some views from writers on musical aesthetics and some data from experimental investigations.

THE VIEWS OF AESTHETICIANS

The two outstanding works on the aesthetic phase of music versus its technical and scientific side are Hanslick's *The Beautiful in Music* and Gurney's *The Power of Sound.*

Hanslick is concerned entirely with combating the widespread notion that the significance of music lies in its power for emotional expression. This he calls a false assumption which has misled musical aesthetics into describing the feelings which music arouses instead of inquiring into what is beautiful in music. The task of aesthetic investigation, he holds, must be the beautiful object, and not the perceiving subject. And he complains that, apparently, it is only in music that this objective approach is lacking, so that the emotions are still as much as ever viewed as the only aesthetic foundation of music and looked upon as defining its scope and function.

The view that the aim and object of music is to arouse pleasurable emotions, or that emotions are the subject-matter which musical works are intended to express or convey, Hanslick vehemently denies. The beautiful, he contends, is a form, and has no aim beyond being a form. Music, likewise, has no aim or object other than as a form, and the mere fact that it is so closely bound up with one's feelings does not justify the assumption that its aesthetic significance and value are dependent upon the life of feeling.

What, then, constitutes the aesthetic hearing of music? Hanslick's answer is that ideas and feelings are extraneous to music, and that in the pure act of listening it is the music itself that is heard and enjoyed. Ideational processes are logical and not aesthetic, while feelings imply a pathological relation.

Hanslick does not, however, deny or underrate the feeling-tone of music. It is, he states, *"one of the most precious and inestimable secrets of nature, that an art should have the power of evoking feelings entirely free from worldly associations, and kindled, as it were, by the spark divine."* (35, p. 26) He protests only against deducing aesthetic principles from such facts, which he calls an unscientific proceeding. Anything can arouse feelings, but anything does not for that reason become an aesthetic object. Feelings, therefore, cannot constitute the substance of the aesthetic response, that is, of beauty. Music is enjoyed aesthetically only when heard for its own sake, and it ceases to be an art the moment it is used as a means to induce some state of mind or some emotion. He writes:

> Now the most essential condition to the aesthetic enjoyment of music is that of listening to a composition for its own sake, no matter what it is or what construction it might bear. The moment music is used as a means to induce certain states of mind, as accessory or ornamental, it ceases to be an art in a purely musical sense. The *elemental properties* of music are frequently confounded with its *artistic* beauty, in other words, a part is taken for the whole, and unutterable confusion ensues. Hundreds of sayings about "music" do not apply to the art as such, but to the sensuous action of its material only.
>
> When Shakespeare's "Henry the Fourth" calls for music on his death-bed (Part II, Act IV), it is most assuredly not to listen attentively to the performance, but to lull himself with its ethereal elements, as in a dream. Nor are Portia and Bassanio ("Merchant of Venice," Act III) likely to have greatly heeded the music which was being played during the ominous choosing of the casket. J. Strauss has composed

charming, nay, highly original music for his Waltzes, but it ceases to be such when it is solely used to beat time for the dancers. In all these cases it is utterly indifferent of what *quality* the music is, so long as it has the fundamental character needed for the occasion, and wherever the question of individuality is a matter of indifference we get a series of sounds, but no music. Only he who carries away with him, not simply the vague after-effect of his feelings, but a definite and lasting impression of the particular composition, has truly heard and relished it. Those impressions which elevate our minds, and their supreme significance both in a psychical and physiological sense, should not, however, hinder the art-critic from distinguishing in any given effect between its sensuous and its aesthetic element. From an aesthetic point of view, music ought to be regarded as an effect rather than a cause, as a product rather than a producing agent. (35, pp. 139-140)

Gurney, like Hanslick, denies that the significant musical factor in music lies in any meanings, whether of an emotional or ideational nature, that it might arouse in the hearer. Furthermore, music cannot directly express or suggest definite emotions, images, or ideas. He insists that "expressiveness of the literal and tangible sort is either *absent or only slightly present* in an immense amount of impressive Music," and that to "suggest describable images, qualities, or feelings, known in connection with other experiences, however frequent a characteristic of music, makes up no inseparable or essential part of its function. . . ." (33, p. 314) Neither definite suggestion nor the portrayal of any special and describable ideas, events or emotions, "can be held accountable for any musical *beauty* which may be present: a tune is no more constituted beautiful by an expression, e.g., of mournfulness or of capriciousness than a face is." (33, p. 318) Musical beauty resides, for him, in the unique musical experience which he describes as the *ideal motion.*

CONCLUSIONS FROM EXPERIMENTAL STUDIES

The results of experimental investigations on the aesthetic musical experience all appear to corroborate the claims of Hanslick, Pater, and Gurney.

Lee (54) concludes from her investigations on the two types of listeners, namely, one to whom music was just music, and the other to whom its significance lay in the message it conveyed, that, "the more musical answerers were also those who repudiated the message, who insisted that music had a meaning in itself, in fact, that it remained for them 'just music.' A certain number of highly musical subjects not only declared this to be the case with themselves, but foretold that we should find it so with every sufficiently musical hearer. Their own experience was that the maximum interest and maximum pleasure connected with music can leave no room for anything else." (54, p. 754) Such listeners often caught themselves thinking of something else while hearing music. But such lapses were regarded by them as irrelevancies and interruptions. Those persons, however, to whom the significance of music lay in what it suggested beyond itself were unaware of such lapses and interruptions. "From some of their answers one might have gathered that no musical person could sit through two hours of a concert with unflagging enjoyment. But further sets of inquiries revealed that although unbroken by boredom, restlessness or the conscious intrusion of irrelevant matters, the enjoyment was not confined to the music. When asked whether the music suggested anything, they abounded in accounts of inner visions, trains of thought and all manner of emotional dramas, often most detailed and extensive, which filled their minds while, as they averred, they were listening to the music; indeed some of which, they did not hesitate to admit, constituted the chief attraction of the music." (54, pp. 754-755)

Lee concludes finally that for the musical person listening to music implies the "most active attention moving along every detail of composition and performance, taking in all the relations of sequences and combinations of sounds as regards pitch, intervals, modulations, rhythms, and intensities, holding them in the memory and coordinating them in a series of complex wholes," and it is these audible forms themselves that constitute the meaning of music. The meaning resides in the music itself and is inseparable from it. The unmusical person, on the other hand, does not listen to music, but only hears or even overhears it. He compensates for his musical poverty with extra-musical matter. He has moments of concentrated and active musical attention, but these are, as Lee well states, "like islands continually washed over by a shallow tide of other thoughts, memories, associations, suggestions, visual images and emotional states, ebbing and flowing around the more or less clearly emergent musical perceptions, in such a way that each participates on the call of the other, till they coalesce and into the blend of musical thoughts there enters nothing which the hearer can recognize as inattention, as the concentrated musical listener recognizes the lapses and divagations of which he complains." (54, pp. 755-756)

Ortmann (72) also confirms the claims of Gurney and Hanslick. The sensorial reaction, he states, is typical of children, untrained adults, untalented pupils, and is the predominant factor in popular music. Of the perceptual and imaginal types in which attention to structural form, or the substance of music as music, is predominant, Ortmann says: "Perceptual response, in all but a very primitive form, is largely absent from the response form of the untalented person. This type of response is preeminently that of the talented person." (72, p. 62) ". . . we may expect to find the auditory imaginal response characteristic essentially of trained musicians and superiorly talented laymen who have frequent associations with auditory stimuli." (72, p. 70)

For the musical significance of the types established by him, Myers concludes that, among the more highly musical, associations are more particularly apt to intrude when the music is felt to be "stagey," unreal, meretricious, or vulgar.

It is by no means strange that associations should appear among the highly musical when music lacks interest or inherent beauty, whereas the less musical tend to appreciate music not so much on the grounds of its inherent beauty as for the enjoyment of the associations evoked. The explanation depends on difference of aesthetic level, the level of the musically gifted person standing higher than that of one averagely musical. So long as the former, attending merely to the music *qua* music, can maintain his high level of aesthetic enjoyment, associations are debarred from consciousness. But when for any reason he fails to maintain that level, *e.g.,* because his aesthetic appreciation ceases, then the products of lower-level aspects enter, *e.g.*, associations more or less incongruous with the enjoyment of beauty. (65, p. 23)

Myers summarizes his general conclusion from his studies as follows:

> We can now see how the various aspects which we have distinguished in the listener may each play a part in the awareness of beauty, and how the different fundamental connections of music with courtship, with dancing, and rudimentary language, may each contribute to aesthetic enjoyment. These different connections may be differently stressed in different persons today, so that one tends specially to sexual, another to dramatic, another to verbal associations with music. But we come to recognize that, apart from these connections, music may be appreciated for its own inherent beauty, that is to say, apart from its sensuous, emotional or conative influences and from associations, symbols and products of "animistic" characterizations. The one common and essential attitude required for aesthetic enjoyment is one of detachment. The listener must view the music, as Bullough rightly insists, from a certain psychical "distance." If that distance be excessive as occurs in listening for the first time to exotic music or to other unfamiliar styles of music, the person feels too remote to get, as it were, to grips with the art material. It is overdistanced. On the other hand, it is underdistanced, when he surrenders himself wholly to its influence in such a way that he is a more or less passive instrument, played upon by the music, without paying any regard to his sensations, images, emotions, or impulses, save in so far as they have immediately personal and "practical" import. (65, pp. 35-36)

Schoen (88) sent out questionnaires and held interviews with several prominent musical artists with the object in view of obtaining from them accounts of their musical experiences. The following question was put to these persons. "When you find yourself in an attitude of intense musical appreciation, what is your general condition of being, physical and mental?"

The answers from a few of the persons to this question follow:

> 1. I am usually in a state of muscular tension—with my hands clenched. If I am really in the aesthetic ecstasy, I am absolutely oblivious of my surroundings. I cannot get to that point except by the piano—that is really the only instrument that can give me the genuine

aesthetic feeling—then everything is black except where the piano is, and I am very tired afterwards. The effect stays with me for a day or two. I feel as though I do not want to be interrupted by anybody or anything rough or harsh, in any sense. I want nothing rough or coarse which could not share that state with me. . . . If I begin to think of any matters of personal interest or any memories while listening, then it is a sure sign that the music is mediocre, that it does not hold my attention as music. There are some associations in situations of this kind. If I hear some dance music, I may feel slightly different in mood, and I can sometimes trace it to a more or less temporary emotional experience, to some association with the dance. Even matters of momentary interest can have that influence upon the music that is not the musical experience at all. I might have the same experience with anything else. The smell of a perfume may have its associations. It is not an aesthetic one, but you can have a very definite association with some girl who has used that particular type of perfume. I have had experiences in which the music had a soothing effect, and I started daydreaming, perhaps extravagantly, of power and mastery, perhaps I dream of doing something which reveals social approval. If I do that, it means that I do not care a rap about the music.

2. When I am in a state of the most intense enjoyment of music, I am never introspective. I never catch myself at it. Looking back on it, I should say that I have rather become the music than remained something apart with some attitude toward it. On the less intense absorption, I should say that music in a very definite way restores me in body, mind, and spirit. I am afraid I am a poor informant though in this case, for I really cannot state confidently any one reaction except that of a wrapt condition, at the end of which I take a deep breath and come back. My enjoyment is derived directly from the music. Associations or imagery, even when suggested by the title, fade from my mind as I listen to the music, and I do little except get my mouth set for the particular kind of taste which I am about to receive.

3. When I find myself in the act of intense enjoyment, it is generally after the experience is over. For such moments, loss of myself is fairly complete. This is, however, for special occasions; the ordinary rhythmic enjoyment of music is very much on the plane of any usual sensuous enjoyment, as eating or drinking. The self is perfectly conscious of the thing being enjoyed. In the supreme moment there seems to be a fusion and I am one with the thing heard. Such moments cannot be but a few seconds in duration, but they raise the whole attitude into a different level. . . . Music that does not affect me strongly often sets

me off into a revery, if it does not roil me. But in the supreme moment the enjoyment seems to come directly as the result of the music, without any suggestion whatever, except that of motion and movement. What I seem to feel is perfection, the realization of an ideal, and perfect harmony between matter and spirit. Why this should move me so, I am unable to tell unless it may be that as in our ordinary consciousness our physical, mental, and spiritual limitations are constantly with us and we are living most of the time, because of our personality, in a state of strife, whenever a perfect moment comes and we forget ourselves, and find the strife giving place to a perfect union, we experience a certain vacation or respite from ourselves.

These speculative and experimental studies just surveyed point to the conclusion that the beautiful in music lies in "listening to music," and not in "hearing music"; not in the associations, images, reflections or emotions that it may arouse, as secondary or derived effects, but in the experiencing of the "thing itself," the musical form. And even this experiencing of the "thing itself" must be direct, spontaneous, detached, and not arbitrary, critical or analytical. That is, it must be "listening *to* music," not "listening *about* music." Myers rightly insists that "To treat the art material as a mere inanimate object having a certain value in reference to the person's standard is . . . merely a last resource in the case of the untrained; while in the case of the technician, it is a consequence of his absorption in the material. It is the refuge of the untrained in the absence of the potentially aesthetic aspects of character, associations, and intra-subjective experience. It is the resource of the artist, in his endeavor by repression to escape from the influence of the other aspects, in order, it may be, to obtain the highest appreciable beauty of music, the beauty of musical meaning which is inexpressible in any other terms." (65, pp. 29-30) The conscious critical attitude is destructive of the aesthetic experience, since analysis destroys the very substance of object being analyzed.

THE BASIS OF THE MUSICAL RESPONSE

Only one study on the basis of the aesthetic response to music is available at present. The problem investigated by Schoen (89) was whether this response was principally the result of training, of habit formation, or whether it depended primarily upon the possession of some native powers in which individuals differ in degree.

Schoen was guided in his experimental procedure by several conclusions he drew from the studies on the nature of the musically aesthetic experience just surveyed. The substance of these conclusions he states as follows:

1. Objectively, a melody consists of a series of discrete tones differing from each other in pitch, intensity, duration, timbre, and two phenomena that arise from timbre, namely, volume and extensity. "Objectively" implies that a photograph of the tones of a melody would reveal no more than sound-waves whose properties vary in frequency, amplitude, length, and complexity of structure or number of overtones. Thus, let a person listen to a melody purely objectively, and he will hear not a melody, but a sequence of tones varying in the four attributes of musical sounds. Consequently, when a person speaks of having *heard* a melody, he is really speaking of a melody he has *formed,* since what he heard was no more than a sequence of musical sounds. A melody is thus not something heard, but something created by the hearer out of the raw tonal material supplied him. To hear a melody is to evolve a form out of a given variety of tonal material, so that what is a melody to one person may be no more than a conglomeration of more or less pleasant sounds to another person.

2. When such a form becomes significant in itself as a form, the experience is aesthetic. That is, the person who has such an experience will label it "beautiful." Beauty in music is a judgment, an evaluation, of an intrinsic tonal experience. When such a form becomes significant not in itself, but for some extraneous cause, such as a flow of ideas prompted by it, or a sequence of pleasant pictures, day-dreams or reminiscences, the experience is non-aesthetic. When a person values all his musical experiences for such extraneous reasons, his attitude to music is non-aesthetic, and he is non-musical. Thus, the conditions for the enjoyment of music by a non-musical person are two: (1) Familiarity: either (a) he has heard the series of tones a sufficient number of times to get accustomed to them so that their originally annoying effect has worn off; or (b) their sequence is so obvious, so like something else to which he has become accustomed, that he can respond to them with the pleasant feeling of "I know you," (2) Concreteness: either (a) music tells him a story or paints a picture, or (b) the structural pattern of the music has been expounded to him and he can follow

it in the course of its development as one follows a game of cards or chess. (89, pp. 348-349)

From the above Schoen concludes that at the bottom of the aesthetic response to music is a power which may be termed *form-mindedness,* and an inquiry into the sources or background of this form-mindedness should reveal the basis of music-mindedness. The key to such an inquiry he finds in the obvious fact that, since form is a construction made out of the raw tonal material, there must be some relationship between form-mindedness and one's sensitivity to this material. If we then find that there is a high correlation between form-mindedness and sensitivity to musical material, we may conclude (1) that the degree of one's aesthetic response to music is in direct proportion to the degree of one's sensitivity to pitch, intensity, duration and timbre, and (2) that since sensitivity to this musical material rests upon innate powers, the aesthetic response to music is also innate, and not acquired. If, however, the data show no such correlation, if differences in sensitivity to musical material do not go hand in hand with aesthetic responsiveness—that is, if we find instances of low sensitivity with high aesthetic responsiveness, and high sensitivity with low aesthetic responsiveness—then it is clear that aesthetic responsiveness is the result primarily of training.

The experimental procedure followed in seeking data on this problem involved three steps: (1) the obtaining of data on a person's attitude towards music, (2) the ascertaining of the person's sensitivity to tonal material, and (3) the correlating of the data from sources 1 and 2.

The experiments were conducted on college students and faculty members. Some of them were studying, or had studied, a musical instrument; others had had no more than the usual musical training of the public school or high school. Altogether, some 70 subjects took part in all the experiments. Each subject filled out a long questionnaire, had an interview with the investigator, listened to and reported his reactions to a program of twelve selections, and was given four music tests. In the questionnaire the person gave information about his mental and temperamental make-up, and his training, experience, interests, and preferences in music. The interview was a check-up on the information furnished by the questionnaire, particularly as to the person's attitude towards music and the rôle that music played in his life. There were 40 questions in the interview, and it was conducted in a very informal, conversational manner, so that the investigator deviated from the set program whenever he thought it advisable. The subject was not questioned directly, but was led along to comment freely and spontaneously on musical matters.

Following are some excerpts from several interviews:

1. The first thing which occurs to me is that musical experience—the musical experience—cannot be described in words; a very, very serious limitation, that of language. I dislike very much to have people tell me the story of a musical selection. I never read it. If I see on the program the story of the composition I won't read it. I may read it afterwards but never before, because that spoils the music for me. If I read it before, I try to imagine things, I try to think where this event fits in the composition, and where that description fits. Of course, if I like the music, it doesn't matter, but otherwise I never listen. I like the harmonic element in music but am rather bored with the melodic element if it is too prominent. There are, however, exceptions to that. The only way in which I could describe the exceptions would be that of hearing the music—I could then say "I like that" or "I dislike that."

I like the piano. I had rather hear one good piano recital than ten vocal concerts, no matter who the singer is. . . . The orchestra—I should probably like the orchestra more than the piano if I understood it, but it tends to be a confused mass of tones which confuses me. I should put the piano first and the orchestra second.

2. I sometimes wonder what other people see in music that I don't. I do not think I have an ear for music. I felt bad as a child because I could not sing. My attention wanders a great deal when I listen to music; sometimes I hardly hear the music at all. Music is an ideal setting for me for dreams. If I know some story connected with the music, I am more interested in it. I don't recognize music very easily. I have great difficulty in distinguishing between "Traümerei" and "The Last Rose of Summer."

3. I am extremely fond of music and I play the piano some. I have no technical knowledge of music. My tendencies are highbrow, my favorites being Brahms, Massenet, and Grieg. My familiarity with these

is the result of my sister's singing of their songs. The piano is least music for me. I prefer the cello and a contralto. I cannot stand high notes and brilliant music.

4. I like music primarily with pronounced rhythm, long continued like the marching tunes of bands. I like this better than anything else, that is, the long sustained rhythm. I once enjoyed a piece by Beethoven. The trouble with music is that it is too choppy; it lacks continuity. It keeps me on the jump. It does not continue what it began. I will not go to high class concerts. I used to be forced to go to them. I day-dream most of the time when I listen to music. Music sets the pace to my thoughts and pictures that it arouses. I revolt against the mental factor in music, that is, for the mind to be active. The majority of music that I like I hardly hear at all. If you would play it again, I would not recognize it. Music is a background for something else that holds the attention. The choppy music is interesting, but the other kind of music is music. When I pay attention to music, it is interesting, but when I don't pay attention I enjoy it.

5. I have a funny attitude toward music. I like Irving Berlin. I don't like extreme jazz. I like sentimental waltzes, songs, and piano and the opera when the singers do not make too much effort to act. I prefer vocal to instrumental; there is more variety in it. My perceptions are not fine enough to get instrumental music. The repetition of themes bores me as it appears in different instruments. The voice appeals to me. Singing appeals to me as a kind of reading.

6. I have liked classical music, because we had it in the family. I was put to sleep with the best music as a child. I had music lessons when young in violin and piano, but got nowhere. I prefer the music of the Masters. I prefer orchestra. I like to follow the themes and melodies as they occur in the composition, and the variety of instruments gives me rich experiences. I get visions of movement in the orchestra, or people moving. It stirs me up emotionally, particularly high notes get me terribly tense, but soft music makes me sorrowful. My enjoyment is more emotional than intellectual. The piano does not stir me up. It lacks shading, connection between notes, and variety of tone. I do not like vocal music, because the tones produced by the human voice are not as pleasing as those of an instrument. I like to hear boys' choirs and the high soprano of a boy.

The program to which each subject listened included music from the most vividly pictorial, such as the "William Tell Overture," to the most strictly formal, such as the "Air from Bach's

Suite in D." It supplied data on the person's actual responses to music. The subject commented freely on each selection, and also filled out a form like the following:

State below, as definitely as you can, your general state of being at the present moment, physical and mental, particularly the mood you are in. For example, "I am tired, and feel like taking a walk or a chat with a friend, need some relaxation, etc."

Do you enjoy the mood you are in at present, or are you eager to change it, or are you indifferent?

If eager to change the present mood what kind of mood would you rather be in? Comment freely.

You will now hear a piece of music. Put yourself in the same attitude as you would adopt at a concert, or, in other words, free your mind of everything and give yourself up entirely to the music. You have absolutely nothing to do now but listen. Do not read what follows.

Now do what you did at the very beginning, namely, comment in full on your present mood and state of being. Do not put down anything that you think will sound nice, but give as accurate a picture of yourself at the present moment as you possibly can.

Below are five numbers. Underscore one of them to indicate the degree of your enjoyment of the music you just heard. oo means you were irritated by the music; o, no effect; 2, enjoyed slightly; 4, moderately; 6, greatly enjoyed.

oo   o   2   4   6

Do you judge the selection you just heard as being good or poor music, irrespective of the enjoyment you get from it? Underscore your judgment below.

very poor,   poor,   fair,   good,   very good

What kind of music would you like to hear now, in preference to any other kind? Describe it as well as you can.

Indicate below your familiarity with the selection you just heard.

new   slightly familiar   familiar   very familiar

Give the name of the selection if you can.

The music tests used were for sensitivity to pitch, intensity, relative pitch, and tonal sequence. These tests indicated the subject's sensitivity to the raw material of music. The questionnaire, interviews, and music programs showed whether a person was an intrinsic or extrinsic listener. A comparison, therefore, of the subject's test-score and his musical response would indicate what relationship, if any, existed between his native musical resources and the kind of effect that music produced upon him. Thus, if the data indicated that the test-score for all intrinsic listeners was in every instance above that for the extrinsic listeners, the conclusion would be warranted that the intrinsic response to music was an inherent, native power. For this critical comparison the subjects were divided into two groups on the basis of their test-score, one group consisting of those whose average was 75 and above, and the other of those whose average was below 75.

The following self-portraits (from the interviews) are taken at random from the material assembled concerning 73 subjects. Each of them had had several years of musical training on the piano. After each portrait the test-score of the subject delineated is given. The comparison thus made possible indicates the general conclusions that may be drawn from these experiments regarding the basis of music-mindedness. The data given are listed in pairs, each of which consists of information about an intrinsic and an extrinsic listener, the two being denoted by (a) and (b) respectively. The pairing helps to stress the contrast between the test-scores made by the two kinds of listeners, and also to emphasize the correlation between the portraits and the scores.

1. (a) When the music is beautiful everything in the room is blotted out except the performer and the instrument. I want to go up and play too, not for the crowd but just to bury myself in the harmony. Usually I think of nothing but the music itself; Strauss and some of the moderns do distract me somewhat. For chamber music I am completely relaxed, for solo instruments I am keyed up.

Test Score 94

(b) When I am enjoying music greatly, I can picture the most beautiful things—waterfalls, trains, battles, country scenes, etc. Something like "The Swan" can just carry me so far away that I do not hear the end of the composition at all.

Test Score 65

2. (a) When I am enjoying music it is hard to understand just what is going on because I do not seem to be there at all—I have disappeared. To me the important thing is WHAT THE MUSIC DOES TO ME—the mood that it leaves, be it joy, sadness, exhilaration, etc.

Test Score 92

(b) I enjoy music not because I listen to it but because it makes me think worth-while things. I am usually the heroine of some grand event and in the background there is beautiful music to urge me on.

Test Score 60

3. (a) Symphony music gives the greatest enjoyment. I like to taste the tone of the instruments. Military music may make me feel like marking time with my hands and feet, but when it is gone it's gone. Popular music should be used when the listeners are mediocre because if they talk it does not make any difference; whereas if it is good music you want to murder them. Music that I like seems to make me swell up inside. I do not remember where I am, or that anyone is beside me; when it is over I just pray that they will not expect me to talk because I want to sit and think about what has happened. Sometimes in listening I am relaxed, often I become tense, sit on the edge of the seat, and my hands perspire. No, decidedly; no stories are needed, just the music and what it LEAVES in me.

Test Score 94

(b) I love stories and descriptions and if I do not get them I make up my own. I like musical comedy with its humor, and plot, and beautiful girls. I also like band music, "God and the Kaiser, and the American Flag." No dreamy stuff for me, nor long drawn out symphonies.

Test Score 55

4. (a) It is the music itself that I enjoy. The title to program music does not distract me for the reason that I promptly forget all about it and become absorbed in the beauty of the music.

Test Score 82

(b) I like Hawaiian music best. The first time that I heard it was in the theatre where four or five sang it in native costume—sort of farewell music, and that was followed by some interesting acrobats. Every time I hear music that is anything like that, the scene on the stage comes back to me and I enjoy it all over again, so you see it is the association that I enjoy and not the music.

Test Score 63

5. (a) Bach, Beethoven, keep me interested in the music itself. Music with a description keeps me busy trying to match the meaning with the tune, but if I really enjoy it I soon forget all about the story. If memories or associations play a part, they distract me from the music itself so that I am just vaguely conscious that it is going on.

Test Score 88

(b) Give me stories, costume, catchy tunes and I can last just as long as I have to. I would rather listen to musical comedy sung out of tune than to the best Symphony that has no meaning. My Grandfather is very musical and has exposed me to the very best music all my life, hoping that it would "take"; he has also spent long earnest hours training me how to listen. If it is hard on him, it's harder on me—I would much prefer going to a Swimming Meet.

Test Score 46

These results indicate quite conclusively, for Schoen, that the conditions for artistic musical responsiveness are the same as those for artistic musical rendition. The true music-lover and the musical artist differ not in kind but only in degree. What the artist can express fully and adequately the music-lover feels but vaguely, and he needs the artist to make the vague feeling articulate for him. The artist utters his conception of the musical composition, the musical form, through the medium of musical tones. Hence, the degree of sensitivity of the listener to this medium will condition his response to what the artist has to say. He can grasp no more than his powers enable him to grasp. What a person finds in music depends upon the degree of his susceptibility to musical form—his form-mindedness. Those who are least form-minded will find the value of music in what it suggests to them. Hence their preference for program music, and their interest in literary musical descriptions.

TESTS OF MUSICAL APPRECIATION

A most thorough discussion of the psychological aspects of the problem of musical aesthetics, with several standardized measures for testing appreciation in music, is presented by Hevner (40).

The aspects of appreciation studied and measured by Hevner

in her series of experiments are the intellectual, perceptual and sensory. The measurements are quantitative rather than qualitative, and deal mostly with those phases of the aesthetic experience that are dependent upon training, environment and experience rather than upon native aptitude. Hevner's definition of appreciation is formulated in keeping with this purpose, and is as follows:

A possible, workable definition of appreciation of art in any field, or more especially appreciation in the field of music, might be as follows: "The highest degree of appreciation is the activity which characterizes a human adult who has good intelligence, auditory acuity, musical memory, good pitch and rhythm discrimination, extended experience in hearing musical sounds and in producing music himself on certain instruments, and a wide experience in other realms of human activity (poetry, business, philosophy, sports, etc.), together with a facility in translating his experiences into verbal symbols for recall and reflection, and who avails himself as often as possible of present day opportunities for hearing music. Appreciation is an activity of such a man in contrast to that of an individual with poor intelligence, poor hearing and discrimination for pitch and rhythm, whose background of experience is barren and unvaried, who never avails himself of any opportunity for hearing music, and who has never given any attention to the music which he has been unable, in the ordinary course of his life, to avoid."

If we could find two such men, set them down side by side and play for them an hour's program of music, obtaining complete objective records of all their reactions all the while, and then cancel out of the records everything which is common to both, the remaining activities would give us a fairly complete and accurate picture of this function called appreciation of music. The activities of these two represent the extremes, and between them we may distinguish activity at many different levels. In other words, we may differentiate appreciation of many degrees, and even of many different kinds. There is the activity, for example, of the very young violinist who has achieved a high degree of skill on his own instrument, who knows its literature very intensively, but whose experiences with other music, voice, or organ, or orchestration in general, is entirely lacking; or the activity of the literary artist whose interests extend into the field of music only as far as the opera, and for whom musical sounds are merely the means for enhancing the meaning, the pageantry, the effectiveness of the drama; or the youth of 1933 whose musical experience has been confined to the rhythmic cacophonies of jazz, or of most of us average men, who have our favorite songs and composers, and who occasionally sit through a symphony program and maintain a fairly high degree of attention throughout. The activities of all these and many other widely differing types are legitimate musical experiences, pleasing and satisfying to the individual in themselves, depending on, and at the same time developing within the human organism, the capacity to appreciate. (40, p. 106)

In this definition four standpoints are taken: first, that appreciation is not a unitary trait, but very complex; second, that there are levels and intensities of appreciation so that no sharp line of demarcation between aesthetic and non-aesthetic activities can be drawn; third, that innate capacities in which human beings differ are only the basis for the superstructure of appreciation built by experience and training, and that there is no innate function of appreciation, an "unerring good taste," although the same degree of appreciation cannot be produced in all; fourth, that there is a difference between "appreciation" and "enjoyment," appreciation lying in attending to music as a rich and complex structure, while enjoyment consists of reactions like humming the tune, nodding in time to the rhythm, vivid and prolonged imagery, and emotional effects. In these studies the measurements are based upon a high degree of attention to the music itself.

From the standpoint of such a view of musical appreciation, there are at least six categories of appreciation to be measured:

1. Sensory capacities by which the stimuli are received and differentiated. Pitch, rhythm, auditory acuity, the traits measured by the Seashore tests.

2. Perceptual habits which enable the subject to receive the stimuli as unified, meaningful wholes. Musical form, the structure, grammar, and syntax of musical statements.

3. Emotional or mood reactions, and affective reactions (pleasantness and unpleasantness) which are best measured by physiological reactions, bodily changes.

4. Methods of symbolizing or crystallizing the experiences for purposes of recall and reflection and creative imagination. Ability to verbalize the experiences and manipulate the concepts.

5. Understanding of the suggestiveness of musical sounds on the basis of their commonly accepted meanings. Relating music to other experiences. Expressing emotions, physiological states, ideas, national idioms, atmosphere.

6. Attitudes or evaluations of music in comparison with other ultimate values of life. (40, p. 109)

The standard for beauty used in devising the measures was determined empirically and experimentally, namely, by accepting the present musical world just as it exists. "We make a survey of musical facts, the music that is being enjoyed, the listeners who are enjoying it, and the musicians who are responsible for both. We do not ask, 'What music can be classified as good, according to our preconceived definition?' but say, 'In the present-day world, these examples are apparently considered as good music. From an examination of their characteristics we will write a definition of good music.' We do *not* ask, 'Which activities may be classified as aesthetic according to our definition?' but say rather, 'Here are the people who appreciate music. Examine their reactions and you will have a fairly clear description of music appreciation.'" (40, pp. 110-111) Beautiful music is, then, the music which is played, studied and enjoyed by the professional musicians of the day.

THE TESTS

There are three series of tests, namely, Music Discrimination Tests, Tests of Musical Concepts, and Tests of Attitude Towards Music.

The Discrimination Tests are constructed on the principle that the creation of an artist whose work is generally acclaimed for its merit is beautiful; and that it is more beautiful than the same creation altered by a deliberate attempt to mutilate its various beautiful qualities. The tests consist of 144 selections from standard musical compositions of wide variety, usually about eight measures in length, and represent a complete musical idea. The selections are played in pairs, one member of each pair being a mutilation of the original in either melody, rhythm, harmony, form, or musical statement. The subject is called upon to decide which of the two versions sounds more pleasing, more musical to him, indicating his preference on a printed schedule blank. The directions to the subjects are as follows:

This is a test to discover what kinds of music you prefer. You will hear two short pieces very much alike, and while you are listening you are to decide which one of them you like better. Sometimes the two pieces are exactly alike except for the rhythm. Sometimes it is the harmony that is different, and sometimes it is the melody or tune. You are to listen carefully and mark on your paper the one you prefer.

The Tests of Musical Concepts deal with the person's understanding and comprehension of musical compositions as complete works of art. The material for the tests consists of phonograph records of compositions representing different types and styles of music, classic as well as modern, symphonies, études, and preludes, as well as descriptive music. The subject listens to these examples first as he would normally listen to any music in his experience, and later answers a number of questions designed to discover how many of the details of the music he has been able to notice, and how well he can relate them to each other and to the larger units of the composition. The tests are thus measures of one's ability to identify certain details by name, determine whether or not they are remembered long enough to be recognized on repetition and recalled to mind in order to understand their relation to the composition as a whole. For instance, one of the nine compositions in this test is the third movement (menuetto and trio) of the Mozart "G Minor Symphony." A four-minute Victor recording made by the Philadelphia orchestra under Stokowski is used. The subject listens to the record three times, and during and after the second and third repetitions, he checks as true or false such propositions as the following:

The first theme begins with an ascending melodic figure.

The theme is introduced first by the cellos.

The trio begins with the same rhythmic idea as the original theme.

The trio is in contrast to the minuet, more lyric in character, that is, less vigorous and spirited, less dynamic in quality.

The first section comes to a resting place or cadence before beginning the repetition.

One is able in this first section to hear five instruments carrying independent melodic and rhythmic lines, each one different from the other.

There are 40 questions of this type, so that these tests measure such factors as: (1) the musical vocabulary of the subject, his ability to recognize and name correctly entities such as theme, motif, rhythm, melody, section, digression, glissando, pizzicato, staccato, cadence, development, coda, introduction, etc.; (2) his "ear," or auditory acuity for such items as changes in key or modulation, major and minor effects, differences in rhythms, distinguishing factors in the tone qualities of the various instruments, cellos, oboes, flutes, horns, etc.; (3) his recognition of the general character of the music as lyric, dynamic, spirited, etc.; and (4) his comprehension of the larger outlines of compositional form, statement and development of theme, digressions and contrasting sections, recapitulation, etc., and even some of the more subtle relationships between the parts of the music, the method of achieving unity, contrast, variety, etc.

The Test for Attitude Toward Music is based upon the fact of individual differences of opinion regarding the worth of music as one of the ultimate values of life. There are those to whom music is of prime significance in that they cannot contemplate an existence without it, others regard it as an occasional source of entertainment, and some are completely indifferent or bored with it. This test is intended as a measure of such personal estimates of music. Hevner does not discuss the basis for these differences in degree of esteem for music, but there can be no doubt that one's conception of the rôle of music in life is an influential, if not a determining, factor in his response to particular musical compositions. There are 50 items in the test consisting of statements each of which is indicative of a certain opinion of music, and the subject is asked to place a check next to the statement if he agrees with it, a double check if he agrees strongly, and a cross if he disagrees. Each statement has a scale value, and the score of a subject is calculated from the scale values of all the statements he had checked.

PART II

The Psychology of Musical Aptitudes

CHAPTER 8

THE PSYCHOLOGY OF MUSICAL APTITUDES

MUSICAL APTITUDES ARE OF TWO KINDS, namely, those for musical reception and those for musical production. The first we may call *musicality* and the second *talent*. The two are supplementary, in that the greater the degree of musicality the finer will be the performance in musical value, provided the requisites for musical production are present. But musicality can be present without much talent, and much talent without musicality. Thus, there are many more very musical persons than good musical performers, and there are musical performers whose production is technically superior but musically only acceptable or even inferior. There is also the relationship between the two, that a highly musical person will have an inner drive to attain increasingly higher technical proficiency in order to give adequate expression to the inner musical experience, while technical aptitude is in itself an encouraging factor because it results in satisfactory accomplishment. In other words, the person of insufficient musicality will have no incentive to push on to technical proficiency, while he of insufficient muscular adaptability will be discouraged from trying by poor results. Satisfactory accomplishment in performance is basically dependent upon muscular dexterity. But it is obvious that without a sufficient endowment in musicality there can be no sufficient incentive for attaining dexterity in performance, and even if such dexterity is attained the performance will be empty.

Consequently, musicality is the primary requisite either in musical receptivity or in musical performance, and the attention of research workers in the field of musical talent has centered in the main on the discovery of the attributes of the musically inclined personality, although the musical production aspect has not been ignored.

THE NATURE OF MUSICALITY

The knowledge we have today regarding the traits of musicality was derived mainly from three sources, namely, general observation on the part of psychologists interested in some phase of the psychology of music and musicians, detailed studies of musical prodigies, and genetic studies of musical families. It is recognized by all students that musicality is a complex power, and it is therefore to be expected that different investigators will differ as to the number of the factors of musicality as well as on the importance they attach to one or another of these factors. This does not involve any contradiction. It rather helps to give us a complete picture of a complex situation.

Billroth (4), who was one of the earliest to present a psychological concept of musicality, defines it as the ability to retain and always recognize and reproduce a short, rhythmical, and definitely organized melody. This ability is possessed by most people, and the person who is deficient in it is unmusical. Meyer (61) designates those persons as unmusical who are but rarely able to analyze out, that is, to hear distinctly, the constituent tones of a simultaneous clang of short duration. Wundt (124) holds that musically gifted persons are those who possess sufficient power of musical hearing and memory to enable them to retain and recognize intervals at least for the duration of an experiment. Crzellitzer (10) calls those persons very musical who are able to reproduce vocally or instrumentally a not too complicated tonal succession presented to them, to retain it for a long time and reproduce it at will, sing at sight, and judge intervals within an error of a semi-tone. The somewhat musical are able to recognize simple melodies without ability to correctly reproduce them. The unmusical are those unable to do either. Stumpf (105) has four criteria for musicality: (1) to sing a given tone correctly, (2) to discriminate higher and lower tones, (3) to judge whether one or two tones are present in a clang, (4) to discriminate between degrees of consonance as to pleasantness.

The earliest investigator to present a comprehensive and elaborate panorama of musicality was Rupp (85). In an extensive study he enumerates the attributes of a musically gifted person, and proposes ways in which the presence or absence of each musical power may be tested. His inventory of musicality includes absolute pitch, interval judgment, melody recognition and reproduction, chord analysis, harmonic feeling, and sensitivity for time and rhythm.

Of investigations that attempted to arrive at the factors of musicianship from a study of highly gifted musical persons, those of Stumpf and Revesz are outstanding.

Stumpf (104) studied a young musical prodigy by name of Pepito Areola. When three and a half years of age Pepito played 20 piano pieces from memory, having learned them by ear. He could play a selection after two or three hearings, and could also reproduce on the piano that which had been sung to him and supply the melody with an accompaniment. What he once played he never forgot. He readily improvised on the piano, and his productions of this type showed a marked feeling for form and structure, while his interpretations of musical works showed unusual musical insight. Intellectually Pepito was developed far beyond his age. When six years old he learned to speak German in a few months and read German and Latin script with ease. He solved problems in addition of two and three figures orally, never having had any formal instruction. He learned his letters and numbers by spelling out the names of streets on street corners and by reading the numbers on house doors. During the tests that were given him he was constantly on the alert, and on no occasion could the purpose of a test be hidden from him. He delighted in the apparatus and wanted to manipulate it. He was very temperamental and restless. On entering a room he seemed to be everywhere at once. At one moment he would be elated, jubilant, and the next moment would come anger and tears to be followed soon by smiles and joy. On the psychological tests Pepito showed to be the possessor of the following musical powers:

1. He could easily judge pitch intervals.
2. He possessed absolute pitch.
3. He had a wonderful musical memory.

4. He could transpose a musical composition with great ease and apparent joy.
5. When a few measures of an improvisation were played for him he would readily continue the musical suggestion and carry it to a logical conclusion. Music seemed to be to him a natural medium for emotional expression.
6. He would reproduce difficult dissonant chords with much ease and with but few mistakes, and he would also easily reproduce a succession of four unmelodic, unrelated tones.
7. His ranking in pitch discrimination was very high.
8. He exhibited a keen sensitivity for the purity of intervals.

The most exhaustive study of the musical equipment of a single individual was made by Revesz (82) of Erwin Nyiregyhazi. Erwin could reproduce melodies sung to him before he could speak. At three years of age he began to play on the piano any music he had heard. At this age he also began to improvise. One half-year later he composed simple melodies with accompaniment. In mental development he was at least three years in advance of his chronological age. He was unusually alert, inquiring, responsive, introspective, particularly so about matters pertaining to music. His comments on music and composers were those of a mature and gifted musician. When ten years of age he stated that "Bach was the composer who brought music to perfection, that Beethoven lowered the standard of musical perfection somewhat because, besides his musical sense, he had strong emotions, while Bach had an enormous sense of music. Schumann is lower than Beethoven because he is finer as a painter of emotional states than as a composer." "Mozart," he said, "stands much farther off from Bach than he does from Beethoven; he is related to Bach only in so far as they were both classical composers. To Beethoven, Mozart stands in much closer relation, for Beethoven's music was not so solid and austere, it was not *music only,* as Bach's was. Mozart was more delicate and light in feeling than Beethoven, but he was not so subtle in music and in his part-writing. Beethoven wrote more serious music than Mozart, for he probably experienced much more sorrow and bitterness than Mozart, and that is why Beethoven's melodies speak to one's heart more than Mozart's." But in spite of his musical mentality Erwin was a child. He played like a child and enjoyed the usual boyish activities.

Revesz subjected the boy to a series of tests on his auditory and musical powers. He found that Erwin could instantly name any tone or chord played for him, and sing any desired note. He recognized every interval and gave its musical name. He would produce any interval called for on a sound variator. He named and analyzed the most complicated chords and dischords, and he could transpose a composition into any key faultlessly. He was excellent in sight-reading, and would play from full score without much trouble. At the age of seven his immediate musical memory was the equal of a gifted mature musician, while his power of retention exceeded that of a good musician.

Haecker and Ziehen (34) conducted an extensive research on the inheritance and development of musical ability. They obtained data from 11,000 questionnaires regarding the mental and musical status of each member of the family, from grandparents to grandchildren. This study yielded some important data as to the factors of musicality and the relationship between them.

The authors feel that there are at least five factors or components in musicianship, namely, sensory, retentive, compositional, motor, and ideational. The sensory component consists of sensitivity and discrimination of pitch, intensity, and duration. In the retentive component there function memory for timbre, pitch, intensity, duration, tonal successions, and tonal combinations. Feeling for the formal elements of music, melody, motif, theme, constitutes the compositional factor. The motor component is the power of vocal or instrumental reproduction of what is heard, and the ideational component refers to the richness of ideas of a non-tonal nature stimulated by tonal forms.

The investigation revealed no relation of any significance between the sensory component and vocal reproduction. For instance, a person may possess fine pitch discrimination and play in correct intonation, and yet sing off pitch or be unable to carry a tune. Consequently, inability of vocal reproduction is no sign of lack of musicality. Tonal memory that attains the degree of absolute pitch is an indication of unusual musicality, in that almost all cases of absolute pitch were also highly musical persons. Very few cases of absolute pitch were found among the musical and somewhat musical. But there is no correlation between memory for melody and chords and absolute pitch, in that there are cases of brilliant musical memory and no absolute pitch, and cases of absolute pitch with only fair or even poor musical memory. Absolute pitch, however, was found to correlate highly with rhythmic ability and imagery. The factor that appeared to have the highest diagnostic value for musicalness was memory for relative pitch, or melodic recognition. Of 208 highly musical, musical, and somewhat musical men and women, only 5 were found to have poor musical memory. But of all cases of unmusical persons only ten had good musical memory, and of all cases of very unmusical persons not one had good memory. The same seems to be true for musical rhythm. Of 175 cases of highly musical, musical, and somewhat musical, all had good or very good rhythmic capacity. But among all the unmusical only a few cases of good rhythmic capacity were found. There is also a correlation between memory for melody and rhythm, but this does not hold for rhythm and melodic memory.

The authors also give a list of symptoms for the presence of musical ability. These are: inclination to a great deal of singing in earliest infancy; early participation in singing; early correct reproduction and imitation of a sung melody; early correct reproduction of played melodies in correct intonation and staying on key till the end; early correct singing of a second voice; early ability to sustain a melody in part singing; early transposition of a melody; early ability to reproduce a heard melody upon an instrument; early ability to retain and play by memory pieces heard but once or seldom; early recognition of intervals or melodies; early invention of melodies; early improvisation on the piano or any other instrument; early recognition of false intonation; early discrimination of tonal quality;

early ability to keep correct time; early imitation of complex rhythms; early manifestation of musical preferences.

Another statistical study on the factors of musicality and their interrelationships was made by Mjøen (62). He obtained data from 2,500 questionnaires on the inheritance of musicality. Of these, 15 per cent were very musical, 33 per cent musical, 30 per cent somewhat musical, and 22 per cent unmusical. In ability for specific musical factors, 65 per cent had good musical recognition, 68 per cent possessed good rhythmic sense, 71 per cent easily recognized false intonation, 62 per cent could easily sing by rote, 60 per cent were able to carry a part in part-singing, 36 per cent could improvise a second voice, 25 per cent could play by ear, 11 per cent had absolute pitch, and 4 per cent composed music.

From his data Mjøen draws conclusions regarding the relative symptomatic values of the various manifestations of musicality. Of the very musical, 33 per cent were composers, of the musical, 1 per cent, and none of the somewhat musical and unmusical composed. Then, 55 per cent of the very musical group, 22 per cent of the musical, 3 per cent of the somewhat musical, and 1 per cent of the unmusical had perfect pitch. Also, 85 per cent of the very musical, 42 per cent of the musical, 11 per cent of the somewhat musical, and 6 per cent of the unmusical could play by ear. The percentages for those who could improvise a second voice were 77, 49, 19, 1. For part-singing the figures were 96, 85, 48, 6. For ability to repeat a melody, 96, 86, 67, 9. For melodic memory, 100, 94, 75, 14. For rhythmic ability, 98, 95, 78, 39. For sensitivity to intonation, 100, 98, 81, 22. From these figures Mjøen constructed a table showing to what degree the possession by a person of a certain ability is indicative of a certain degree of musicality as a whole.

Mjøen further made a special study of his data to see the diagnostic value of the ability to carry a lower voice in part-singing. One of his statistical computations shows that 96 per cent of the very musical, 85 per cent of the musical, 48 per cent of the somewhat musical, and 6 per cent of the unmusical had the ability to sing a lower part. Of those who could not carry a lower part 4 per cent belonged to the very musical group, 15

TABLE V

	Very Musical in %	Musical in %	Somewhat Musical in %	Unmusical in %
Composing	92	8	0	0
Absolute pitch	51	42	6	1
Playing by ear	42	44	13	1
Improvising second voice	35	47	17	1
Singing second voice	26	48	24	2
Repeating melody	18	46	33	3
Good memory for melody	21	46	29	4
Good sense of rhythm	18	40	32	10
Good feeling for intonation	16	46	32	6

Table showing with what certainty the presence of a certain criterion is indicative of degree of musicality. Thus, if a person readily hears false intonation the probability of his being unmusical is 6/100, somewhat musical 94/100, musical 62/100, very musical 16/100. Of those who compose the probability is 92/100 that they are very musical.

per cent to the musical, 52 per cent to the somewhat musical, and 94 per cent to the unmusical. These results indicate that there is a close relationship between ability to carry a lower part and degree of musicality. This ability also correlates significantly with other musical aptitudes, as is shown by the figures in the accompanying table.

TABLE VI

(L+ indicates ability to carry lower voice, L— no ability)

	L+	L—	L+ : L—
Number of persons	1,471	981	60:40
Good musical recognition	85%	36%	79:21
Good sense of rhythm	81%	50%	71:29
Good sense of intonation	92%	39%	78:22
Can sing easily by rote	86%	26%	83:17
Can improvise second voice	60%	1%	99:1
Can play by ear	37%	5%	92:8
Has absolute pitch	17%	1%	96:4
Can compose	6%	0.2%	98:2

Thus, to take a single instance, 17 per cent of the L+ persons and 1 per cent of the L— persons had absolute pitch. This gives a proportion of L+ to L— persons who had absolute pitch of

96:4. Of the subjects investigated, therefore, 96 per cent of those who had absolute pitch belonged to the L+ group and 4 per cent to the L— group, indicating that an L+ person had a 96:4 chance of also possessing absolute pitch as compared with an L— person. Similarly 98 per cent of those who composed, 92 per cent of those who could play by ear, 99 per cent of those who could improvise a second voice, 83 per cent of those who could readily sing by rote, and 78 per cent of those who easily recognized false intonation, belonged to the L+ group. The ability to carry a lower part is therefore indicative of a high degree of musicality.

From his data Mjøen also established the relative symptomatic values for musicality of the different musical aptitudes in his list. Ability to sing, or a good sense of rhythm, is possessed even by the unmusical, so these powers by themselves have no significance for musicality. But musical recognition plus singing ability or a good sense of rhythm, or good sense of intonation plus two of the preceding aptitudes, are indications of being somewhat musical. Those who can carry a second voice and also possess any four of the preceding aptitudes, or who can improvise a second voice and in addition possess any five of the preceding aptitudes, are musical. The earmark of the very musical is ability to play by ear plus six of the preceding aptitudes, or absolute pitch and seven other aptitudes, or composition plus eight other aptitudes.

MUSICALITY AND MUSICAL TALENT

When we examine what outstanding teachers of instrumental music and musical artists have to say concerning the requisites for artistic musical performance we find that, taking the motor factor of virtuosity for granted, they emphasize the basic importance of the same gifts found by psychological investigation to constitute musicality. Thus, Leopold Auer (2) mentions the qualities needed by a musician to be a keen sense of pitch, a strong feeling for rhythm, fine sensitivity for tonal quality and tonal nuances, and a ready aesthetic comprehension of all shades of musical meaning and fine points of the art.

Likewise, Elman insists that the fundamental requisite for a perfected violin technique is perfect pitch, that anyone who can play a single phrase in perfect intonation has the great and first essential of musical artistry.

A brief analysis of the conditions that must be met before a musical performance can attain any degree of artistic worth will show quite clearly why musicality must be the basis for talent.

Artistic musical performance calls, above all, for perfect *intonation,* and intonation depends, first of all, upon an ear that recognizes readily and accurately slight pitch deviations. A person whose pitch discrimination is poor might play off pitch without being aware of the fault, since he does not hear it. A second equipment functioning in correct intonation is the motor or muscular, which is conditioned upon the proper confirmation of hand and fingers. Poor motor control, coordination, and adjustment mean that a performer might be aware of producing faulty pitch and yet not be able to make the necessary muscular adjustments to correct the fault. The fingers refuse to obey the dictates of the ear. But the ear is the guide for the fingers.

A second essential of artistic performance is good *tonal quality,* and here also the ear is the crucial factor. It must be sharply sensitive to differences of timbre before the hand can produce them. In other words, when the performer does not feel a need for a singing tone, or his conception of a singing tone is crude, the hand naturally will not produce any better effect than what the ear calls for. On the other hand, the ear might call for a beautiful tone and the hand be unable to produce the desired effect. The items then that function specifically in the production of tonal quality are, first of all, an ear sensitive to timbre, and the muscular control that enables the performer to produce the desired effect.

A third large factor is *tone inflection.* This implies the ability to produce such musical effects as piano, forte, crescendo, diminuendo, and all other intensity variations without which a performance is dull and monotonous. The factors upon which the production of these effects is conditioned are, as in the previous cases, an ear that can detect very fine dynamic inflections, fine muscular sensitivity, and coordination of ear and hand.

A fourth essential is *phrasing.* The phrase is the structural and aesthetic unit of music, and the interpretation of a musical composition rests upon the performer's conception and rendition of the constituent phrases. As the phrase, so the entire composition. Now, a phrase is a rhythmic unit, made up of a sequence of tones of varied pitches, durations, all combining to produce a symmetrical, balanced, aesthetic whole, and also arousing an expectation for a sequential phrase. Each phrase has an individuality all its own, and yet is not sufficient unto itself. It is an individual in a society of individuals, having its own earmarks, its distinguishing characteristics, but depending for its full realization upon the other unities or individuals that constitute the composition as a whole. It must stand out by itself, and yet be submerged in the whole. Furthermore, some phrases are more important than others, have a more important place in the composition than others. From the point of view of phrasing, then, an artistic rendition is conditioned upon (1) the performer's musical understanding of, and his aesthetic response to, the musical composition as a whole; (2) his evaluation of the constituent phrases of the composition as regards their relative importance and significance; (3) his aesthetic response to the individual phrase; (4) his response to every tone in the phrase as regards its intonation, duration, intensity, timbre, consonance; (5) his muscular ability to produce the above effects.

THE NATURE OF TALENT

We may now attempt a summary of the nature of musical talent. Musical talent is first an inborn capacity. Artistic musical performance rests ultimately upon innate, inborn equipment. It is not something that is acquired in one's lifetime, but the person is born with it or without it. All that training can do is to develop that which already exists potentially. We therefore speak of musical capacity and not of musical ability. Ability is that which one has attained through training, practice or experience; capacity is that which enables one to attain a certain degree of ability. Capacity is inborn, while ability is acquired on the basis of capacity. Two persons differ in ability because they differ in capacity, and if we can determine the capacity of a person along any one line before training is begun, we can predict the degree of ability that person will attain.

Furthermore, talent for music is not a single power or capacity, but consists of several groups of talents, each group performing a specific and definite function in the making of the artist. In other words, when the musician works his miracles in his audience through the medium of his voice or instrument he is exercising not one single power or capacity possessed by him, but a cluster of powers functioning together to produce the single effect.

Musical talent as a whole, then, consists of scores of individual, elemental, specific capacities, each contributing its share to the making of the artist. These specific talents may be summarized under four heads, viz., *Musical Feeling, Musical Understanding, Musical Sensitivity,* and *Musical Virtuosity*—forming the affective, the intellectual, the sensory, and the motor bases of musical artistry. This means that an artistic rendition of a musical composition is conditioned upon the intensity with which the artist experiences its affective content, his intellectual grasp of the composition in content and structure, the sensitivity of his ear to intonation, timbre, and dynamics, and finally, upon his technical equipment by means of which the other factors of musical interpretation are enabled to function. Where there is no technique there is no art, but where there is no feeling and understanding, that is, musicianship in general, technique is but an empty shell. Thus it is only when the affective, the intellectual, the sensory, and the motor equipments exist to a marked and somewhat uniform degree in the same person that artistic accomplishment is possible.

Finally, talent for music is a gift bestowed by nature upon different persons very unequally. In the first place, we have the extremes of very marked talent, of the musical genius on the one hand, and no talent at all on the other, and all the degrees of talent between these two extremes. Then again, there is the person who is equipped by nature with the sensory, the affective and the intellectual basis of talent, but is deficient in the motor or technical requisites for effective musical production. Again, we find the reverse of this condition in the person who possesses a marked motor equipment and who can attain marked technical proficiency, but who is short in one or all of the other three capacities. This is the person who would express himself adequately through some musical medium, but who has little or nothing to express. It is but rarely that we find an individual equally gifted, and to a high degree, with all the capacities that function in artistic performance, a fact supported by the scarcity of shining lights in the firmament of music.

AN INVENTORY OF MUSICAL TALENT

We are now in a position for a schematic inventory of musical talent. The inventory will consist of two types of factors—primary factors and secondary factors. By secondary factors are meant those capacities or powers that are of value only provided the primary factors are present.

PRIMARY FACTORS

Auditory Sensitivity. As has already been noted, the first general requisite of musical talent is a keen ear. The potential musical artist must be keenly sensitive to minute variations in matters of pitch, intensity, timbre, and duration. Without a keen ear for these factors his performance may be faulty in such vital artistic effects as good intonation, a singing tone, a tone of varied dynamic contrasts, and fine rhythmic balance and symmetry. These four items form the very basis of musical talent. Where there is no keen auditory sensitivity to these four attributes of tone that constitute the basic material of music a satisfactory degree of artistic musical performance is impossible.

Musical Feeling and Musical Understanding. Under this general heading function the following specific affective and intellectual musical gifts: absolute pitch, relative pitch, tonal memory, tonal sequence, consonance, harmonic sequence, tonality, and rhythm. These factors constitute the general musicianship of the person. A person's response to these items is an indication of the degree of his aesthetic sensitivity to the material of music, both melodic and harmonic.

Musical Virtuosity. The factors thus far mentioned indicate the musical constitution of the mind as a whole. They form the basic conditions in the making of a musical artist, for they determine whether the prospective performer possesses the essential sensory, affective and intellectual equipments which will enable him to have something to say through the medium of his instrument or voice. But one most essential general factor functioning in musical artistry still remains, namely, granted that the individual possesses the musical capacities already enumerated, does he also possess natively the muscular equipment which will enable the musical mind to express itself articulately? Musical expression is conditioned basically upon adequate technical equipment, for where there is no technique there can be no art. Technique is ultimately a matter of native muscular equipment. It has been established experimentally that not only are there measurable differences between the reactions of the several fingers in speed and accuracy for the same person, but there are very marked individual differences, so that there are persons who with unlimited practice can never attain the speed or the accuracy which others show at the very beginning. Motor capacities upon which technique is based remain fairly constant into old age under normal conditions.

SECONDARY FACTORS

Intelligence. We have evidence that in intelligence the musically talented person ranks above average. Specifically, he has a quick comprehension, a retentive memory, wide interests, power of concentration, ambition, alertness, originality, and conscientiousness. The implication is that the possession of musical capacities above the average carries with it a high degree of general intelligence. It is a fortunate provision of nature that those she endows with musical powers shall also possess sufficient intelligence to develop these powers to the utmost point of perfection.

There are, however, several specific phases of general intelligence that function more directly than others in the making of the musical artist. The first of these is the power of musical reflection. The artist must be able to think clearly and deeply on all matters pertaining to music, to possess insight to a marked degree into human nature as it functions in music, and to broaden his outlook on his art by bringing to bear upon it the spheres of literature, art, and science.

Perhaps only second to the power of musical reflection is the capacity for musical adaptation. This refers to the ability of the artist to adapt himself and his art to the particular needs of a particular situation. An illustration of the significance of this point is the relative success of different artists with the public. There are some artists whose success is limited to a certain sphere or section of society. Thus one artist succeeds only in interesting the highly musical. He is a musician's musician, and is to that extent limited in his influence. Another succeeds only with the musical plebeian, his standing with the highly musical public not being very high. A third succeeds with all types and kinds of hearers. This means that the third type of artist is more adaptable to all sorts of conditions, and to that extent possesses more intelligence. Let us take the specific matter of program making. While one artist seems to possess unusual intuition in the selection and grouping of the numbers for his program and succeeds in every instance to carry his audience with him and to put across every number on his program, irrespective of the type of audience, another has to depend more upon one part of his program getting across with one section of his audience, and another part with another section. The first artist plays music, the second plays for his audience. There are other instances illustrative of this difference of musical adaptation, as, for instance, the fact that there are artists who sell themselves and their music to the audience, while there are others who sell only their music.

Musical Memory. More than any other profession, the musician must have a dependable memory, particularly for tones. Contrary to popular belief, it is not true that a slow learner retains the learned material for a longer period than a fast learner, but there are indications that the opposite is true, namely, that the more rapid the acquisition the longer the retention. Accuracy of memory and rapidity of acquisition are indispensable assets to the artist, for not only must he have at his finger tips a large and extensive repertoire, but must also be able to depend upon his memory in order not to encounter embarrassing situations at crucial moments.

Will Power and Resolve. Many a potential musician falls by the wayside because of the lack of sufficient will power to submit to the grueling discipline demanded for artistic perfection. The lives of composers and artists supply ample evidence of the numerous difficulties and obstacles that are encountered by those who wish to serve the cause of art, and it is only the sternest and boldest that can survive.

Self-Confidence. While over self-confidence makes the braggart and is often the sign of a lack of the possession of the genuine article, the lack of sufficient self-confidence has, on the other hand, nipped in the bud many a promising talent.

Temperament. The musically talented person is temperamental and follows the sway or feeling rather than that of cold reasoning. He is highly sensitive to all types of manifestations that are beautiful, and feels the need and urge for a medium of emotional expression. He feels a drive to become familiar with the life, labors, and purposes of the great masters of art, literature, and particularly of the masters of his own art.

CHAPTER 9

TESTS OF MUSICALITY AND TALENT

The survey just made of the studies and comments on musicality and musical talent enables us to make the following classification of the factors of musical equipment:

- I. Auditory Factors
  - a. Sense of Pitch
  - b. Sense of Intensity
  - c. Sense of Duration
  - d. Sense of Timbre
- II. Musical Factors
  - a. Melodic
    1. Absolute Pitch
    2. Relative Pitch
    3. Tonal Memory
    4. Tonal Sequence
    5. Sense of Rhythm
    6. Melodic Reproduction
    7. Melodic Judgment
  - b. Harmonic
    1. Consonance
    2. Chord Analysis
    3. Chord Recognition
    4. Chord Sequence
    5. General Harmonic Sensitivity
- III. Muscular Factors
  1. Control
  2. Motility
  3. Precision of Movement
  4. Strength and Endurance
  5. Timed Action

6. Free Action
7. Motor Discrimination
8. Reaction Time

The auditory factors concern the keenness of the ear in its response to the attributes of tone, and auditory tests are intended to reveal the smallest difference in the pitch, loudness, duration, and quality of two tones which a person can recognize. The musical factors refer to musicianship, and the tests serve the purpose of indicating a person's aesthetic responsiveness to the elements of musical form. The muscular factors bear upon musical performance, and the purpose of motor tests is to show how well a person is equipped by nature with the requisites for technically artistic production.

The tests that have been suggested, devised, and standardized for a number of these factors are for the purpose of indicating the degree to which an individual is endowed by nature with the particular power as compared with other individuals. All the tests are musicality tests rather than talent tests. But since musicality is the prime condition for artistic musical performance, tests of musicality can be used as tests of talent. From the standpoint of talent these tests answer the following question: Given the necessary prerequisites for technically artistic rendition, is the person sufficiently endowed by nature with musicianship so that his performance will also have a satisfactory degree of musically artistic value? It is of course assumed that the tests indicate native capacity rather than the results of training. And the assumption is valid, in that it is true that the degree to which a person profits by experience along a certain line depends upon his native endowment.

TESTS NOT STANDARDIZED

The original extensive test program, as has already been mentioned, was proposed by Rupp (85). Rupp, however, only pointed the way for others to follow. The first tests were devised by Revesz (81) as a result of his study of his musical prodigy. Revesz was concerned with devising a test procedure by means of which musical ability could be identified before the beginning of musical instruction even in cases less exceptional than that of genius, and which could be used with children and adults. He devised eight tests on auditory and musical factors and tried them out on 63 boys and girls ranging in age from seven to twelve years.

The tests were of the following: rhythm, absolute pitch, octave recognition and transposition, relative pitch, harmony, melodic memory, and playing by ear. For the rhythm test he arranged twelve rhythmic groups in order of difficulty. In the first part of the test the rhythms were given monotonically and the child was asked to reproduce the rhythm by handclaps. In the second part of the test the same rhythms were presented melodically and the child was called upon to clap the rhythm. For absolute pitch a tone was sounded on the piano which the child was to reproduce on the instrument. In the relative pitch test an interval was sounded and the child was given a new tone and asked to form the interval vocally. In the harmonic tests the child was to reproduce vocally the component tones of a chord. The melodic memory test called upon the child to reproduce vocally a simple melody played for him, while for playing by ear a known tune was to be picked out on the piano. The test on octave recognition and transposition was abandoned because it proved to be too easy.

Revesz found that melodic memory as tested by him had the highest prognostic value, and by correlating the other tests with the memory test he concluded that sense of rhythm does not have much musical significance, but that spontaneous reproduction of a known tune, absolute pitch, vocal transposition of an interval, and the ability to hear tones out of chords are characteristic manifestations of musicality.

Another series of tests was proposed jointly by a group of psychologists, musicologists, and music teachers (99). This group proposed a battery of eight tests on rhythm, absolute pitch, relative pitch, chord analysis, tonal sequence, melodic reproduction and judgment, harmonic sequence, and what they call final tests.

The tests are as follows:

I. Rhythm Test.

1. Non-melodic rhythm

   a. Reproduction test. A certain rhythm is to be reproduced by tapping.

   b. Discrimination test. The rhythms in (a) to be judged the *same as* or *different from* other rhythms.

2. Melodic rhythm. The tests under (1) given melodically.

II. Absolute Pitch.

A tone is given on the piano, then after an interval of distraction, as for instance, going through another test, the given tone is to be selected out of a series of tones.

III. Relative Pitch.

a. Recognition of successive intervals. An interval is given and the person called upon to identify it in a series of five intervals.

b. Recognition of simultaneous intervals. Same test as (a) using simultaneous intervals of two tones.

c. Recognition of three-clangs.

d. Reproduction of successive intervals. An interval is given which is to be reproduced vocally. Then a different initial tone is given and the interval is to be built with the new tone.

IV. Chord Analysis.

1. Giving the number of tones in a chord.
2. Naming tones in a chord or reproducing them vocally.

V. Tonal Sequences.

This is a test of sensitivity for tones in a definite tonal environment. The subject is given a tonality, after which he hears a pair of tones and is called upon to designate which tone is stable and which unstable in relation to the established tonality.

VI. Melodic Tests.

a. Subject is asked to sing a familiar melody to see whether the reproduction is correct in tonal detail or only in general melodic outline.

b. A melody is played on the piano to be reproduced vocally. Two melodies without accompaniment and two with accompaniment are used.

c. Subject hears a melody, then a modified version of the melody in tonality or modality is presented to him, followed by the original melody, and the subject is to state which of the two is the original melody.

VII. Final Tests.

1. Identification of a melody in true and false accompaniment.
2. A melody played with several accompaniments, subject to state which accompaniment is most satisfactory.
3. Subject called upon to complete a melody, or invent a melody for a given text, or invent melodies without texts.

Drake (14) devised four tests each of which he carefully studied with respect to validity and reliability. The tests are on *musical memory, interval discrimination, retentivity,* and what he calls *intuition.*

The musical memory test consists of 24 original two-bar melodies. Each melody serves as a standard of comparison for four possible variables: change of key, change of time, change of note, and the original melody repeated. Only one of these changes occurs in any one variable. The subject is to identify each variation, whether the same as or different from the original melody. The standard melodies increase slightly in difficulty from one trial to the next. The test is given on the piano and can be used as a group test.

The test on interval discrimination calls for a judgment as to whether the second of two musical intervals is longer or shorter than the first. There are 80 intervals in the test. The first interval of each pair always begins in the region of the octave below middle C on the piano, and the second interval is always above the first interval. The intervals all proceed in an upward direction, increasing in difficulty in the first half of the test, and decreasing in the second half. The difficulty is based on the ratio of the difference in length of the two intervals, the smaller the ratio between two intervals the more difficult being the discrimination between them.

The retentivity test was constructed as a measure of absolute pitch, or memory for isolated tones. The test consists of 20 trials, each trial being made up of two sections. In the first section the person first hears a musical interval on the piano, then a metronome beating at the rate of 164 beats per minute, then a sequence of three tones. These three items the person is asked to keep in mind. In the second section of each trial the person hears another musical interval and he is to judge whether it is longer or shorter than the interval he heard in section one. Following this he hears the metronome again and he is to judge whether the rate of beating is faster or slower than the rate in the first section. Finally, one note is sounded on the piano, and the person is to judge whether it is none, the first, second, or third of the three tones he heard in the first section.

The test on intuition "attempts to measure some of the more subtle aspects of musical talent through the medium of expression and feeling for musical form. . . . The name comes from the belief that the musical response, or the desire to express feelings through music, is derived from an intuition which is in general opposed to intellect." (14, p. 144) This intuitive power is measured by the ability to supply an answer to a given unfinished theme. "The successful accomplishment of this task is said to depend upon an intuitive feeling for three things: (1) phrase-balance, whereby the answering phrase should be of the same length as the initial phrase; (2) key-centre, whereby the answering phrase should return to the central point (key) from which it started; (3) time-balance, whereby the answering phrase should end in the same time as that in which the first began." (14, p. 145) The test is made up of 72 trials, each trial consisting of two given phrases without harmony. The person is to judge whether the second phrase does or does not make a satisfactory answer to the first phrase. Each answering phrase is a test for one of the intuitions, namely, either phrase-balance, key-centre, or time-balance.

Lowery (57) constructed a test of musical memory, a test of cadence, and a phrase test. In the memory test an initial phrase is played, after which several other phrases are given, some of which are improvisations on the initial phrase. The person is to state after each example whether or not it is founded upon the initial phrase. In the cadence test a judgment is to be made as to which of two cadences is more complete. In the phrase test a series of tones is repeated with the same or a different phrasing, and the listener is to state whether or not a change in phrasing has occurred.

STANDARDIZED TESTS

A standardized test is one for which rankings have been established, so that a person's standing in the factor tested can be definitely indicated, and whose reliability as a measure of that particular factor and validity for diagnostic and prognostic purposes have been demonstrated. Of such tests there are at present four batteries, those of Seashore, Schoen, Kwalwasser-Dykema, and Ortmann.

THE SEASHORE TESTS

The Seashore battery (95) includes six tests: pitch, intensity, time, memory, consonance, and rhythm.

The pitch test indicates a person's threshold of pitch discrimination, or the least difference in the pitch of two tones that the person can perceive. The test is made up of 10 pitch increments within a frequency range of 30 cycles. The standard tone has a frequency of 435, and the increments are 1/2, 1, 2, 3, 5, 8, 12, 17, 23, and 30 cycles above the standard frequency. At the level of 435 cycles, one cycle is equal to approximately 1/54 of a tone. There are 100 trials in the test, each increment being compared ten times with the standard tone. The person is called upon to make a judgment as to whether the second tone he hears is higher or lower than the first tone. Seashore offers evidences that the results from this test are unaffected by age or training. It is a test of basic capacity.

The intensity test does for loudness discrimination what the pitch test does for pitch discrimination. It is a test of the least perceptible difference in loudness that a person can detect.

There are ten series of trials with 10 trials in each series, making 100 trials in all. The difference in the loudness of the two tones in each series of 10 trials is the same. The test covers five degrees of loudness, with the difference of the first series of 10 trials being greatest and the fifth series smallest. Series 6-10 are repetitions of series 1-5. The instructions to the subject are that he is to judge whether the second tone is weaker or stronger than the first. Seashore offers evidences that loudness discrimination, like that for pitch, is an elemental capacity, and specialized training after early childhood does not result in improvement. The test is therefore one of basic capacity.

In the time test the listener hears three clicks, marking off two time intervals. The second time interval is always either longer or shorter than the first. The test consists of 100 trials divided into ten series of 10 trials in each series. In series 1 and 2 the difference between the two time intervals is 20/100 of a second, in series 3 and 4 it is 14/100, in series 5, 9/100, in series 6 and 7, 2/100, in series 8 and 9, 5/100, and in series 10, 9/100. The subject is called upon to make a judgment as to whether the second interval is longer or shorter than the first.

The consonance test is constructed out of 100 two-tone combinations of various degrees of consonances. Consonance is defined, for the purpose of the test, as smoothness, blending, and fusion. The 100 combinations are arranged into pairs, so that the entire test consists of 50 trials. The subject is called upon to make a judgment as to whether the second combination he hears is better or worse than the first. He is told that a good combination is one in which the two tones are smooth and blend, tending to fuse together into one. Seashore writes that "It was rather surprising in our first experiments to find how largely elemental this test is; that is, to what extent it embodies a simple direct judgment which is developed early in childhood outside of specific training. The 'sense of harmony' which we have defined here more accurately as the sense of consonance, is undoubtedly a specific talent which one may have quite apart from special education or keen intelligence very early in childhood." (96, p. 157)

In introducing his memory test Seashore states that "Everything taken into account, the best single and fundamental test of capacity for a musical memory that we have been able to devise is the test of memory span." (96, p. 239) The test is therefore constructed to indicate one's memory span for a succession of non-melodically related tones, similar in the language field to a test of memory for nonsense syllables. The shortest span in the test is of two tones and the longest of six tones. In each span there are 10 trials, making 50 trials in all. The subject hears a sequence of tones and immediately following another sequence. The second sequence is like the first excepting in one tone, and the subject is called upon to indicate by number which tone in the second sequence was changed. "The most striking result of this test," Seashore writes, "is that a span of 6 is difficult enough for practically all of a normal community. A person who, in an extended series of trials, is able to get all records right would have an extraordinary capacity for this kind of memory. Other things being equal, the child in the fifth-grade room who ranks 85 gives promise of a memory for as extensive a repertory as any musician may need, and persons who now play programs of several hours entirely from memory may not rank higher than 90 on this scale." (96, pp. 239-240)

The rhythm test consists of two rhythmic patterns, the second pattern being either the same as the first or different from it. There are 50 pairs of patterns in the test of varying length and complexity.

THE SCHOEN BATTERY

In this battery (87) there are three tests, a test of relative pitch, a test of tonal sequence, and a rhythm test. These, according to their author, are tests of general musicianship. The person's ranking in these tests is supposed to indicate his aesthetic response to the structural material of music. The relative pitch test is a measure of one's power to judge the difference between two successive pitch intervals as to their distance. This capacity has been found to be a fairly certain criterion of musicalness. Most persons can, with sufficient and adequate training, learn to judge musical intervals with fair accuracy, but the degree to which this ability is acquired depends on native equipment, and this native equipment can be determined before training. The test consists of 60 pairs of intervals grouped into six series of 10 pairs of intervals in each series, and increasing in difficulty from series A to F.

Series A. Comparison of two intervals of opposite direction, with second tone of first interval in common with first tone of second interval.

Series B. Comparison of two intervals of same direction, with first tones in common.

Series C. Comparison of two intervals of same direction, with second tones in common.

Series D. Comparison of two intervals of opposite direction, no tones in common.

Series E. Comparison of two intervals of same direction, no tones in common.

Series F. Comparison of two intervals of opposite direction, with first tones in common.

The subject is called upon to judge whether the second interval is larger or smaller than the first.

The tonal sequence test was designed to reveal a person's sensitivity to a melodic line. A melody is defined as a succession of tones differing from each other in pitch and duration and giving the effect of an aesthetic unity. That is, the tones as they succeed each other seem to belong to each other, to give the feeling of relationship, one tone seeming to follow and to grow out of the preceding tone, all falling into a definite rhythmic pattern, and giving the effect of balance, unity, variety, and completeness. Here we have the several factors of tonal sequence, firstly, the effect of belonging-togetherness; secondly, the effect of balance, rhythmic sequence, or phrasing; thirdly, the effect of unity and variety; and finally the effect of finality, or of coming to rest. The test consists of four two-phrase melodies, all standard compositions. For the second phrase of each melody there are three alternative phrases as possible endings, in addition to the original ending. Each of the three alternative phrases is inferior to the original phrase as an ending, one being just a shade poorer, another noticeably poorer, and the other entirely inappropriate. The listener is asked to evaluate the relative appropriateness of the four endings. The four melodies are arranged according to difficulty, the most obvious being placed at the beginning, and the most complex at the end, of the test.

The rhythm test measures one's sensitivity to slight variations in rhythmic patterns. The test consists of 25 pairs of monotonic rhythmic phrases, each phrase containing two fairly distinct, and in some cases entirely alike, rhythmic patterns. The second phrase of each pair is entirely like the first phrase, excepting that a slight change occurs in the duration of one of the constituent tones of the first or second pattern, without, however, destroying the rhythmic sequence of the phrase. The rhythms are arranged in a scale of increasing difficulty as to length, similarity of the two motives, complexity of meter, and minuteness of variation. The rhythms were chosen from standard musical compositions instead of being arbitrarily devised by the experimenter. The subject is called upon to make a judgment as to whether the second phrase is the same as or different from the first, and, if different, whether the change is in the first or second pattern of the repeated phrase.

THE KWALWASSER-DYKEMA TESTS

There are ten tests in this battery (53) to measure tonal memory, quality discrimination, loudness discrimination, feeling for tonal movement, time discrimination, rhythm discrimination, pitch discrimination, melodic taste, pitch imagery, and rhythm imagery. The authors hold that experimental investigations in the field of psychology of music have established the importance of these traits as indicative of music talent and achievement. They represent significant attributes of musicianship and lend themselves readily to objective measurement. These tests reveal, therefore, reliable information for the guidance of student, teacher, and parent.

Tonal memory is tested by pairs of tonal patterns, the shortest patterns consisting of four tones and the longest of nine tones. There are 25 pairs of patterns in the entire test. The listener hears each pair once, and is to judge whether the pair of patterns is the same or different.

For testing quality discrimination the same two tones are produced by different instruments of the orchestra. There are 30 trials in the test. In one-half of the trials the two tones are played by the same instrument twice in succession, in the other half by two different instruments in succession. When the tones are played twice by the same instrument the tonal quality is the same. When repeated by two different instruments the tonal quality is different. The subject is to judge this sameness or difference in quality.

In the loudness test intensity discrimination is measured for single tones and chords. There are 15 trials for single tones and 15 for chords. The same single tone and the same chord occur throughout the test. Fifteen different degrees of loudness are used, with the contrast varying from very marked to very slight. The subject is to judge whether the second tone or chord is weaker or stronger than the first.

Tonal movement is a test of the feeling for tonality. The test material consists of 30 melodic patterns of four tones, each pattern calling for a fifth tone for its completion. The person hears the four tones and is to state whether the fifth tone called for by the melody for its completion is *up* or *down* from the last of the four tones heard.

Time discrimination is measured by 25 items of three consecutive tones in each item. Of the three tones, the first and third are always of equal duration, while the second tone is in some of the items of longer duration and in some of the items of the same duration as the first and third tones. The longest time variation is 0.30 second, the shortest 0.03 second. The judgment called for is whether the three tones in each item are the same or different in length.

The rhythm discrimination test is a measure of the ability to detect the presence or absence of variations of time or loudness in a rhythmic pattern. The test is made up of 25 paired rhythmic patterns, in some of which the second pattern is identical with the first, in some of which there occurs a change in time, and in some a change in loudness or accent. The patterns consist of two pitches, the last tone of each pattern being C′ and the other tones a half-step below. The trials increase in difficulty in the number of tones they contain and in complexity of the rhythmic pattern. The judgment to be made is whether the paired rhythms are the same or different.

Pitch discrimination is measured by 40 items consisting of a tone sustained for about three seconds. The beginning and end of every tone are always of the same pitch, whereas in the middle part of the tone there occurs at times a pitch change. Two pitches are used, a tone of 500 cycles in the first twenty trials and a tone of 1,000 cycles in the last twenty. The smallest pitch change is 0.01 tone, the largest is 0.40 tone. The pitch changes are both above and below the standard pitch. The judgment called for is whether the tone heard is the same throughout or whether a part of it is different.

The melodic taste test was devised to indicate sensitivity for melodic structure, balance, and phrase. Two melodies of two phrases each are played in succession for comparison. The first phrases in both melodies are identical, while the second phrases are different. The judgment to be made is which of the two melodies is better, that is, which of the two concluding phrases makes better musical sense. There are ten trials in the test.

In the tonal imagery test the person is supplied with the notation of 25 tonal patterns containing all the chromatic characters used in music, that is, sharp, double sharp, flat, double flat, and cancel. On this test blank the subject is to indicate whether the tones he hears produced by a record are the same as or different from the tones called for on the printed page. The test contains 25 items, ranging from two to four tones.

The rhythm imagery test is similar to the tonal imagery test. The person indicates on a test blank whether the rhythms on the printed page are the same he hears produced by a record or different. The test consists of 25 rhythms of various lengths and complexities.

THE ORTMANN BATTERY

Ortmann (70) devised seven tests as objective, scientifically acceptable, measures of the fundamental auditory and musical capacities of students entering the Peabody Conservatory of Music. The tests are of pitch discrimination, pitch memory, time discrimination, fusion, rhythm memory, melodic memory, and harmonic memory.

In the pitch discrimination test there are 50 pairs of tones arranged into five series of 10 pairs in each. The pitch differences in the series are, respectively, 8, 5, 3, 2, and 1 cycles. The standard tone is of 435 cycles. The subject judges whether the second tone is higher or lower than the first.

The pitch memory test consists of five series of tones, each beginning with a standard tone to be remembered and a number of other tones to be judged as higher, lower, or the same as the standard tone.

Time discrimination is measured by 50 pairs of five-click patterns. One member of each pair is a pattern of even clicks, the others consist of ten each of five degrees of unevenness. The judgment to be made is whether the second pattern of each pair is more even or more uneven than the first.

In the fusion test five tonal combinations of varying degrees of fusion are given. The combinations are: one of two tones, one of three tones, and three of four tones. Each combination is given ten times. The subject is to judge the number of tones in each combination.

Rhythm memory is tested by five series of five-click patterns, each series containing a standard five-click pattern and a number of other five-click patterns. The subject is to remember the standard pattern and to judge several of the other patterns as more even, uneven, or the same as the standard.

The melodic memory test consists of 25 pairs of 2-, 3-, 4-, 5-, and 6-tone melodies. There are 5 pairs of each. The subject is to indicate the tones in the second member of each pair that differ from the corresponding tones in the first member of each pair.

In the harmonic memory test there are five series of chords

each beginning with a standard chord, followed by a number of other chords. The subject is to judge several of the chords as being the same as or different from the standard chords.

THE VALIDITY OF THE TESTS

The first question the psychologist raises about any proposed test is in regard to its reliability, namely, whether it can be depended upon to measure the factor it proposes to measure. The interest of the musician, however, is not so much in the reliability of the tests offered to him as measures of musical talent, as in their validity for predicting accomplishment. This problem has been investigated for all the standardized music tests.

THE VALIDITY OF THE SEASHORE TESTS

The Seashore tests have had the most severe trial as to their validity at the Eastman School of Music (100). The project has been carried on for a period of over ten years under the direction of trained psychologists.

In one study the test results were classified into A, B, C+, C—, D, and E, each letter indicating an estimate of the student's talent, with A representing the highest talent. The classification was then compared with the teachers' estimates of talent, using the same letter classification. The results showed striking similarities not only between test results and one teacher's estimate of talent, but between test results and many teachers' estimates of talent for various instruments and voice.

In another study a comparison was made for 99 pupils between three classifications of talent, one by the tests, another by the director of the school, and a third by the teacher of the pupil. Again, considerable consistency appeared between the three estimates of talent, with the tests placing fewer cases in the D and E and more cases in B and A groups than did the director and the teachers. This study was followed by one on the highest and lowest 10 per cent of a group of 300 students who were tested the year before. The teachers of these students rated them on musical talent, musical feeling, and rhythmic action, and the ratings were compared with the test results for the same students. The results showed that for each of the three factors rated by teachers there was a paucity of ratings in D and E for those who tested high and a paucity of ratings in A and B for those who tested low. For those who tested high, teachers' ratings bulked in the upper part of the rating scale (C+, B, and A). For those who tested low, teachers' ratings bulked in the lower part of the rating scale (C—, D, and E).

Another study indicated the value of the tests in predicting how long the pupil was liable to last in the school, according to his talent classification. The period used was two years. Of those who tested D and E none lasted out the two years. Of the C— talents about one-fourth lasted out, of the C+ talents, two-fifths, of the B talents over one-half, and two-thirds of the A talents.

A further study comparing test ratings with teachers' estimates was made with two selected groups, 149 who tested A and B and 149 who tested D and E. Of the D and E talents, about one-eighth remained in school. The teachers' ratings for this group showed 21 per cent D and E and 1 per cent A. Of the A and B talents about five-eighths remained, and the teachers' ratings for this group were 46 per cent A and B and 2 per cent D and E.

In 1928 a standardized comprehension test was added to the music tests, and a five-fold classification of Safe, Probable, Possible, Doubtful, Discouraged, was made for the music degree students as a basis for predicting achievement. Of 565 students who graduated within four years, 60 per cent came from the Safe group, 42 per cent from Probable, 33 per cent from the Possible, 23 per cent from the Doubtful, and 17 per cent from the Discouraged.

Stanton, who made all the studies summarized above, makes the following comments on the results in their bearing on the significance of differential musical capacities:

Generalizations from the type cases and the numerous cases within the range of investigation, suggest various aspects of the significance of the different degrees of fundamental talent. For students to make progress in a broad program of music education, their fundamental musical capacities need to be average or above. Those with capacities below average rarely accomplish in any musical outlet other than voice and preliminary work on an instrument. A natural voice, facility in playing by ear, or muscular dexterity in performance, may go a long way in compensating for poorer fundamental capacities. It is probable that the usual vaudeville entertainer requires little in specific musical capacities. Those with average capacities are known to find outlets in various music fields such as teaching privately or in public schools, singing, playing in orchestral and band ensembles, and playing the piano. Those with capacities above the average are known to have survived a long period of musical progress. Here are found the violinist and other performers on stringed instruments, pianists of ability, some private music teachers, college and university music teachers, some supervisors in public school music, first chair men in orchestras, conductors, and composers.

From the viewpoint of either the field of music or the instrument, it is found that although there may be a range of capacities from great to small in any field of music, one can predict from the samples of information at hand that voice pupils usually rank lower in musical capacities than most violin pupils and lower than the majority of piano pupils. Many of the ensemble players in orchestras and bands, and teachers in public school music, have average capacities; those who lift themselves out of the mass of ensemble players, public school music teachers, et cetera, are usually those with greater fundamental musical capacities. In other words, the extent of musical growth and the advancement to higher levels of achievement are in proportion to the differential levels of fundamental capacities. Therefore the superior students, who accomplish beyond the elementary and intermediate stages of musical development, have potentialities such that their musical interests are not limited and their pleasures are found in a variety of musical outlets. All those with greater capacities are not expressing their talent necessarily through the medium of music, but those who achieve the higher levels of musical development are found to have fundamental musical capacities above the average. (100, p. 27)

OTHER STUDIES OF THE SEASHORE BATTERY

The Seashore tests have been the subject of numerous other studies as to their reliability and validity. Farnsworth (22) gives a summary of these investigations, together with his own experiments on the tests, and draws several general conclusions based upon the findings of all these researches.

The pitch test, Farnsworth concludes, is quite high in reliability. There is some evidence, however, that the test might be just as reliable if it were reduced by at least one-half its present length. It is also claimed that the 5-cycle trials function little, if any, in the test, and that finer increments between the 2- and 8-cycle range are desirable. Seashore's advice regarding the significance of the results from this test, namely, that those who rank in the best 10 per cent should be encouraged enthusiastically to study music, the next 20 per cent encouraged freely, the next 40 per cent encouraged, the next 20 per cent questionable, and the next 10 per cent discouraged, Farnsworth considers to be probably the best advice that can be given today, if time and money are limited.

The loudness test is somewhat less reliable than the pitch test, but most of the conclusions on the pitch test are equally applicable to the intensity test.

The reliability of the time test Farnsworth considers to be low, one of its disadvantages being that its unmusical manner of judging time is decidedly disturbing to many students who have had musical training. It is also sometimes difficult to make the directions clear.

The consonance test has been most severely criticized by investigators. It is found to be of questionable value, for one thing, because different subjects understand the directions in different manners. Its criteria for consonance have also been seriously questioned. The loudness factor is not constant, with the result that certain of the combinations are rated higher or lower than would be the case normally. Again, a few of the combinations are at times so hideous that they cause laughter and thus interfere with the succeeding pair of combinations. Farnsworth feels, however, that for all its faults and unreliability, it is well to keep in mind that the errors made by groups of subjects are quite consistent.

The tonal memory test, like that of pitch, is the most reliable member of the battery, according to Farnsworth. One of its disadvantages is that as the number of tones increases, murmurs of discouragement are often heard. The rhythm test is found by Farnsworth to be the poorest in standardization and to be very low in reliability—should be used with caution.

Farnsworth's conclusion concerning the use of the tests is that the pitch and memory tests would appear to possess sufficient reliability for certain diagnostic purposes. The others should be employed only with extreme caution. The reliability of the entire battery is 0.885, with that for pitch being 0.75, loudness 0.66, time, 0.51, consonance 0.65, rhythm, 0.47, and memory, 0.83.*

STUDIES OF THE SCHOEN, KWALWASSER-DYKEMA, AND ORTMANN BATTERIES

The only study of the validity of the Schoen (90) tests is one made by the author himself in combination with five of the Seashore tests—pitch, loudness, time, consonance, memory.

* The Seashore Test Battery has been completely revised (97), with the consonance test omitted and a test of timbre added. The revision provides three sets of test material, one for an unselected group, one for a musical group, and one for most refined measurement in individual testing. Other significant changes in each test have been made. For pitch and loudness pure tones are used, while for time the duration of a pure tone has been substituted for the original time intervals between clicks. In tonal memory, the smallest interval of the changed tone is a whole-step instead of a semi-tone, and in the rhythm test a short tonal impulse is used instead of a click. The rhythmic patterns are also graded in the order of difficulty.

The new timbre test was constructed by using a tone having a fundamental pitch of F#, and composed of six adjacent partials of equal energy. By taking certain amounts of energy from the third partial and adding them to the fourth partial, a series of deviations from the original timbre of the tone was obtained. The problem then became one of determining what was the smallest amount of change in the tone the subject could detect. The tests are presented in two forms, one for an unselected group, the other for a musical group or individual testing. Norms are given for fifth and sixth grade pupils, seventh and eighth grade pupils, and for adults, including high school students, in terms of number correct judgments on a block of 50 or 100 trials covering the entire range.

The investigation was made in cooperation with several music teachers. The teachers were asked to permit the author to give the tests to several of their pupils selected by them, some of their most talented, some of their least talented, and some between the two extremes. Altogether, ten pupils were used. At the time the tests were given the investigator knew nothing about the status of these boys and girls as to degree of talent or accomplishment, excepting that the ten pupils represented various degrees of endowment and attainment. A report was issued for each pupil giving his ratings in the tests, and on the basis of the test results a prediction was made as to the pupil's probable accomplishment, given proper instruction and adequate application, in six factors of artistic musical performance namely: intonation, tonal quality, shading, variety in performance, phrasing, time and rhythm. A blank was then sent to each teacher, asking for an evaluation of the actual attainment of the pupil in these factors. The purpose of this procedure was to test the predictive value of the tests by determining the degree to which actual accomplishment, as judged by the teacher, would agree or disagree with the predictions of accomplishment based upon the test results.

TABLE VII. RANGE OF AGREEMENT BETWEEN TEST RATINGS AND TEACHER'S RATINGS

	0	1	2	3	4	5	6	7	8	9
Intonation	7	2	1							
Tonal quality	8	2								
Tonal shading	7	3								
Variety of performance	6	3	1							
Phrasing	7	2	1							
Time and rhythm	8	2								
Talent as a whole	6	4								

Figures 0-9 represent the possible extent of a disagreement between the two ratings. 0 means no disagreement; 1, disagreement of one step; 2, disagreement of two steps, etc. The predictive value of the tests is indicated by the clustering of the figures in columns 0, 1, and 2. If the tests were unreliable, the figures would be scattered all over the nine columns.

In Table VII, the reader will find a summary of the ratings of the tests and those of the teacher for each of the items, plus an estimate from both sources as to the pupil's talent as a whole. The teacher and the investigator both used the following scale of ratings: very inferior, inferior, poor average, below average, average, good average, high average, superior, very superior.

In estimating the significance of the figures in the table in their bearing upon the validity of the tests, the reader should bear in mind that there was room for divergence between the teacher's ratings and the test ratings in five directions, as follows: (1) the disagreements between the two ratings might be very extensive and numerous, (2) extensive and few, (3) of small extent and numerous, (4) of small extent and few, and (5) total agreement. Thus, for any one of the pupils, the teachers' ratings and the predictions based upon the tests might be in perfect accord for all seven items, or they might disagree to the extent of nine grades for all the items, or there might be perfect agreement on some and various degrees of disagreement for others. The extent and frequency, then, of the disagreements ought to serve as a measure of the validity of the tests, the smaller and the fewer the disagreements, the more valid the tests.

A study of this table gives us the following results.

For intonation there is complete agreement between tests and teacher for seven of the ten pupils, while for the other three pupils there is a disagreement to the extent of one grade for two of the pupils and two grades for the other. For the next item, tonal quality, we have complete agreement for eight of the pupils and disagreement of one grade for two. For tonal shading there is agreement for seven of the pupils, a disagreement of one grade for the other three. For variety of performance there is complete agreement for six pupils, disagreement of one grade for three, and two grades for one. For phrasing there is complete agreement for seven pupils, disagreement of one grade for two, and two grades for the other. For time and rhythm there is complete agreement for eight pupils and disagreement of one grade for the other two. For talent as a whole there is agreement for six pupils and disagreement of one grade for the other four.

Summarizing these results, we note that out of a total of 70 evaluations there are 49 complete agreements between teacher and tests and 21 disagreements, and that of these 21 disagreements, 18 are only of one grade, and 3 of two grades.

The K-D test battery has been investigated by Farnsworth (23), whose major point of interest rested in their utility as psychological tools. In the K-D battery there are five tests which overlap five of the Seashore tests in that they supposedly measure the same capacity, namely, pitch, rhythm, loudness, memory, and time. In one of his investigations, Farnsworth was concerned with finding out how the pairs of similar tests correlated with each other. He gave these tests to sophomores in Stanford University and found that, with the exception of the tests of tonal memory, the tests are not measuring at all perfectly the same behavior variables. These findings are verified by a somewhat similar investigation by Tilson on college students enrolled in the music supervisors' course. Several other studies on the relation between the two test batteries seem to confirm the findings of Farnsworth and Tilson.

The reliability of the tests has been found by practically all investigators to be small. The tonal memory test proves to be the best of the battery. The reliability of the K-D battery is 0.77, whereas that of the Seashore battery is 0.89. Farnsworth states that the only possible conclusion to be made on the subject of reliabilities would seem to be that, with the possible exception of the test of tonal movement, the Kwalwasser-Dykema tests are too unreliable for individual prognostication. Comparing the K-D with the Seashore tests, Farnsworth's study clearly indicates that the Seashore tests are superior psychologically to the K-D tests, and also decidedly more reliable, but the K-D tests, he claims, do offer a few advantages. They are shorter and less tiresome. The stimuli are more musical and so, perhaps, more pleasing to musical groups. As the items are announced by number, the testing procedure is made more fool-proof. Certain of these improvements, however, have been made at the expense of reliability. Farnsworth concludes that the K-D tests should probably be employed solely in studies of group differences.

Drake (15) made a study of the validity and reliability of twenty tests, namely, four by himself, the cadence test by Lowery, the K-D and Seashore batteries, and the tonal sequence test by Schoen. Of all these tests he finds that only three are satisfactory in both validity and reliability. These are his own musical memory test, and the pitch and tonal memory tests by Seashore.

The validity of the Ortmann battery was studied by an analysis of the accumulated data from the tests at the end of a ten-year period. During that period 500 students had taken the tests. The purpose of the study was to see (1) what relation each pupil's test scores had to his success in music, (2) how closely a pupil's scores made on the test at one time agreed with his scores made on the same tests a year or so later, (3) whether any of the tests might be omitted, (4) how the tests might be improved, and (5) differences in test performance between pupils majoring in piano, organ, voice, composition, string instruments, and school music.

The validity of the Ortmann tests is reported by Ortmann to be higher than that obtained for the Seashore tests in twenty investigations. Their reliability, as indicated by the results from 50 students who took the tests twice, 44 after an interval of one year, 7 after two years, 3 after four years, and 1 after five years, is reported to be fairly high and adequate for individual measurement in the case of the average test score and the score on memory for a simple tone. The others would be considered low and inadequate for individual measurement, although useful for group averages and school surveys. The uniformity of the score made by students of different musical branches was more striking than any diversity that was evident. But the string instrument students scored higher on pitch discrimination than did the other groups, and the composition students higher on memory for a chord than the other groups. The composition students as a whole made higher scores on the tests than did the other students.

A careful study of the reliability and validity of his test-battery inclines Ortmann to believe that his tests compare favorably with all other aptitude tests of the present in practically all features except that they can be given only at the Peabody laboratory; and that their primary importance lies in being a step forward in musical talent testing rather than as instruments for differential prognosis in individual cases. He feels that few aptitude tests of the present can be used for individual prognosis with greater safety.

SUGGESTED USES OF THE TESTS

From the investigations just reviewed on the reliability and validity of existing standardized music tests it is clear that these and similar other tests do have considerable value as aids in the discovery and guidance of special musical aptitudes. The makers of the tests are more skeptical of the ultimate value of their tests than even their most severe critics. Thus, Seashore, in speaking of the Eastman experiments, states that, "Only six talent measures and only one brief intelligence measure were used. If to these had been added the corresponding motor tests and some affective responses, the predictive value would, of course, have been greatly increased." He insists, furthermore, that, "I have never advised the use of such measures alone, but have constantly urged that they be used as aides, especially in connection with auditions and analyzed records of achievement." All tests of any sort are but prognostic and diagnostic aides, and, when used discriminately by a competently trained person, are useful tools for the advancement of adequate educational procedures. When used in such manner, standardized musical aptitude tests have at least three very specific applications, namely, (1) the early discovery and evaluation of special musical powers, (2) the diagnosis of difficulties encountered in the course of training, (3) guidance in the public school program.

Every teacher, in order to promote his own good, as well as that of his students, is eager to do justice to each individual entrusted to him for instruction. Justice to the pupil means developing his own peculiar resources to the maximum point of efficiency through the most efficient and economical procedure available. The prerequisite condition for such a procedure is that the teacher know the resources of the individual student and then adopt a method to suit the individual case. "I know," states Professor Auer, "that there is a theory somewhat to the effect that I make a few magic passes with the bow by way of illustration, and—presto—you have a Zimbalist or a Heifetz! But the truth is I have no method—unless you want to call purely natural lines of development, based on natural principles, a method—and so, of course, there is no secret about my teaching. The one great point I lay stress on in teaching is never to kill the individuality of my various pupils. Every pupil has his own inborn aptitudes, his own personal quality as regards tone and interpretation. I always have made an individual study of each pupil, and given each pupil individual treatment. And always, always I have encouraged them to develop freely in their own way and to guard inspiration and ideals, so long as this was not contrary to aesthetic principles and those of my art. My idea has always been to bring out what nature has already given rather than to use dogma, to force a student's natural inclinations into channels I myself might prefer." (2)

In music education there are several items involved in knowing the resources of each individual student. Firstly, how much talent as a whole the pupil possesses, whether superior, excellent, average, poor or no talent at all. By determining at the very outset the degree of talent possessed by the person the aim of the teaching as well as the method of procedure can be determined upon to the great advantage of both student and teacher.

Secondly, having determined the amount of talent possessed by the individual, it is important to know for what instrument the talent is best suited. The requisites for all instruments are not the same. The master violinist would probably have made a poor pianist, and the great pianist but a mediocre violinist. There are numerous cases on record of persons who failed entirely or accomplished little on one instrument and then attained marked proficiency on another.

Thirdly, of great aid in developing talent would be a knowledge of the general direction or trend of the talent. Each talent leans more or less in one direction, being either more intellectual than emotional, or more technical than emotional, or more emotional than either intellectual or technical, and so forth. By discovering the tendency of the talent in this respect before the beginning of training or during the period of training, the teacher can exercise his ingenuity in an effort to develop a well-balanced performer.

Fourthly, in order to attain best results, the instruction should be guided by the peaks and valleys of the talent. As we have already seen, talent is not a single capacity, but a complex or cluster of capacities, each performing a definite and essential function in artistic performance. It is but rarely that any one person, no matter how talented as a whole, possesses all the specific factors of talent to the same degree. It is for this reason that we find artists who excel in some one point of artistic performance and are weak in another. Thus, one violinist has perfect intonation, but not a very superior technique, another, a singing luscious tone, but somewhat faulty intonation. A pianist might have a wonderful technique but a poor tone, and so forth. Artists themselves comment on the strong and weak spots in their own performance, as for instance, Mischa Elman, who states that double-stops on the violin have always been easy for him, whereas he has had to work very hard to attain a satisfactory staccato bowing. By having an inventory of the weak and strong points of each pupil, the teacher is able to determine what phases of the talent need special care and stress, and what can be left to take care of itself.

In sum, the tests offer several kinds of service to parents, teachers, students and school officials. For parents they are a valuable means for ascertaining the musical status of a child. The private music teacher can have a musical profile of each of his students and use it as a guide in his teaching. The music student himself is bound to be helped by a knowledge of his own peculiar musical resources. School officials can use the tests for making music surveys in their schools to discover unusual talent and to section pupils for general musical instruction according to ability.

CHAPTER 10

THE PSYCHOLOGY OF ARTISTIC SINGING

In 1902 Scripture (93) wrote that "Songs are never sung—or intended to be sung—exactly as written. Even the most mechanical popular tune is rendered differently by each individual, the difference lying mainly in the duration of the elements, in the stress assigned to them, and above all in the attack by the voice and the utterance of each sound. In artistic performance all these sources of variation are employed, mainly unconsciously, to express the thought or emotion of the singer. Concerning just how they are varied and how they are employed there are at present no experimental data." (93, p. 485)

Today the situation is quite different. We have a large accumulation of data on many of the conscious or unconscious variations mentioned by Scripture, and on many other phases of artistic vocal rendition. These data were gathered objectively, mainly in the psychology laboratory of the University of Iowa, by means of recording instruments possessing high degree of precision and accuracy. Specimens of singing under normal conditions have been analyzed into their structural and functional elements, and classified, described, and explained in a thoroughly scientific manner. This procedure is made possible by the fact that whatever is conveyed vocally or instrumentally by the performer to the listener as music reaches the listener through the medium of sound waves. These sound waves can be recorded with a very high degree of precision and analyzed and studied from every angle.

The first such objective study of what actually goes on when a song is rendered by a great artist was made by Schoen. His study concerned itself with pitch intonation, and with the nature and significance of the much disputed vocal phenomenon known as the *vibrato*.

PITCH INTONATION IN ARTISTIC SINGING

The main apparatus used by Schoen (86) in this investigation was the Seashore tonoscope, an instrument that visualizes the voice so that a person can actually see himself sing. It works on the principle of moving pictures, technically known as stroboscopic vision. The machine converts sound vibrations into pictures on a screen. This screen has 18,095 holes so placed that, when acted upon by a sensitive flame, these holes arrange themselves in characteristic figures for every possible pitch within the range of the human voice. The holes are arranged into 110 rows, the first row having 110 holes, the third 111 holes, and so on, each successive alternate row having one more hole than the preceding one, up to the last, which has 219 holes. When a tone is sounded the row which has the hole frequency that corresponds to the vibration frequency of the tone will stand still, while all other rows move and tend to blur. The row that stands still, or nearly still, points to a number on a scale which designates the pitch of the tone. The tonoscope thus produces for the eye a picture of the vibrations of a tone, a picture which reveals details of pitch faithfully and far more finely than the ear can hear. It thus affords a most sensitive, objective measurement of pitch. Every pitch movement of the voice is pictured on the screen, and the observer can tell at the very moment a tone is produced whether an error is involved, even down to a small fraction of a vibration.

With this instrument the recorded voices of five world-famous opera singers were analyzed in the act of rendering the same composition. The Bach-Gounod "Ave Maria" was chosen for study on account of the prevalence in it of long-sustained tones and the numerous phonograph records of it available as sung by famous artists. The renditions of the following singers, all sopranos, were selected: Nellie Melba, Alma Gluck, Frances Alda, Emma Eames, Emmy Destinn.

Under the general term "pitch" the following specific items for each tone of the composition were observed and recorded for each singer:

1. Attack: how a tone is attacked when preceded by (a) a higher tone, (b) a lower tone, (c) a rest, (d) when the sung tone is of long duration, and (e) when it is of short duration.
2. Release: how a tone is released when succeeded by (a) a higher tone, (b) a lower tone, (c) a rest, (d) when the sung tone is of long duration, and (e) when it is of short duration.
3. Predominant pitch: if the tone undergoes several pitch changes while sustained, on which one of the several pitches is it mostly held, and what are the number and extent of the deviations above and below this predominant pitch?
4. Vowel: the effect of the vowel on which the tone is sung on the pitch of the tone.
5. Tonal movement: how the singer moves from tone to tone, whether by glides or leaps, and to what degree. Thus, in the case of a glide, the movement may be heavy and slow, the voice dwelling upon every vibration intervening between the two tones, or it may be light and quick so as hardly to be perceptible to even the most acute ear.
6. The crescendo: the effect of a rise in the intensity of the tone upon its pitch.
7. Successive predominant pitches: when the same tone is sung several times in the course of the composition, how do the predominant pitches of the tone in the repetitions compare with one another?
8. Deviations: how the deviations above and below the predominant pitch compare with one another in number and extent in a given tone.

If the phonograph disk gives a true picture of what goes on as a singer attacks, sustains, and moves from tone to tone, then the following results for each of the five sopranos can be accepted as being typical of pitch intonation in artistic singing.

Destinn. 1. The low attack predominates, and is of large extent. The tone is never attacked high, irrespective of the position of the preceding one.

2. The release is predominantly above, and is of comparatively large extent.

3. A predominant tone is slightly present, the fluctuations being large in extent and numerous, with the deviations above the predominant tone outnumbering those below the predominant tone.

4. The effect of the vowel on the pitch of the tone is erratic.

5. A pitch rise in the crescendo is almost always present.

6. The tonal movement is a marked portamento.

7. The deviations from each other of the predominant pitches for the same tone are marked and numerous. Thus, the tone d″, sung twelve times, occurs on five different pitches within the range 545-573 cycles.

8. A tendency to sing sharp, in terms of the predominant pitch, is manifest.

Gluck. 1. When the tone is sung after a rest or after an inspiration, or is approached from an interval more than a major second below, it is invariably initiated on a pitch somewhat below the desired tone, the extent of the error in attack depending on the distance, below, of the preceding tone. The low attack is more marked in extent when the tone is preceded by a rest, and is also more marked in a tone of long duration than in one of shorter duration. When the preceding tone is above, the attack is invariably accurate.

2. The release is predominantly high, irrespective of the succeeding tone, and is of marked extent.

3. The fluctuations in the tone are few, of small extent, and are more numerous above than below the predominant pitch. A predominant pitch is present to a marked degree.

4. There is a tendency for the vowels *i, a, e,* to be sung higher than *o* and *u.*

5. The movement from tone to tone is mostly in the form of portamento.

6. In the crescendo tone there is invariably a rise in pitch of marked extent.

7. The deviations from each other of the predominant pitches for the same tone, as sung in successive occurrence, are very small in extent and few in number.

8. The maximum deviation below the predominant pitch is greater than the maximum deviation above, but the general tendency is to sing sharp in terms of the predominant tone.

Melba. 1. The low attack is almost constantly present and is of large extent.

2. The release is unusually accurate.

3. A predominant tone is conspicuously present, the fluctuations are very few and of small extent, with the departures above and below the predominant tone about evenly divided in number.

4. Vowel *e* is sung higher than the other vowels, *i* and *a* next, and *o* and *u* lowest.

5. The tonal movement is very smooth and legato.

6. There is rarely a rise in pitch on the crescendo, and when it does occur it is of small extent.

7. The deviations from each other of the predominant pitches for the same tone are small in number and extent.

8. The tendency to sing above or below the predominant pitch is very slight.

Alda. 1. The low attack predominates, but is of comparatively small extent. The attack from above is accurate, irrespective of the position of the preceding tone.

2. The presence of a predominant tone level is not marked, while the fluctuations are numerous and of large extent, being about evenly divided in number above and below the predominant pitch.

3. The high release is almost constant and is of large extent.

4. The vowel tendency is erratic.

5. The portamento tonal movement is markedly present.

6. Pitch rise in the crescendo is not very frequent, but is of large extent when present.

7. The deviations from each other of the predominant pitches for the same tone in successive repetitions are very numerous and of large extent. Thus, out of twelve repetitions the tone d″ is sung on nine different pitches within a range of from 565-589 cycles, and the tone e″, out of eleven repetitions, is sung on seven different pitches within the range of 639-659 cycles.

8. The maximum deviation below is larger than that above the predominant pitch, but the general tendency is to sing sharp in terms of the predominant tone.

Eames. 1. The attack as a whole is accurate, excepting after a rest, in which case it is initiated markedly low. A high attack occurs once and is of very small extent.

2. The release is mostly accurate, but when a deviation does occur there is a slight rise in pitch.

3. The presence of a predominant tone is unusually marked and continuous, the fluctuations being few, but of large extent, the deviations above outnumbering those below.

4. No constant vowel tendency is present.

5. The tonal movement is a slight portamento.

6. No pitch rise in the crescendo is noticed.

7. The deviations from each other of the predominant pitches for the same tone in successive repetitions are large in extent but few in number.

8. The tendency to sing off pitch in terms of the predominant tone is very marked.

These data for individual singers point to the following general conclusions on the nature of pitch intonation in singing:

1. A tone is almost invariably attacked below the pitch intended when it is preceded by a lower tone, and in the majority of cases it is released above. The size in the error of attack depends on the distance below of the preceding tone,—the greater the distance, the greater the error. The largest error occurs when the tone is sung after a rest. The size of the error also depends on the duration of the tone, the longer the duration the larger the error. When the preceding tone is above the tone sung, the attack is accurate. The high release is independent of the succeeding tone.

The cause for the low attack may lie in the fact that a time interval elapses before the intensity of breath pressure requisite for the production of a tone of a certain pitch is fully established. In other words, the singer does not immediately, on striking a tone, set up a tension in the vocal chords adequate for the production of the desired pitch. Though this swooping up to a tone is no doubt at times intentional, particularly under great emotional stress, it is evident from its universality that the phenomenon is to a certain extent beyond the singer's control.

The high release may be due to an attempt on the part of the singer to maintain a steady pitch to the very end of the tone, with the result that with the waning of breath the final effort is somewhat overreached.

2. A tone is very rarely sustained on the same pitch for an

interval of time beyond half a second, the number and extent of the deviations depending on the individual characteristics of the singer.

3. Two tones of the same pitch and of equal duration are never sung twice the same way, but vary in the number and the extent of the fluctuations as well as in the pitch of the predominant tones.

4. The vowel quality seems to have but an insignificant effect on the pitch of the tone, though a slight tendency is present to sing the vowels "i" and "e" highest, "a" next, and "o" and "u" lowest.

5. The five singers are divisible into three classes in the matter of tonal steadiness and the number and extent of the fluctuations: Melba and Gluck having the steadiest voices with the fewest and smallest fluctuations, Eames having a steady tone with few fluctuations, but of marked extent when they occur, while Alda and Destinn manifest unsteady tones with fluctuations large in number and extent.

6. The movement from tone to tone is predominantly in the form of glides, but varies in degree for the different singers, being heavier for some than for others.

7. A tendency for a rise in pitch with a rise in intensity is manifest throughout.

8. There exists a tendency for all the singers to sing sharp in the sense that the deviations above the predominant tone are more numerous than those below, but the maximum deviations below the predominant tone are always larger than those above.

Schoen's findings regarding the pitch factor in artistic singing have been extended and refined upon by other studies along the same line. All results show that the pitch of a sung tone fluctuates irregularly, and that what the listener hears is neither the correct pitch of the tone, nor the pitch fluctuations, but a pitch movement or trend above and below the correct pitch level. The singer produces not a straight pitch-line throughout a tone, but one that is curved. Levels occur within the curved pitch-line, and these may be *on* or *off* the correct pitch, and if *off* the correct pitch they may be below or above it. In other words, a tone of constant pitch *on* pitch, or a tone of constant pitch *off* pitch, is not produced by the human voice. The most common phenomenon in this irregularity of vocal tonal production is that of rising inflections. The tone begins on a certain pitch level, whether *on* or *off* correct pitch, and rises progressively throughout its duration. For one singer studied, rising inflections occurred in 37 per cent of the tones, whereas falling inflections were rare. The rising inflections were characteristically present in longer tones and occurred more often when the melody was descending than did the logically expected falling inflections. In short tones rising inflections occurred in 25 per cent of the cases. Most of the upwardly inflected tones began below correct pitch. They began flat and rose to, or beyond, the correct pitch of the tone.

Regarding attack, transition from tone to tone, and release, the data from the studies made of numerous singers show that about 40 per cent of all intertonal movements are made with a continuous pitch glide, about 35 per cent are cleanly attacked, and about 25 per cent are attacked with gliding pitch inflection, usually rising. In gliding attacks 97 per cent begin below the proper tone and rise up to it, irrespective of the direction of the melodic line. That is, even when the melody drops several steps in pitch the singer will begin the lower tone with a long pitch glide from below its pitch level. Such gliding attacks occur most frequently at the beginning of phrases. Of all the phrases investigated almost 62 per cent were begun with gliding attacks. Rising gliding attacks may occur irrespective of whether the tone to be sung is preceded by a tone that is higher, lower, or the same, in pitch. They are most common, however, when the melody is rising and when the succeeding tone is of the same pitch as the one just sung. Two-thirds of the rising gliding attacks occur when the tone is of long duration. The average extent of the gliding attack is about one whole musical step.

The release of a tone is, in about 40 per cent of cases, that of a portamento glide to the succeeding tone, in another 55 per cent it is a level release followed by a pause, while only in 5 per cent does the tone end on a gliding release, usually falling, followed by a pause.

The aesthetic significance of the pitch perambulations found in artistic singing, whether they are an asset or a liability, is an open question. Singers and singing teachers no doubt consider a tone of constant pitch a *sine qua non* of a good tone. But no such tone exists, and therefore the tendency among investigators is to interpret the data concerning the way singers actually do sing as a device used by them for the conveyance of artistic effects. On the other hand, all these pitch phenomena are certainly involuntary. Neither the singer nor the listener is aware of their occurrence, and therefore the singer does not consciously produce them and the listener is not consciously aware of them. So the situation at present is that we have the facts, but their aesthetic significance is still to be determined. It is certain, however, that a scientific treatment of the aesthetics of song must be based upon a consideration of both the physiological and psychological factors involved in the act of phonation, for, when a combination of tones, or even a single tone, is pronounced beautiful as emitted by the human voice, it means that the vocal mechanism is functioning in a manner such as to result in an emotionally favorable auditory stimulus. In other words, song cannot be grasped by the ear alone, no matter how well trained and schooled, or by a consideration of the organs involved, no matter how thorough and complete the treatment, for the one involves the other. It is only when the vocal organs are working properly that an aesthetic result is forthcoming; and vice versa, when an aesthetic effect is produced it is a sign that the vocal mechanisms are adequately functioning. The muscular and the aesthetic are one and the same, and must be considered together. It is then essential that the investigator into the beautiful in singing should begin with a voice whose aesthetic effect is established and search minutely for its physiological and psychological characteristics in order to arrive at standards for artistically effective pitch intonation. What is needed most urgently at present is some rigidly controlled experimental work on the physiology of tone production.

THE VIBRATO

Schoen's observations on pitch intonation in his pioneer study were but incidental to his main interest in the vocal phenomenon known as *vibrato*. That the vibrato was present in every voice possessing any artistic quality had not gone without notice. But whether it was a vice to be deplored and eradicated or a virtue to be praised and cultivated was a matter of dispute. Thomas Edison (17) stated that out of some 3,800 records of singers examined in his laboratory there were about 22 who sang without "the almost universal tremolo effect," which he considered a serious defect. He meant, of course, the vibrato, and not the tremolo, since the tremolo is rare in singers. He felt that if this defect could be eliminated no instrument would exceed the human voice in beauty. The same point of view is held by many singers and teachers of singing. One of them calls it an affliction possessed by five out of every six singers, "and consequently there is a great deal of make-believe that the tremolo is a splendid vehicle for the expression of sentiment and passion." Here also the vibrato is misnamed as a tremolo, for it is certain that five out of six singers do not have a tremolo. The opposite opinion maintains that "the vibrato is a desirable vibration of pulse which should be in every tone and which gives it life. The vibrato is the natural pulse or rhythmic vibration of the tone, and in the attempt to keep the voice steady this must not be lost; any control which prevents this natural vibrato or life-pulse from entering the tone is as bad, though not so obvious, as the tremolo itself."

In order to throw some light on the disputed status of the vibrato Schoen set out to investigate scientifically what it is, what is its significance in the singing voice, what is its physiological seat, and what is the secret of its psychological effect.

THE NATURE OF THE VIBRATO

Schoen's preliminary step was to imitate the vibrato artificially. This can be done in one of three ways: (1) by a tone that oscillates periodically in intensity; (2) by a tone that oscillates periodically in pitch within certain frequency limits; (3) by a combination of both.

An intensity oscillation is produced by sounding two tuning forks with a difference of 5 cycles between them into a resonator, thus producing the phenomenon of beats, or by sounding a single tone into a resonator and passing the hand in front of its mouth at the rate of five or six times a second. By using the same two forks and sounding them alternately into a resonator at the rate of five or six times a second the pitch analogue to the vibrato will be heard. An experiment conducted on a class containing twelve musicians of experience indicated clearly that within certain limits the human ear cannot distinguish easily between a pitch and an intensity oscillation, especially when the fluctuations take place rapidly and periodically.

In so far, then, as its effect on the ear is concerned, the vibrato could be either a pitch pulsation, an intensity pulsation, or a combination of both. When registered on the tonoscope, the pulsating tone disclosed to the eye a periodic up and down movement of several adjacent rows of dots, the movement being synchronous with the audible pulsations. This indicated that the pulsations consisted of rhythmical pitch changes of a certain extent. Another piece of apparatus showed that the pulsating tone also contained periodic intensity fluctuations. By these means Schoen concluded that the vibrato was a periodic pitch and intensity fluctuation. The tone, instead of being of comparatively constant pitch, glides periodically up and down within certain pitch limits at the rate of about six times per second. These pitch changes are accompanied by intensity changes, the pitch and intensity changes being coordinated and therefore simultaneous.

The next step was to determine the extent of the pitch fluctuations in the vibrato of the voices of artists. The tones of the Bach-Gounod "Ave Maria" were used, sung by the same singers as in the study on pitch intonation. An analysis of the individual characteristics for the vibrato for the five singers gave the following results:

Melba. The vibrato was constantly present, with an average extent of 10 cycles. The voice has a marked uniformity and constancy of timbre and pitch throughout the entire range of the composition.

Gluck. The vibrato was constantly present in every tone with an average extent of 13 cycles. Its presence was most marked in the middle and low ranges and least in the highest range of the composition.

Eames. The vibrato was intermittent, being present in some tones and absent from others, as well as present in one part of a tone and not in another part. When the latter case occurred the tone usually began without the vibrato and ended with a vibrato. The average range was 6 cycles. The voice as a whole, as well as single tones, lacked uniformity in timbre. The vibrato was mostly absent from the highest tones.

Alda. The vibrato was present in every tone, but intermittently. It had an average extent of 8 cycles, but was quite variable in the same tone. This gave the tone an effect of constantly changing timbre.

Destinn. The tone almost invariably began minus the vibrato and ended with the vibrato. The effect on the ear was that of a tone beginning with one timbre and ending on another. The average extent of the vibrato was 16 cycles.

THE SIGNIFICANCE OF THE VIBRATO

For the purpose of determining the significance of the vibrato in vocal expression the voices of twenty persons were studied, ranging in age from fourteen years to middle age, and in vocal ability from the monotone to a celebrated concert artist. These observers were divided into four classes, as follows: (1) the monotone; (2) untrained non-musical voices; (3) untrained musical voices; (4) trained musical voices. A careful study of these classes of voices on the tonoscope with regard to the vibrato showed that the voice of the monotone, which sounds dull, hard and strident to the ear, registers rigid in pitch. There is no sign of vibrato in it. The untrained, non-musical voice sounds dull, but not as hard and strident as the monotone. The tonoscope showed the tone from this voice to fluctuate irregularly above and below a predominant pitch within two to four vibrations, but no vibrato.

The untrained, musical voice sounds bright in comparison with the monotone and the non-musical voice and a slight pulsation is clearly heard. The pulsation has a marked periodicity of about 6 beats per second. Only in the case of one singer did the rate of the pulsation reach 13 per second. When observed on the tonoscope, the following phenomena were seen to take place in this type of voice: (1) a progressive fluctuation in pitch above and below a predominant pitch, and (2) a periodic rise and fall in pitch ranging in extent from six to twelve vibrations, and synchronous with the audible pulsations. Not every tone sung, however, showed the periodic pulsation. But, whenever a pulsation was heard the periodic fluctuation was also invariably present. The observations on the trained musical voice were like those for the untrained musical voice, with the addition that both the pulsations and the pitch fluctuations were more markedly present and were more constant and regular.

To summarize: In the musical tone of both trained and untrained voices a periodic pulsation is heard. When the pulsating tone is registered on the tonoscope it is seen to undergo a periodic pitch fluctuation of from six to twelve vibrations in extent. This pitch fluctuation is synchronous with the audible pulsations. The periodic pitch fluctuations appear above, and in addition to, an irregular fluctuation. When the singer was told to control the pulsations in the voice, that is, to try to eliminate them, he could do so only for a fraction of a second, and reported that it was very difficult to sing a tone under such conditions. From these observations Schoen concluded that the vibrato was a basic, fundamental attribute of an effective singing voice.

FURTHER STUDIES OF THE VIBRATO

Since Schoen's first study, his conclusions on the vibrato have been subjected to rigorous examination by a host of investigators who were able to obtain more accurate and detailed results with improved apparatus. By far the most significant contributions made to the improvement of devices and techniques, as well as to more precise measurements of the extent and rate of the vibrato, are those of Metfessel (60). Metfessel confirmed Schoen's principle that the vibrato is a fundamental attribute of the artistically effective singing voice. "The fact that the vibrato is an ingredient of celebrated voices should be regarded as settled. Anyone who will listen to artistic tones on a slowed down phonograph can discover for himself that 95 per cent of artistic tones, long and short, gliding and steady, high and low, pianissimo and fortissimo, register vibrato." But not all vibratos are beautiful, although all beautiful voices have a vibrato. The disagreeable vibratos, he suggests, could be called tremolos, for emphasis. He found, furthermore, that the vibrato contains not only a pitch and intensity factor, but also one of timbre. In rate the artistic vibrato varies from 5.5 to 8.5 pulses per second, the average rate being 7. In pitch it varies from a tenth to over a whole-step, with an average of a half-step. The artistic factor in the vibrato lies, however, not so much in its absolute extent as in the fact that the extent varies from tone to tone. When the vibrato becomes prominent to the point of being unduly noticeable the defect lies not so much in its extent as in its slow rate, excessively wide intensity, bad timbre, and a variety of irregularities in production.

A trill differs from a vibrato mainly in its wider extent, varying from three-quarters to two whole-steps. The tremolo is a disagreeable vibrato due to the presence in it of some factor which interferes with either the pitch salient of the vibrato or the evenness of the vibrato pulsations. Metfessel also feels that some kinds of vibratos are more expressive of emotional factors or climactic tones than others. For instance, a tone expressing great passion would probably better be fitted with a vibrato approaching the trill, and likewise a calm tone might be quite out of place with the vibrato three-quarters of a step.

From a study of the voices of ten prominent singers, male and female, Tiffin (110) concluded that the presence of rather large individual differences was one of the most significant facts about the extent of the pitch factor in the vibrato. He found that among his tenor singers the pitch extent ranged from an average of 0.99 of a step for one singer to 0.49 of a step for another. For the women singers the individual differences were not so large; the widest extent being an average of 0.59 of a step, the smallest, 0.41. For the rate of the vibrato the individual differences were found to be less marked.

The results of Tiffin's analysis of the pitch vibrato in his group of ten artistic voices show this type of vibrato to be present approximately 95 per cent of the phonated time, with an average extent of about 0.6 of a step and an average rate of about 6.5 pulsations. Averages are, however, only of general interest. The significant facts are that there are rather large individual differences in the extent of the vibrato, and significant but smaller individual differences in its rate. "Since it is not true that all artistic singers have a vibrato of the same pitch extent or the same rate, the artistic vibrato cannot be defined in terms of a general average. Such an average does not even indicate the type of vibrato which most great singers use, as the majority of such singers will fall either above or below the average, few if any agreeing with it exactly. This fact is exceedingly important and should be kept in mind by anyone evaluating the specific type of vibrato present in a given singer's voice." (110, p. 146)

Tiffin further investigated the question as to whether the vocal vibrato is primarily a pulsation of pitch or of intensity. Schoen held it to be both. But Tiffin gives three reasons for his conclusion that it is primarily a fluctuation of pitch, and that the intensity fluctuation, when present, plays a relatively small rôle in the total effect. The three grounds for this conclusion are, first, that the intensity vibrato, even when it is present, is less prominent, in that its average extent is about one-eighth the average extent of the pitch vibrato; second, that it is present during a much smaller percentage of the duration of the tone than is the pitch vibrato; and third, that when students were asked to exaggerate the vibrato deliberately it was found that the extent of the pitch vibrato invariably increased whereas the extent of the intensity vibrato showed no significant change. Tiffin does not claim, however, that a vibrato cannot be produced by an intensity fluctuation. His point is only that in the vibrato of the normal singing voice, whether of students or artists, it is pitch rather than intensity that produces the characteristic vibrato effect. But there may be voices in which both are equally prominent. He further insists that the vibrato, as we know it today, is not necessarily the final word about its aesthetic significance. It may possibly be true that the vibrato is in its present form only a fad, and that artistic voices would be improved if it were made less prominent, or even eliminated. His study, he maintains, "simply shows that the vibrato is, at this time, an essential part of what is now considered artistic singing, and it describes the phenomenon in objective terms. No attempt is made to prophesy future artistic taste nor to justify current preferences in terms of ultimate aesthetic principles." (110, p. 165)

An interesting problem in the vibrato phenomenon is the relationship of the pitch and intensity fluctuations that actually occur in the voice to what is heard by the listener. On this point Seashore (98) obtained some interesting data. He produced by means of a synthetic tone producer vibratos that closely simulated actual vocal and string instrument vibrato tones, and asked observers, who were told that they would hear a tone that fluctuated periodically in pitch or intensity, to estimate the extent of the fluctuations. His data show that only a fractional part of the actually occurring physical changes of pitch and intensity—one-fourth to one-half—is heard. It seems, therefore, that the mellowness and richness of vibrato tones is perhaps due to some form of successive tonal fusion which seems to occur in rapidly recurrent pitch changes, rather than to the pitch and intensity fluctuations themselves.

Two questions of considerable interest to singers and teachers of singing have been investigated by Easley and Wagner.

Easley (16) studied the vocal renditions of five opera singers and five concert singers in order to see whether these two types of singing exhibited a characteristic type of vibrato. Opera singing, it was assumed, is probably more expressive of excitement than concert singing, and consequently the study would show whether or not the rate and extent of the vibrato is affected by emotional intensity. Data were obtained, for this purpose, on concert songs by concert singers, concert songs by opera singers, and opera songs by opera singers.

A small but reliable difference between the average rates of the vibrato for concert songs sung by concert singers and opera singers was found to exist, the opera singers having a slightly faster vibrato. In opera singing, however, the vibrato rate was much more rapid than in concert singing, even when the two types of singing were by the same artists. The difference in vibrato rate for concert and opera singers singing concert songs is so small as to be of no real significance. But for opera songs rendered by opera singers the average extent is considerably greater. In other words, when concert and opera singers sing concert songs there is little, if any, difference in vibrato extent between them. But when opera singers render opera songs a somewhat wider vibrato is present. Opera singers, then, have a wider and faster vibrato in singing opera songs than concert songs. Concerning these results Easley makes the following comment:

> This tendency among the opera artists to use faster, wider vibratos in opera songs than concert songs seems to indicate that there is some difference in the nature of the songs themselves. The fact that the concert artists and the opera artists, when singing concert songs, use similar vibratos would further indicate that such vibratos are adequate to achieve the effects required in these songs. It is reasonable to suppose that since the opera artists, when singing opera songs, use faster and wider vibratos than they do in concert songs; and since, for some reason, the concert singers have not been popular in opera, the vibrato is one of the factors necessary for an adequate presentation of opera songs. It is obvious from the results of this study that the opera singers are more versatile in this respect than are the concert singers." (16, pp. 273-274)

The study by Wagner (115) on the artistic development of the vibrato is perhaps of most direct and immediate practical significance. Wagner calls attention to the fact that the dispute among writers and teachers of voice regarding the artistic value of the vibrato arises from the failure to distinguish clearly between vibrato and tremolo. There are irregular vibratos, and when such a vibrato becomes conspicuously fast or slow in rate, or conspicuously wide in extent, it is commonly called *tremolo*. Tremolos are therefore undesirable vibratos, the desirable vibrato being a regular and inconspicuous voice pulsation, and therefore pleasing. He suggests that the term tremolo be dropped, and that all periodic voice fluctuations be designated as a beautiful vibrato or a badly controlled vibrato, or a vibrato of too wide extent, or too fast or too slow in rate, or a fluttering vibrato, and so on. The position taken in his study, based upon the analysis of the vibratos of great artists and those of students and amateurs in various stages of vocal development, is that properly controlled, refined vibrato adds beauty and emotional quality to the voice and is usually associated with good tone; that badly controlled or unduly conspicuous vibrato is ugly and is usually associated with bad tone; and that a voice without vibrato is cold, dead, and uninteresting. He admits that in most naturally fine voices the vibrato is naturally present and does not have to be taught. Nevertheless, refinements in rate and extent of oscillation in natural vibratos are often necessary, and would unquestionably improve the voices of many of our well-known concert and operatic singers. The purpose of his experiments was therefore to test methods of production and refinement of this essential of good singing on the grounds that a singer should be able to increase or diminish his rate and extent of oscillation at will to suit the composition.

Wagner's first step was to set up standards of attainment for use in teaching the control of the vibrato. For this purpose he selected as models tones from Red Seal phonograph records of nine well-known concert and operatic artists. For these nine artists all the tones selected as models exhibited vibratos whose pitch extent in calm singing ranged from 0.20 to 0.40, with an average centering around 0.34; in agitated singing it ranged from 0.26 to 1.04, with an average of 0.58. The rate of the vibrato for calm singing ranged from 5.7 to 6.6, with an average of 6.3 oscillations per second, and for agitated singing from 5.9 to 6.9, with an average of 6.5. With these facts about artistic tones as models, Wagner undertook the training of 43 of his own vocal students in the control of the vibrato. The method of procedure is best given in the words of the investigator.

It was found that many of the singers taking part in the experiments were unaware of the presence or lack of vibrato in their voices. Approach to the experiments was made in the following manner. A phonograph record containing a "model tone," the rate and extent of vibrato oscillation of which were known, was played. The singer's attention was directed to the vibrato in the model and a graph of the tone was shown and explained. The model tone was again played and the vibrato of the artist compared with that in the voice of the instructor. The student was then asked to sing and to notice whether he himself sang with vibrato and if so, how it compared with that of the artist's tone in extent, regularity, and rate of oscillation. Next, before any training in control of the vibrato was attempted, the student's voice in selected tones was photographed. Before making the photograph of his control tone, he was given practice in singing into the horn of the phonophotograph camera. The pitch for all tones in the study was taken from a 435 d.v. tuning fork. The singers were, in every case, told to make as good, smooth tones as possible while intoning the sentence, "The night is clear and calm," sustaining the vowel of the word "calm" until told to "stop." The phonophotographs of these tones represent tones about 0.75 sec. in length.

After the singer had been shown in a graph the discrepancies in rate, regularity, or extent of oscillation between the vibrato in his own voice and that of the model tone of the artist, the training proper began.

While no attempt was made to attain the exact rates and extents of any of the model tones, the average rate of 6.3 oscillations per second and average extent of 0.34 of a step shown in the artists' voices in the examples of calm singing were kept in mind in teaching refinements of vibrato.

Control of amount and character of training. Since this study was in the main carried on with the private vocal students of the writer, the subject of control of the vibrato was deferred from the third to the twentieth lesson depending upon the state of advancement of the student and his attitude toward the experiment. The length of the training period for improvement in control of the vibrato varies therefore as is shown in the tables from a few days to several weeks. In no case, however, are results shown which required a training period longer than a semester of eighteen weeks.

One of the most potent factors in the training in all cases seemed to be the incentive gained from the objective evidence shown by the control phonophotograph of the faults to be overcome, and the evidence in subsequent tests that improvement was being made.

The singers. The forty-three singers who are reported in the experiments ranged from pre-adolescent boys to university professors; and from men and women vocal students to professional singers.

The experiments. The experiments undertaken come under the following general heads:

1. Teaching production of the vibrato—
   (a) To pre-adolescent boys,
   (b) To men vocal students,
   (c) To women vocal students.

2. Teaching control of rate of vibrato oscillation—
   (a) Correction of too slow a rate,
   (b) Correction of too fast a rate.

3. Teaching control of extent of vibrato oscillation—
   (a) Correction of too wide an extent,
   (b) Correction of too narrow an extent. (115, pp. 177-178)

For production of the vibrato Wagner reports that out of the eleven cases who received the training all but one learned to produce vibrato within periods varying from one to seventeen weeks, depending upon the degree of vocal advancement and the perseverance of the individual. The one exception was tone deficient.

Training in increase of vibrato rate resulted successfully for all the singers who took part in the experiment. They were all able to attain faster rates by learning to "harness" the vibratos to rhythms. Regarding decrease in rate it was found that too fast vibratos of wide extent were not difficult to control. But vibratos of the fluttering type were difficult to check or modify as to rate until the center of control was shifted to the region of the diaphragm.

Wagner also found that his singers could learn without much trouble to decrease the extent of their vibratos. "The simple suggestion to hold firmly, though not rigidly, the muscles discovered through the 'warm breath exercise' to function in control of forced expiration, was usually all that was necessary to bring about the desired refinement in extent of vibrato oscillation. The time required for establishment of the corrective habits was from three to thirteen weeks." (115, pp. 207-

208) The experiments on increasing the rate yielded similar results. With the exception of thoroughly established fast vibratos of the throat-controlled, fluttering type, the desired amount of increase in extent was comparatively easy to acquire. The singer simply had to learn to shift the center of control from the throat to the heavier respiratory muscles. This procedure never failed to produce desirable results. The control of slow vibratos with very narrow extents was largely a problem of convincing the singer through comparison of his own graphs with those of the artist models that a wider extent was desirable.

Wagner's general conclusions regarding the control of the vibrato are worth giving in full because of their practical significance.

The experience of the author during twenty years of vocal teaching, supported by the results of the present study, leads to the conclusion that most singers with naturally fine voices associate vibrato with good tone and acquire it either by conscious or unconscious imitation without having to be taught. The fact that singers with pleasing voices who took part in the experiments were often unaware of the existence of vibrato, as such, in their own voices, leads us to believe that the imitation had been unconscious, or that the habit of singing with a passable vibrato had been learned so easily or so gradually as to have escaped notice both of themselves and their hearers. On the other hand, a student with a conspicuous vibrato was usually found to be aware of its presence either as "tremolo" or "poor tone." In some few cases, students admitted that they had acquired vibrato deliberately, usually by imitation of phonograph records.

Critical listening to the voices of great vocal artists shows that not all vibratos even in the tones of our most celebrated singers are by any means equally pleasing to the ear. The causes for the differences in esthetic effect are made evident through phonophotography which makes possible objective analysis of various types of vibrato. By comparison of phonophotograms of tones with the originals heard on the phonograph records the desirable and undesirable aspects of vibrato become evident in terms of rate, extent, and regularity of vibrato oscillation. The artists' tones herein selected as models in the use of vibrato in calm and agitated singing were subjected to phonophotographic analysis and later used in connection with the training as standards of attainment in learning to sing with beautiful vibrato.

In all cases a potent factor in the training was the incentive gained from the objective evidence available to the students of the faults to be overcome, as shown in their control phonophotographs and the proof in subsequent tests that improvement was being made. Another incentive, equally strong, was furnished by the metronome technique, for students who were working for control of rate; without this device they were unable in their daily practice to know how slow is too slow, how fast is too fast or what constitutes a satisfactory rate.

It was found that so-called "diaphragmatically controlled" vibratos could be refined as to rate and regularity by "harnessing" them to rhythm. The results also show that fast vibratos of the throat-controlled, fluttering type can be made slower by developing a firm open throat and shifting the control of the vibrato to the larger respiratory muscles in the region of the diaphragm.

It is moreover proven by objective evidence that changes and refinements in extent of vibrato oscillation can be effected by focusing attention, until the necessary habits are formed, upon control of the abdominal muscles used in expiration.

These scientifically proven facts in regard to control of the vibrato should be of value to the student of singing. It is a satisfaction to the serious student to know that his vibrato compares favorably in rate, extent and regularity, with that of the great concert singer whose tones he admires, or if not, that improvement can be made through use of a practice exercise. It is also a satisfaction to the singer who is musical but who has no vibrato to know that by use of scientifically proven methods a desirable vibrato can be developed.

To the teacher of singing these facts in regard to the nature and control of the vibrato should be of great significance, not only for training of pupils for public performance, but on account of the demands of radio, talking pictures, and other methods of recording where refined and inconspicuous vibrato is essential.

For these various reasons the procedure used in the experiments has been described with detail and with considerable care. It is not to be inferred that certain teachers of singing have not in the past recognized and attempted to teach production and control of the vibrato, some surreptitiously and others openly; but that scientific knowledge on the subject has not heretofore been made available either to students or teachers of singing.

The author is aware of the fact that the application of exact science or scientific methods to the art of music is offensive to some musicians. Since, however, mere observation of vibrato has in the past led to such divergent and tangled opinions, the phonophotographic method was herein resorted to in order to answer the questions of serious-minded students as to the nature and control of this essential of good singing. (115, pp. 211-212)

STUDIES ON SOME OTHER PHASES OF ARTISTIC SINGING

Wolf, Stanley and Sette (123) made a study of the voices of some fifty singers in order to obtain objective data on intensity as a function of pitch and time, vibrato, vibrato-tremolo, and tremolo and quality. Their singers included baritones, tenors, sopranos, contraltos with untrained voices, beginners and successful professional artists. The fundamental aim of their work was to evaluate the caliber of a voice as completely as possible in so far as its external physical manifestations were concerned.

Pitch-intensity measurements were made over the entire pitch range of the singer as a test of ability to maintain a high level of intensity over a wide range, on the grounds that such ability is an indication of high efficiency in voice production, and is one criterion for evaluating a voice. They first investigated the relative intensities of the different vowels with regard to pitch, in order to find the best vowel to use as the standard throughout the experiments. For this purpose they took measurements over the range of five good baritones singing on the vowels "ah," "ay," "oo," and "ee," and found that "ah" and "ay" were at a somewhat higher level than "oo" and "ee."

They also found that there is a relatively smooth rise in intensity with pitch for "ah," "ay," and "oo," while for "ee" there occurred a sudden drop of intensity centering at the pitch of A below middle C. Whereas this effect was extremely pronounced for some of the singers, it was not, however, consistently present in the same voices. This drop was accompanied by a noticeable change in the quality of the vowel, so it would seem that whether or not the drop occurs depends upon the initial quality with which the vowel is sung. On the basis of these findings the vowel "ah" was used for all subsequent measurements.

The results of the pitch-intensity measurements showed consistent increase of intensity with rise in pitch. Several explanations for this phenomenon are offered by the investigators. One is that as the pitch rises the tension on the vocal cords and on the muscles of the thorax increases, resulting in an increase in breath pressure. This should partly account for the rise in intensity. Another possible explanation lies in the fact that as the pitch rises the lower harmonics generated by the larynx more nearly coincide with the resonance frequencies of the vowel sounds. And when the lower partials of a high tone are accentuated through resonance, a higher level of energy results. Another possibility is that, if the amplitude of vibration remains constant with frequency, the energy should increase according to the square of the frequency. It is possible that all three factors operate in some proportion, and it is well known that a great deal more exertion is involved in singing a high tone than in producing a lower one. It is a common observation that when speaking loudly one raises the pitch of the voice.

The voice movements which impart a live, pulsating character to sung tones, these investigators classify as vibrato, tremolo-vibrato, and tremolo. They believe that in the vibrato there occurs a movement of the thorax as well as of the laryngeal and pharyngeal muscle, whereas in the other types of movements there is no such thorax action. The rate of the vibrato is from about 4.5 to 6.4 per second, whereas that for the tremolo and tremolo-vibrato is from about 6.5 to above 8 per second. The movement is a tremolo-vibrato when there is considerable variation in pitch and intensity at the higher rates of speeds. Otherwise it is a tremolo.

The intensity variations that accompany the movement of the voice differ for individuals as well as for different tones of the same individual. There are medium and wide vibratos, having a relatively even form, and others that have a sort of square characteristic. Others are quite irregular.

Measurements of the rate of voice movements of some of the world's greatest artists showed that, out of 115 measurements, fluctuations in the vicinity of 6.0 per second occurred 31 times and predominated over all other rates. The investigators take this to mean that 6.0 is an optimum rate from the point of view of the person producing the tone. Less than about 4.5 per second is not as pleasing as a higher rate.

The pitch oscillations occurring in the voice movements were also shown to be various. In the vibrato they may be very wide or relatively narrow. In the tremolo-vibrato they are relatively wide. In the tremolo of a successful radio "crooner" of the better type of music, the pitch changes were so small as to be negligible. In the trill the pitch changes are very wide.

Regarding good and bad voices, these investigators report that the "outstanding difference between the better and the bad singers is the lack of vibrato frequency spread which characterizes the poor voices. In regard to harmonic distribution, there is no pattern which may be indicative of a good singer." (123, p. 263) "Another requirement for good singing concerns the ability of the singer to hold a constant mean pitch as long as the tone is sustained. If the pitch varies, apart from the vibrato fluctuations, the quality is not pleasant. It is not improbable that good musical quality, from the acoustical standpoint, lies primarily in accuracy of intonation and in proper vibrato variation, provided that the harmonic distribution is not abnormal." (123, p. 264)

The rôle of the vibrato in artistic vocal production has also been investigated by Bartholomew (3), together with other attributes of good voice-quality. Bartholomew limited himself to the male voice. The study extended over five years and included the recording of more than a thousand vocal tones. Besides the vibrato, at least three other major attributes were found to characterize a good voice. These are absolute vocal intensity, a predominance of resonance at a low point, and a predominance at a high point.

The vibrato is the first characteristic, in that a smooth and fairly even vibrato is inseparable from good voice-quality. In a good voice, the vibrato is more marked the louder the tone. "The importance of an even vibrato to the satisfying quality of a voice appears to be considerably greater than formerly realized. Tone qualities which are quite disagreeable when sustained without a perceptible, even vibrato can be made passable if given artificially a proper amount of an even variation at a proper vibrato speed. This does not mean that the vibrato is necessarily heard as a variation. Instead it imparts to the total complex tone a certain richness, to which we react unconsciously as a part of the timbre, unless we learn to direct attention to it." (3, p. 26) Bartholomew feels that physiologically the whole vibrato involves a large group of muscles rather than one particular muscle. Sometimes it is entirely unconscious in the singer, sometimes partly conscious, and in some individuals it can be made entirely conscious and voluntarily controlled. The tremolo is an inartistic extreme of one or more of the three variables of the vibrato, pitch, intensity, and timbre. The tremolo is caused by uncoordinated muscular tension.

Total intensity as a factor of good voice-quality manifests itself in the fact that an individual with good quality is usually able to produce a tone of considerably more intensity than an individual with a poor quality. The total intensity of a voice is a function of the size of the throat. "The relatively large throat which is generally necessary to good tone makes possible this increase in intensity by permitting a more vigorous action of the cords, a free egress through the lower pharynx and over the tongue and a greater degree of resonating by tensing of the walls." (3, p. 27) Laryngoscopic studies have shown that in poor voices there is either a constricted pharynx or a partly closed epiglottis forcing the sound to go through a very narrow opening in getting to the mouth.

Good male voices further possess a low formant, or a predominance of resonance at a low point. There is a decided tendency in such voices to strengthen a low partial somewhere in the general range of 500 cycles or lower. The records of good voices singing middle C had relatively strong second partials, while the poorer voices shifted to thirds, fourths, or fifths. As evidence of the reality of the low formant in good tones Bartholomew cites the fact that the teacher of voice can obtain a better quality of tone in singing the vowel "ah" by asking the student to add "oh." This happens because "oh" has a lower formant than "ah," and therefore a change from "ah" towards "oh" causes a larger resonator with tense walls, giving a somewhat lower pitch and larger amplitude at this lower pitch.

Bartholomew found further that a high formant, usually lying between approximately 2,400 cycles, was present in varying amounts in all male voices he tested, as well as in an overwhelming majority of the total number of records taken. In some poorer male voices the range ran up higher, occasionally as high as 5,000 or 6,000. The data showed that, as a general rule, this high formant increases in prominence with the better voice and the louder tone, at least during some part of the vibrato cycle. The pitch average of the formant, for the most part, is around 2,800-2,900 cycles, whether the voice is that of a tenor or baritone, a good voice or a poor one, and regardless of the fundamental pitch, the vowel, or the intensity. Convincing proof is offered that this high formant is produced in the larynx itself, and its prominence usually varies with the excellence of the voice. But this formant "is not the *sole,* nor even the most important, determinant of good quality. Voices which possess it at the proper point and even which possess it in large degree, may still be of poor quality due to the lack of a suitable vibrato, of a low enough formant, or of sufficient power. If these latter are present, the addition of a strong high frequency at the point for which the hearer's ear is most susceptible will have the effect of adding a very desirable 'ring' or brilliance." (3, p. 31)

The same four attributes of a good voice are reported by Bartholomew to be characteristic of the female voice, but with two modifications. One of these is that the high formant is higher than in the male voice, centering around 3,200 cycles, corresponding to a somewhat smaller larynx. The other is that some types of tones of female voices having a much smaller percentage of high formant are nevertheless of good tone quality. Thus the coloratura voice sometimes has practically no high formant at all, but is of good quality precisely because of its purity and its agility. The high formant tends to drop out in the female voice, as the pitch rises.

In sum, a voice of good quality, according to Bartholomew's investigations, possesses a vibrato which gives life or warmth to the tone, has a high and low formant, the former giving the tone a "resonance" or sonority, the latter a "ring" or shimmer, and is capable of producing great intensity, making it dynamic.

CHAPTER 11

THE GROWTH OF MUSICAL POWERS

The scientific studies on the stages of development of musical powers are not numerous, but the few we have are quite significant. These studies deal with the development of the child's singing voice, the development of musical reproduction and recognition, growth in attitude towards music, and types of listeners among children.

THE DEVELOPMENT OF THE SINGING VOICE

Fröschels (27) conducted an investigation with 380 children of both sexes, ranging in age from four to fifteen years, on the development of the vocal range. Each child was called upon to sing the C scale, ascending and descending. The keytone was sounded by a tuning fork and the scale was first sung for the child either by the experimenter or by the teacher. The child was then called upon to sing the scale. If he could not do so because of lack of training or vocal deficiency a song was attempted. If this also failed the assistance of a child of similar age was called upon, since it is well known that some children can imitate the voice of another child better than that of an adult. Only seven children failed in this attempt also. Five of these seven could only utter one or two tones. Some of the smallest children sang only a few tones, but it was quite evident that they only needed training to do better. The vocal range, then, as given for four- and five-year-old children should be taken with some reserve.

Those children who had to sing a song because of inability to sing the scale used only vowels, since singing with words is more difficult, and the vocal range was therefore best determined by the use of vowels only. All children sang either the scale or the song on various vowels, since different vowels have a considerable effect on the tone. The vowels used were *a, i,* and *u.*

The upper limit of the vocal range was determined by the highest tone that a child could produce without evident strain of vocal muscles. In other words, the tone below the forced tone was taken as the upper limit of the vocal range. It was found that 308 of the children were able to complete the test on the vowels. Of these 308, 161 produced the tones within their vocal range equally well whether using *a, i,* or *u.* In 65 cases *u* sounded free in tones that were forced on *i* and *a.* In 50 cases *u* and *i* sounded free when *a* was forced. Only 11 times was *i* superior to *a* and *u,* with *u* being more difficult than *i* three times, but easier than *a. U* and *a* were superior to *i* two times, and *a* sounded free four times when *u* and *i* were forced. As a whole, then, *u* had higher value 132 times, *i* 76 times, *a* only four times.

The vocal pitch range for these 380 children was as follows:

Age	Boys	Girls
4th year	c′ — g′ sharp	c′ — a′
5th year	c′ — a′ sharp	c′ — b′
6th year	b — a′ sharp	c′ — a′ sharp
7th year	a sharp—c″	b — c″
8th year	a — c″ sharp	g sharp—d″ sharp
9th year	g — d″ sharp	g sharp—d″ sharp
10th year	g — d″ sharp	g sharp—c″ sharp
11th year	d sharp—d″ sharp	f sharp—d″ sharp
12th year	e — e″	f — f″
13th year	e — d″ sharp	f — f″
14th year	d — f″ sharp	f — f″

The most recent and significant study on the child voice in song is that of Jersild and Bienstock (48). They gave tests of vocal reproduction of pitch to 407 children aged two to ten years, and to 65 adults. The purpose of the tests was to obtain a record of the range of tones that the child or adult was able to sing. The experimenter sounded a tone from the C major scale, sang it, asked the subject to reproduce it, and made a record as to whether or not the given tone had been correctly reproduced.

The most impressive result of the tests is the indication that the development of the ability to sing a wide range of tones is rapid. From the second to the sixth year the development is decidedly greater than it is from the sixth year to maturity. Children, particularly girls, attain in the first three grades of the elementary school a large portion of their potential pitch range as adults. This finding, the investigators point out, means that vocal training should be emphasized in the lower grades, so the child shall form the habit of using his voice, as well as acquire skill in how to use it.

Regarding the particular tones within the range of a child at a particular age, the results show that at six years of age children possess a relatively wide tonal repertory. Of the children of that age 50 per cent had a range from a to g″. It seems, then, that six-year-olds are able to sing lower tones than the limits given in some manuals on the musical training of children. At all ages, the data show, from two years and on, 50 per cent of the children were able to produce one or more tones below e′. At two years the range was found to be from d′–a′, at three, c′–a′, at four, b–c″, at five, a–d″, at six, a–g″, at seven, a–g″, at eight, g–g″, at nine, f–g″, at ten, f–g″. These are the ranges produced by approximately 50 per cent of the children tested.

In a further experiment by the same investigators, in which the pitch range covered in spontaneous humming and singing of 18 children, aged thirty-one to forty-eight months, was studied, it was found that out of a record of 920 tones, 915, or 99 per cent, were within the range from e′ to e″, only 50 per cent of the tones occurred within the range from c′ to a′, while 50 per cent were above a′. These findings suggest that in free vocalizing children are more likely to sing tones within their high than their low register. But the data indicate clearly that children have the ability to sing low tones. Thus, in a study of 95 children aged four and a half to eight years, Hartwick found that the mean pitch used by them when singing songs spontaneously was significantly lower than that found for these songs as printed in song books for children of those ages.

Furthermore, experimental results do not support the rule set forth in some manuals that half-step intervals should be used sparsely in songs for young children. On the contrary, in an investigation of interval singing on 47 children, aged thirty-one to forty-eight months, and 27 children aged three to eight and a half years, it was found that seconds and thirds were reproduced more readily than fourths and fifths by the younger children, while the older group reproduced major and minor seconds, thirds, and the perfect fourths more frequently than wider intervals. The differences were, however, small, and training practically eliminated them.

Jersild and Bienstock also conducted experiments on 36 children, ranging in age from thirty-one to forty-eight months, and on 23 children aged three to eight and a half years, in order to ascertain the effects of training on ability to sing tones, intervals and songs (47). The gains from practice were large even for the short period of training, which consisted of 38 twenty-to-thirty-minute periods distributed over six weeks. The average gain made by the children during the practice period was over 30 per cent in the number of tones they could sing. The gains were greater for high than for low tones. On the basis of their observations on the children during the period of training the investigators make the following practical suggestions for procedure in singing.

At the beginning of training, when songs are first introduced, it seems best to select songs that are well within the child's tonal range. A test of his ability to reproduce tones is helpful in discovering what this range is. When a child seems unable to sing, this may mean that the song that is assigned is not suited to his voice and should be transposed to a higher or lower key. If a child has only a limited tonal range, chromatic intervals should be introduced as a means of providing greater variety and as a means of avoiding too much monotony in the materials he is asked to sing. Many children who at first seem either inhibited or incompetent respond favorably to opportunities to sing in unison with others and to the example of hearing another competent child perform. After the child's cooperation has been won, the songs introduced for the purpose of training should include not only tones that are within the child's range but also tones which he hitherto has been unable to reproduce; the former should, however, be more numerous and should serve as the foundation of the tune. It is helpful also to drill the child in the singing of particular tones. In the case of preschool children, it may be helpful at times to utilize songs dealing with and accompanied by activity (such as putting the baby to sleep, imitating animals, etc.). Monosyllables rather than polysyllabic words are recommended for the songs first presented to very young children so that the emphasis may be on the tune rather than the mastery of words. In the case of children who are able to sing a wide range of tones, songs incorporating a wide range of tones should be used to encourage them to make full use of their abilities. On the same ground it is also recommended that a variety of wide as well as narrow intervals be included in songs designed for children who are capable singers. (48, pp. 499-500)

MELODIC INVENTION AND MELODIC REPRODUCTION

Werner (122), who was the first to investigate the earliest melodic inventions of children, found that when children make up their own melodies they use small intervals. The first melodic structure consists of a repetition of a descending minor third motif and its derivations. This is characteristic of children up to the third year. The second melodic stage, continuing till about three and a half years of age, consists of ascending or descending motifs of 3 to 4 tones, of a range up to a minor third, ending on the most often repeated lowest tone of the melody. In the third stage, lasting till about age four, the melody is made up of ascending-descending motifs of many tones, with repeated cadences, of a compass up to a diminished fifth, ascending regularly and descending irregularly, with intervals of a minor third to semi-tones, and ending on the most common lowest tone. The fourth stage, up to four and a half years, is typified by a rising and falling many-toned motif with ascending repetition, regularity in ascending and descending, having a range up to a diminished fifth, and closing on the middle tone. In the fifth stage, till the fifth year, there occur double-phrased, many-toned motifs, the smallest interval used being a quarter tone, with rising-falling continuity, and a maximum range of a diminished fifth.

In an experiment on melodic invention by children, Vater (113) asked 16 girls thirteen to fifteen years of age to make up a melody to (1) a given rhythm, (2) a given text, (3) a suggested mood, color, or story. For rhythm the children fell into two groups: those whose inventions were melodic and those whose inventions were non-melodic. The non-melodic renditions consisted of a repetition of a portion of the rhythm, most often one measure, out of which the whole rhythm was pieced together, using one tone or one interval. Children who did this did not seem to know when they reached the end of the rhythm, often asking the experimenter whether they were through. The second group sang the rhythm to a melodic whole, using many tones of the scale. This shows that they conceived the melody from the outset as a form, a configuration. For the text the results were quite different, in that here even those children whose production was non-melodic for rhythm could form melodies to the text. This suggests that the text, presenting a complete idea, influences the invention of a melodic sequence of tones. Melodic inventions to happy stories prompted fast, crisp, high vocalization and of large pitch range, while sad stories were sung to slower time, smaller pitch range, smaller steps, and lower pitch.

Meissner (59) found some typical phenomena in the mistakes made by children, eight to fourteen years of age, in reproducing melodies. There were rare cases of children who kept singing on the same tone. But there were frequent cases in which the general melodic outline was correctly sung, but the single intervals were sung only with approximate accuracy. This was particularly true of half-steps. Thirds were repeatedly interchanged with fourths or fifths, while the rest of the melody was correctly sung. In general, descending intervals were sung more accurately than ascending intervals, this being particularly so with the minor second. Among thirteen- and fourteen-year-olds, an attempt to produce a tone of good quality and to sing with expression was noticeable. Puberty seems to be the period at which an interest in singing as an expression of mood and feeling appears. This is also the age when a marked improvement in melodic memory occurs, following the slow improvement until the twelfth year.

Meissner's finding that for a time children grasp mainly the general outline of a melody, its up and down movements, and not the single intervals, is corroborated by other investigators, particularly Stern (101) and Brehmer (7). The small child is guided in rote singing by the changes in the brightness of the ascending and descending tones rather than by the pitch changes that occur from tone to tone. Details of structure are either beyond his grasp, or he has no interest in them up to a certain age. Brehmer also noticed the tendency among his 76 children, six to fourteen years of age, to overemphasize in their melodic reproductions the parts of motifs that occupied a prominent place in the melody. Such prominent parts are more correctly reproduced than are the less prominent portions. All this indicates that, at least up to the sixth year, the child grasps tonal relationships only as a general mass impression, so that the reproduction of a melody tone for tone is difficult before that age. During the seventh year signs of a feeling for tonality begin to appear, and it is at this age that children begin to reproduce melodies with correctness of detail, because it is tonality feeling that makes possible the perception, and therefore the correct reproduction, of the simplest formal melodic units.

THE DEVELOPMENT OF PITCH RECOGNITION

The response to melody begins, as we have already seen, as a mass impression, without much differentiation, or "hearing out," of single tones and intervals. This may be due either to the child's inability, before a certain age, to differentiate between the short pitch steps that are most common in music, or to lack of sufficient experience in such differentiation. Several investigations on the ability of children to recognize pitch differences of various sizes at different ages are at hand.

In one of several investigations Meissner (59) asked children eight to fourteen years of age to state which one of two given tones was the higher. The given interval was the semitone. His results show that the judgments of the younger children were fairly uncertain, although when these same children were asked to judge whether the two tones heard were the same or different the answers were mostly correct. Judgments of *higher* or *lower* are then more difficult than judgments of *same* or *different*. For judgments of *higher* or *lower* the interval must be larger than for *same* or *different*. The children who could produce the tones most correctly also gave the most correct judgments. Ten per cent of the eight-year-olds failed in the judgment of the interval of the third. Meissner holds that the perception of pitch differences depends upon the delicacy and memory for more or less definite sensations of muscular tension, this being perhaps the reason why development of improvement in pitch discrimination runs a parallel course with improvement in melodic memory, which, according to this investigator, also has its basis in sensations of tension.

Pitch discrimination in terms of *same-different* judgments develops in three stages, according to Meissner's data. The first stage is from years six to nine, the second from ten to fourteen, the third from fifteen to twenty. This result is somewhat different from Seashore's, who holds that development of pitch discrimination culminates at age twelve, and from Gilbert's, who found a continuous improvement from years six to nineteen. For six-year-olds Meissner found the differential threshold to be 18 cycles. At the beginning of systematic music instruction in school, children hardly perceive a difference of a quarter tone. A significant rise in improvement occurs during the next three years. During the tenth and eleventh years no improvement takes place. At the twelfth year another stage of development sets in, which reaches a peak at fourteen. In the course of the six years from age eight to fourteen there is an improvement of about 50 per cent. This does not mean that development ceases at fourteen; it probably continues and reaches its maximum at twenty. As a rule, children of high mental endowment also have better pitch discrimination. It also appears quite certain that improvement in pitch perception is a result of improvement in attention and memory as a whole, and not of any physiological changes in the organ of hearing.

An experiment of successive interval judgment was conducted by Hentschel (39) with 491 children, nine to fourteen years of age. The intervals judged were the prime, major second, minor third, augmented fourth, fifth, major seventh, and the octave. Each interval was presented three times ascending and three times descending. The children were instructed to state whether the second tone was higher, lower, or the same as the first. The interval judged correctly most often was the prime, while the tones of the major second were pronounced to be the same more often than any other interval, excepting the prime. The greatest progress in correct judgments of the major second and minor third occurred for boys from the eleventh to fourteenth year, and for girls from the twelfth to fourteenth year. For the minor third and augmented fourth the greatest progress in correct judgments occurred for boys from the ninth to tenth year, and for girls from the ninth to eleventh year. No improvement in the judgment of the intervals from the fourth to the octave was noticed for the three upper years. The number of false *same* judgments decreased with increase in age.

At the pitch level of 800 cycles a pitch difference of 8 cycles was very poorly judged by children of ages ten to fourteen. Half the judgments were that the tones were the same, one-fourth were correct, and one-fourth named the wrong direction or gave uncertain answers. The older children gave more correct judgments than the younger. There was marked improvement in the judgments of the more gifted children of twelve to thirteen years of age. For 10 cycles the number of correct judgments doubled, and for 20 cycles it rose to 70 per cent. More correct judgments of the minor second occurred in tests with unmusical or micro-intervals than of the major second in tests with musical intervals. This the investigator explains on two grounds: first, that judgments of micro-intervals call for closer attention, and second, that in the series of unmusical intervals the minor second was the largest, while in the musical series the major second was the smallest. Furthermore, the intervals between the prime and the minor second were novelties for the subjects, while the minor second struck them as familiar. In all these tests boys excelled girls.

THE DEVELOPMENT OF THE HARMONIC SENSE

The feeling for consonance-dissonance and harmonic fitness is shown by research to be a slow development. Valentine (112) has shown that at the ages of six and seven children show no consistent preference for consonance over dissonance. At seven all the discords are liked more than the octave or minor sixth, probably due to love of noise. A slight preference for the concords begins to appear among a few of the eight-year-old children, and at nine years there is a decided preference for concords. At ten and eleven the discords become still less pleasing, and by the age of twelve and thirteen children have reached a stage at which their preferences for the various intervals are remarkably like those of adults. Valentine also reports that after the age of eleven greater musical capacity is correlated with much greater aversion to discords, and that, on the average, boys are much more critical than girls of musical intervals.

Concerning sensitivity to harmony, a German investigator reports some very significant results from an experiment with a few six-year-olds. A melody familiar to the children was played with the correct harmonization, excepting that it was ended on a false chord. The children, all of whom could sing the melody correctly, and could recognize any change in the familiar melody, were entirely indifferent to this change in the harmony.

To investigate the matter more intensely a more drastic harmonic change was used. The following melody was played

for the children and their preferences for the correct and false harmonizations called for. Most displayed no definite preference; a few preferred the false harmonization.

Next the following melody was played, using successively the bass accompaniments as indicated:

Here also the children were altogether indifferent as to which accompaniment was used. Once in a while, however, they showed signs of displeasure at the most painful dissonances in the performance. It seems, then, that there is a period of growth when a melody is correctly recognized and sung, but harmonic sensitivity is still lacking. For the child up to a certain age, a melody does not carry or imply a certain definite harmonization.

THE DEVELOPMENT OF THE RESPONSE TO MUSIC

Students of child psychology agree that of all the arts music is the first to appeal to the child. The nursing infant localizes auditory stimuli before it does visual impressions. It listens intently to tones and noises, which might indicate that hearing is biologically more primitive and vital than vision. But the earliest musical appeal is probably essentially motor, in that it is the rhythm rather than the tonal sequence that impresses the child. Later comes joy in the music, but this joy is seldom aesthetic. Stern holds that it is a motor activity of the entire body and not primarily an auditory effect. It is therefore a matter of general and practical interest to discover at what age music first begins to produce a musical impression, and how the musical response develops.

According to studies by Walker (116), there are four stages of development. In the first stage, lasting through the eighth year, the dominant appeal is that of tonal beauty and rhythm. In the second stage, from the tenth to the twelfth year, there is a preference for strong rhythms as found in marching songs, hunting songs, spring songs, and wandering songs. From the thirteenth to the fifteenth year preference for strong marching rhythms is gradually displaced by the appeal of sentimental folk songs and songs of patriotism. At sixteen, the fourth stage, there begins the appreciation of the art song and artistic forms as an expression of different moods. These results indicate a gradual differentiation with age of the musically aesthetic experience of children. The response becomes increasingly more subjective and deep in feeling. Till about the tenth year the rhythmic or motor element predominates, and the feeling or expressive aspect of the musical experience is secondary. A dance melody has a greater appeal during these years than a song of sentiment or mood. From this period on there begins a progressive deepening of the feeling response, including a differentiation of the feelings, plus a sensitivity to musical form as such, which is markedly absent in the earlier years.

The factors that influence the depth of the musical experience are tempo, rhythm, interval size, intensity, and mode. The preference develops from wider to narrower intervals, from faster to slower tempo, which means from exciting to calm melodic movement, from the motor to the mental, and from louder to softer dynamics. In the later years loudness is no longer pleasant in itself as excitement, but becomes in an increasing manner the basis for feeling differentiation. Whereas sudden changes in dynamics are highly valued by the younger children, among the older, at about the age of puberty, a demand arises for a more gradual transition.

Children of six to seven years of age do not seem to differentiate between the major and minor modes. Both produce the effect of joy. When such differentiation begins to appear it occurs as a result of the minor melody lacking in brightness, which the children experience as unpleasant, dull, and therefore sad. Beginning with the tenth year the minor is characterized increasingly as being sad. When not described as sad it is called unpleasant. But an identification of the major with pleasure and the minor with displeasure does not occur with sufficient frequency among children six to fifteen years of age to indicate any consistent differentiation between the two modes.

Walker claims that, as regards major and minor music, children fall into two groups: a small group that prefers minor to major, and a larger group whose preference is the major. The grounds given by the children for their preferences seem to indicate temperamental differences, or differences in depth of feeling. The minor is preferred by those to whom musical experience does not mean only sensory and motor excitation, but an expression of longing, sorrow, or any other feeling or mood. The larger group has no such deep-seated feeling-tone, and prefers therefore the more exciting, faster moving music. The minor type begins to appear about the eighth year, and becomes quite distinct at twelve. It leans towards melodies with small intervals, soft tones, and slow rhythms. For the major type music is a source of entertainment, and it dislikes melodies of narrow intervals, calling them monotonous. It also wants loudness and speed to produce the effect of liveliness. The result is that this type hardly distinguishes between major and minor, because it does not possess the requisite refinement of emotional resonance called for by the minor. This type is found, according to Walker, at all ages, whereas the minor type undergoes a process of development. If the minor response appears at an early age it is a sign of a marked musical inclination. The major type preponderates over the minor from the eleventh to the thirteenth year in the proportion of three to one. Walker holds, further, that there is also a group which, while recognizing the better music, nevertheless prefers the poorer.

TYPES OF LISTENERS AMONG CHILDREN

Children's responses to music fall, according to Walker, into four types, the sensory, the motor, the emotional, and the imaginative. For the sensory the appeal is that of the brightness of pitch movement. For this type the musical experience has little subjective content. The motor type is very numerous. The music is significant as a stimulus for motor impulses and movements. For the emotional type music is primarily a vehicle for feeling. The imaginative type finds in music a stimulus for some ideational content. These types are not permanent. In the course of growth a transition may occur from some one attitude to another. Nor are these types exclusive of each other. In any one person there is only a predominance of one attitude over the others. The sensory attitude is characteristic of the first school year. Tonal beauty produces its effect even when there is no response to the melody, and even when the performance is in false intonation. In the second school year, individual differences begin to appear. Most of the children are sensory-motor, but signs of the emotional and imaginative attitudes are in evidence. In the third school year a distinction can be noticed between the sensory and the motor, as well as between the emotional and the imaginative. In the fourth year the sensory attitude has mostly disappeared, the motor is still prominent, and the emotional and imaginative begin to come to the fore. In the fifth year there is a further decline in the sensory type and also a decrease in the motor, but an increase in the emotional and imaginative. The sixth school year is characterized by a marked shift in the proportion of types. The sensory has disappeared, the motor has markedly decreased, the emotional increased, and half the children are of the imaginative type. It is noticeable that from the sixth to the eighth school year the formal aesthetic attitude becomes prominent, but it is seldom present without an admixture of the others. In the seventh year there is again a predominance of the emotional and imaginative attitudes, while in the next year more than half the children are of the imaginative type, and one-third predominantly emotional. The more musical children develop more rapidly in these attitudes than their less musical classmates.

Another classification of types is given by Alt (1), based on a study of 434 children. There is the sensory type, in which the tonal material is appreciated primarily as a source of pleasant excitation by producing a mental or physical change in the listener's condition. The interplay of tones, harmonies, and rhythms arouses a kaleidoscopic flow of feeling, and attention is absorbed in the pleasurable functioning of unobstructed vital processes. There is a naïve joy in the stimulating effect of the tonal material. The hearer is passive, and the stimuli operate freely and fully upon the physiological processes. The sensory has three sub-types, namely, one in which the sensory effect gives rise to imagery of various sorts, another in which the concomitants are organic motor processes, and a third where the sensory stimulation produces emotional effects such as longing, sorrow, joy or sadness.

Then there is the aesthetic type, in which attention is focused upon the exciting object rather than upon the excitation. In aesthetic hearing the inner effects are objectified and localized in the musical stimulus, so that the hearer is engrossed in the stimulus rather than in himself. The aesthetic listener is not passive in his attitude, permitting the music to produce its effects upon him, but his attention is actively fixed upon the musical stimulus as an object of contemplation. And it is not the effect that interests him, but the aesthetic object. Here intellect plays a higher rôle than in the sensory attitude. But it does not act in a critical manner as a judgment of the music. The response is rather that of a joyful spontaneous experiencing of value coming from the object of contemplation. The tonal structure engrosses the hearer as such.

In the third type the hearer experiences the music as a medium of expression for the composer. The music is felt as an expression of grief, sadness, or longing; as a bearer of messages; or as depicting some event or situation. Here also the hearer projects himself into the music, and is interested in the music rather than in his own feelings or mental processes. But the interest in the music is not as music, as an aesthetic object having significance as such, but as the bearer of a content or meaning intended by the composer.

The three types use different criteria for musical evaluation. For the sensory type the criterion of value is the subjective impression or effect, a heightened consciousness of living. ("I like the piece because it arouses me, makes me joyful.") The aesthetic type bases the evaluation on the impression produced by the artistic object in parts or as a whole. ("It is so 'clear,' 'simple,' 'soft,' 'full of various moods,' 'rich,' 'so unique in its harmonies.' ") For the third type the evaluation is ethical. ("The music inspires one with ideals. It leads one to the higher and nobler.")

BIBLIOGRAPHY OF WORKS CITED

(1) Alt, M. Die Erziehung zum Musikhören. Leipzig, Kister and Siegel, 1935.

(2) Auer, L. (in) Martens, F. H. Violin Mastery. New York, Stokes, 1919, 15-16.

(3) Bartholomew, W. T. A physical definition of "good voice-quality" in the male voice. J. acoust. Soc. Amer., 1934, 6, 25-33.

(4) Billroth, Th. Wer ist musikalisch? Berlin, 1896.

(5) Binet, A. and Courtier, J. Recherches graphiques sur le musique. Année psychol., 1895, 2, 201-222.

(6) Bingham, W. V. D. Studies in melody. Psychol. Monogr., 1910, 12, no. 3, whole no. 50.

(7) Brehmer, F. Melodieauffassung und melodische Begabung des Kindes. Beiheft, Ztsch. f. ang. Psychol., 1923, 36.

(8) Brues, A. M. The fusion of non-musical intervals. Amer. J. Psychol., 1927, 38, 624-638.

(9) Corning, J. L. The use of musical vibrations before and during sleep. Med. Rec., 1899, 55, 79-86.

(10) Crzellitzer, A. Zur Methodik der Untersuchung auf Vererbung geistiger Eigenschaften. Ztsch. f. ang. Psychol., 1910, 3.

(11) Dogiel, J. Über den Einfluss der Musik auf den Blutkreislauf. Arch. f. Physiol., 1880, 416-428.

(12) Downey, J. A musical experiment. Amer. J. Psychol., 1897, 9, 63-69.

(13) Downey, J. E. and Knapp, G. E. The effect on a musical programme of familiarity and of sequence of selections. (in) Schoen, M. (ed.) The effects of music, New York, Harcourt, Brace, 1927, ch. 12.

(14) Drake, R. M. Four new tests of musical talent. J. appl. Psychol., 1933, 17, 136-147.

(15) Drake, R. M. The validity and reliability of tests of musical talent. J. appl. Psychol., 1933, 17, 447-458.

(16) Easeley, E. A comparison of the vibrato in concert and opera singing. Univ. Iowa Stud. Psychol. Mus., 1932, 1, 269-275.

(17) Edison, T. A. An interview with Thomas Edison regarding the imperfections of the human voice. Amer. Magaz., March, 1921.

(18) Edmonds, E. M. and Smith, M. E. The phenomenological description of musical intervals. Amer. J. Psychol., 1923, 34, 287-291.

(19) Faist, A. Versuche über Tonverschmelzung. Ztsch. f. Psychol., 1897, 15, 189-205.

(20) Farnsworth, P. R. Atonic endings in melodies. Amer. J. Psychol., 1915, 36, 393-400.

(21) Farnsworth, P. R. The effect of repetition on ending preferences in melodies. Amer. J. Psychol., 1926, 37, 116-122.

(22) Farnsworth, P. R. An historical, critical and experimental study of the Seashore-Kwalwasser test battery. Genet. Psychol. Monogr., 1931, 9, 291-393.

(23) Farnsworth, P. R. The Kwalwasser-Dykema tests as psychological tools. Genet. Psychol. Monogr., 1934, 15, 50-84.

(24) Féré, C. Travail et Plaisir. Paris, 1900, ch. 11.

(25) Féré, C. and Jaël, M. L'action physiologique des rythmes et des intervalles musicaux. Rev. scient., 1902, 18.

(26) Foster, J. C. and Gamble, E. A. The effect of music on thoracic breathing. Amer. J. Psychol., 1906, 17, 406-414.

(27) Fröschels, E. Untersuchungen über die Kinderstimme. Zentralbl. f. Physiol., 1920, 34, 477-484.

(28) Gatewood, E. L. An experimental study of the nature of musical enjoyment. (in) Schoen, M. (ed.) The effects of music. New York, Harcourt, Brace, 1927, chs. 4, 5.

(29) Gilman, B. J. Report on an experimental test of musical expressiveness. Amer. J. Psychol., 1892, 4, 42-73; 1893, 5, 558-576.

(30) Guernsey, M. The role of consonance and dissonance in music. Amer. J. Psychol., 1928, 40, 173-204.

(31) Gundlach, R. H. An analysis of some musical factors determining the mood characteristics of music. Psychol. Bull., 1934, 31, 592-593.

(32) Gundlach, R. H. Factors determining the characteristics of musical phrases. Amer. J. Psychol., 1935, 47, 624-643.

(33) Gurney, E. The power of sound. London, Smith, Elder, 1880.

(34) Haecker, V. and Ziehen, Th. Zur Vererbung und Entwicklung der musikalischen Begabung. Leipzig, Barth, 1923.

(35) Hanslick, E. The beautiful in music. London, Novello, 1891.

(36) Heinlein, C. P. An experimental study of the Seashore consonance test. J. exp. Psychol., 1925, 8, 408-433.

(37) Heinlein, C. P. The affective character of the major and minor modes in music. J. comp. Psychol., 1928, 8, 101-142.

(38) Helmholtz, H. L. F. Sensations of tone. Longmans, Green, 1912.

(39) Hentschel, M. Die Beurteilung musikalischer Intervalle durch Kinder. Ztsch. f. ang. Psychol., 1913, 7, 55-69.

(40) Hevner, K. Appreciation of music and tests for appreciation of music. Univ. Oregon publication, 1934, 4, no. 6, 83-150.

(41) Hevner, K. Experimental studies of the elements of expression in music. Amer. J. Psychol., 1936, 48, 246-268.

(42) Hevner, K. Expression in music: a discussion of experimental studies and theories. Psychol. Rev., 1935, 42, 186-204.

(43) Hevner, K. The affective character of the major and minor modes in music. Amer. J. Psychol., 1935, 47, 103-118.

(44) Hevner, K. The affective value of pitch and tempo in music. Amer. J. Psychol., 1937, 49, 621-630.

(45) Huber, K. Der Ausdruck musikalischer Elementarmotive. Leipzig, Barth, 1923.

(46) Hyde, I. M. Effects of music upon electrocardiograms and blood pressure. (in) Schoen, M. (ed.) The effects of music. New York, Harcourt, Brace, 1927, ch. 9.

(47) Jersild, A. T. and Bienstock, S. F. The influence of training on the vocal ability of three-year-old children. Child Develpm., 1931, 2, 272-290.

(48) Jersild, A. T. and Bienstock, S. F. A study of the development of children's ability to sing. J. educ. Psychol., 1934, 25, 481-503.
(49) Karwaski, T. F. and Odbert, H. S. Color Music. Psychol. Monogr., 1938, 50, whole no. 2.
(50) Katz, M. Die Schilderung des musikalischen Eindrucks bei Schumann, Hoffmann und Tieck. Ztsch. f. ang. Psychol., 1911, 5.
(51) Kemp, W. Methodisches und Experimentelles zur Lehre von der Tonverschmelzung. Arch. f. d. ges. Psychol., 1913, 29, 139-257.
(52) Külpe, O. Outlines of psychology. London, 1895.
(53) Kwalwasser, J. and Dykema, P. W. Kwalwasser-Dykema music tests. New York, Fischer, 1930.
(54) Lee, V. The varieties of musical experience. North Amer. Rev., 1918, 207, 748-757.
(55) Lipps, Th. Das Wesen der musikalischen Harmonie und Disharmonie. Psychol. Stud., Heidelberg, 1885.
(56) Lipps, Th. Zur Theorie der Melodie. Ztsch. f. Psychol., 1902, 27, 225-263.
(57) Lowery, H. Cadence and phrase tests in music. Brit. J. Psychol., 1926-27, 17, 111-118.
(58) Maltzew, C. v. Das Erkennen sukzessiv gegebener musikalischer Intervalle in den äussern Tonregionen. Ztsch. f. Psychol., 1913, 64, 161-257.
(59) Meissner, H. Beitrag zur Entwicklung des "musikalischen Sinnes" beim Kinde während des schulpflichtigen Alters. Berlin, Trowitzsch, 1914.
(60) Metfessel, M. The vibrato in artistic voices. Univ. Iowa Stud. Psychol. Mus., 1932, 1, 14-117.
(61) Meyer, M. Ueber Tonverschmelzung und die Theorie der Konsonanz. Ztsch. f. Psychol., 1898, 17, 404-421.
(62) Mjøen, J. A. Zur psychologischen Bestimmung der Musikalität. Ztsch. f. ang. Psychol., 1926, 27, 217-273.
(63) Moore, H. T. The genetic aspect of consonance and dissonance. Psychol. Monogr., 1914, 17, 1-68.
(64) Moran, H. and Pratt, C. C. Variability of judgments on musical intervals. J. exp. Psychol., 1926, 9, 492-500.
(65) Myers, C. S. Individual differences in listening to music. (in) Schoen, M. (ed.) The effects of music. New York, Harcourt, Brace, 1927, ch. 2.
(66) Ogden, R. M. Hearing. New York, Harcourt, Brace, 1924.
(67) Ortmann, O. Interval frequency as a determinant of melodic style. Peabody Bull., Dec. 1937, 3-10.
(68) Ortmann, O. On the melodic relativity of tones. Psychol. Monogr., 1926, 35, no. 1, whole no. 162.
(69) Ortmann, O. Some tonal determinants of melodic memory. J. educ. Psychol., 1933, 24, 454-467.
(70) Ortmann, O. Tests of musical talent. Peabody Conservatory of Music (unpublished).
(71) Ortmann, O. Tonal intensity as an aesthetic factor. Mus. Quart., 1928, 14, 178-191.

(72) Ortmann, O. Types of listeners: genetic considerations. (in) Schoen, M. (ed.) The effects of music. New York, Harcourt, Brace, 1927, ch. 3.
(73) Ortmann, O. What is tone-quality? Mus. Quart., 1935, 21, 442-450.
(74) Pear, T. H. The experimental examination of some differences between the major and the minor chord. Brit. J. Psychol., 1911, 4, 56-88.
(75) Power, E. Elements of the beautiful in music. (in) Gurney, E. The power of sound, 319.
(76) Pratt, C. C. Comparison of tonal distances. J. exp. Psychol., 1928, 11, 77-87.
(77) Pratt, C. C. Some qualitative aspects of bitonal complexes. Amer. J. Psychol., 1921, 32, 490-515.
(78) Pratt, C. C. The meaning of music. New York, McGraw-Hill, 1931.
(79) Pratt, C. C. The spatial character of high and low tones. J. exp. Psychol., 1930, 13, 278-285.
(80) Redfield, J. Music—a science and an art. New York, Knopf, 1928.
(81) Revesz, G. Prüfung der Musikalität. Ztsch. f. Psychol., 1920, 85, 163-209.
(82) Revesz, G. The psychology of a musical prodigy. New York, Harcourt, Brace, 1925.
(83) Rich, G. J. A preliminary study of tonal volume. J. exp. Psychol., 1916, 1, 13-22.
(84) Ruckmick, C. A. Rhythm and its musical implications. Proc. Mus. Teach. Nat. Ass., 1924, 53-62.
(85) Rupp, H. Ueber die Prüfung musikalischer Fähigkeiten. Ztsch. f. ang. Psychol., 1919, 9, 1-76.
(86) Schoen, M. An experimental study of the pitch factor in artistic singing. Psychol. Monogr., 1922, 31, 230-259.
(87) Schoen, M. Tests of musical feeling and musical understanding. J. comp. Psychol., 1925, 5, 31-52.
(88) Schoen, M. The aesthetic attitude in music. Psychol. Monogr., 1928, 29, 161-183.
(89) Schoen, M. The basis of music-mindedness. Mus. Quart., 1935, 21, 348-355.
(90) Schoen, M. The validity of tests of musical talent. J. comp. Psychol., 1923, 3, 101-121.
(91) Schoen, M. and Gatewood, E. L. Problems related to the mood effects of music. (in) Schoen, M. (ed.) The effects of music. New York, Harcourt, Brace, 1927, ch. 8.
(92) Schoen, M. and Gatewood, E. L. The mood effects of music. (in) Schoen, M. (ed.) The effects of music. New York, Harcourt, Brace, 1927, ch. 7.
(93) Scripture, E. W. Elements of experimental phonetics. New York, Scribner, 1902.
(94) Scripture, E. W. Thinking, feeling and doing. New York, 1907.
(95) Seashore, C. E. Seashore measures of musical talent. New York, Col. Phon. Co., 1919.

(96) Seashore, C. E. The psychology of musical talent. New York, Silver, Burdett, 1919.

(97) Seashore, C. E., Lewis, D. and Saetveit, J. G. Seashore measures of musical talent. (1939 revision.) Camden, RCA, 1939.

(98) Seashore, H. G. The hearing of the pitch and intensity in vibrato. Univ. Iowa Stud. Psychol. Mus., 1932, 1, 213-235.

(99) Serejski, M. and Maltzew, C. v. Prüfung der Musikalität nach der Testmethode. Psychotech. Ztsch., 1928, 3, 103-107.

(100) Stanton, H. M. Measurement of musical talent: The Eastman Experiment. Univ. Iowa Stud., 1935, no. 291, 1-140.

(101) Stern, W. The psychology of early childhood. New York, Holt, 1924, ch. 25.

(102) Sterzinger, O. Rhythmische Ausgeprägtheit und Gefälligkeit musikalischer Sukzessintervalle. Arch. f. d. ges. Psychol., 1916, 35, 75-124.

(103) Sterzinger, O. Rhythmische und ästhetische Characteristik der musikalischen Sukzessintervalle und ihre ursächlichen Zusammenhänge. Arch. f. d. ges. Psychol., 1917, 36, 1-58.

(104) Stumpf, C. Akustische Versuche mit Pepito Areola. Ztsch. f. ang. Psychol., 1909, 21, 1-11.

(105) Stumpf, C. Die Unmusikalischen und die Tonverschmelzung. Ztsch. Psychol., 1898, 17.

(106) Stumpf, C. Konsonanz und Konkordanz. Ztsch. f. Psychol., 1911, 58, 321-385.

(107) Stumpf, C. Tonpsychologie. Berlin, 1900, 1.

(108) Tarchanoff, J. L'influence de la musique sur l'homme et les animaux. Arch. Ital. de. biol., 1894, 21, 313-317.

(109) Thurstone, L. L. The problem of melody. Mus. Quart., 1920, 6, 426-429.

(110) Tiffin, J. The role of pitch and intensity in the vocal vibrato of students and artists. Univ. Iowa Stud. Psychol. Mus., 1932, 1, 134-165.

(111) Updegraf, R. A preliminary study of the nature of finality in melody. Proc. Iowa Acad. Sci., 1926, 23, 279-282.

(112) Valentine, C. W. The aesthetic appreciation of musical intervals among school children and adults. Brit. J. Psychol., 1913, 6, 190-216.

(113) Vater, H. Musikalische Produktion, ihr Wesen, ihre effektive Leistung, ihr intentionaler Gehalt. Arch. f. d. ges. Psychol., 1934, 90-160.

(114) Vescelius, E. G. Music and health. Mus. Quart., 1918, 4, 376-400.

(115) Wagner, A. H. Remedial and artistic development of the vibrato. Univ. Iowa Stud. Psychol. Mus., 1932, 1, 166-212.

(116) Walker, E. Das musikalische Erlebnis und seine Entwicklung. Göttingen, Vanderhoeck and Ruprecht, 1927.

(117) Washburn, M. F., Child, M. A. and Abel, T. M. The effects of immediate repetition on the pleasantness or unpleasantness of music. (in) Schoen, M. (ed.) The effects of music. New York, Harcourt, Brace, 1927, ch. 10.

(118) Washburn, M. F. and Dickinson, G. L. The sources and nature of the affective reaction to instrumental music. (in) Schoen, M. (ed.) The effects of music. New York, Harcourt, Brace, 1927, ch. 6.

(119) Washco, A. The effects of music upon pulse rate, blood-pressure and mental imagery. Philadelphia, Temple Univ., 1933.

(120) Watt, H. J. The psychology of sound. Cambridge University Press, 1917.

(121) Weld, H. P. An experimental study of musical enjoyment. Amer. J. Psychol., 1912, 23, 245-308.

(122) Werner, H. Die melodische Erfindung im frühen Kindesalter. Phil.-Hist. Klasse. Sitzungsberichte, 1917, 182, 4. Abhandlung.

(123) Wolf, S. K., Stanley, D. and Sette, W. J. Quantitative studies on the singing voice. J. acoust. Soc. Amer., 1935, 6, 255-266.

(124) Wundt, W. Grundzüge der physiologischen Psychologie. Leipzig, 1910.

SELECTED BIBLIOGRAPHY

1. Abraham, Otto and Hornbostel, E. M. v. Zur Psychologie der Tondistanz. Ztsch. f. Psychol., 1925, 98, 233-249.
2. Adler, M. J. Music appreciation: an experimental approach to its measurement. Arch. of Psychol., 1929, 110.
3. Agnew, M. The auditory imagery of great composers. Psychol. Monogr., 1922, 31, 279-287.
4. Anschütz, G. Untersuchungen zur Analyse musikalischer Photismen. Farbe-Ton Forschungen, Leipzig, 1927.
5. Arreat, Lucien. Observation sur une musicienne. Rev. Phil., 1903, 28.
6. Auer, Leopold. Violin playing as I teach it. New York, Stokes, 1921.
7. Baerwald, R. Zur Psychologie der Vorstellungstypen, mit besonderer Berücksichtigung der motorischen und musikalischen Anlage. Leipzig, Barth, 1916.
8. Bahle, J. Psychologie des Einfalls und der Inspiration in musikalischen Schaffen. Acta Psychologica, 1935, 1, 7-29.
9. Baier, D. E. The loudness of complex tones. J. exper. Psychol., 1936, 19, 280-307.
10. Bean, K. L. An experimental approach to the reading of music. Psychol. Monogr., 1938, 50, 80.
11. Bean, K. L. Reading music instead of spelling it. J. of Musicol., 1939, 1, 1-5.
12. Beaunis, H. L'Emotion Musicale. Rev. Phil., 1918, 86, 353-369.
13. Belaiew-Exemplarsky, S. Das musikalische Empfinden im Vorschulalter. Ztsch. f. ang. Psychol., 1928, 27, 177-216.
14. Belaiew-Exemplarsky, S. Die Auffassung melodischer Bewegung. Arch. f. d. ges. Psychol., 1934, 92, 370-422.
15. Belaiew-Exemplarsky, S. Grundsätzliches für die Untersuchung der Musikalität und ihre Elemente. Psychotech. Ztsch., 1928, 3, 107-111.
16. Belaiew-Exemplarsky, S. Zur Psychologie der Musikwahrnehmung. Moscow: Russky Knischnik, 1924.
17. Belaiew-Exemplarsky, S. and Jaworsky, B. Die Wirkung des Tonkomplexes bei melodischer Gestaltung. Arch. f. d. ges. Psychol., 1926, 57, 489-522.
18. Bernfeld, S. Zur Psychologie der Unmusikalischen. Arch. f. d. ges. Psychol., 1915, 34, 235-254.
19. Blind, E. E. An experiment with monotones. Music Educators J., 1938, 24, 37-39.
20. Bogen, D. The significance of tonal memory and sense of pitch in musical talent. Psychol. Bull., 1933, 30, 599.
21. Borchers, O. J. The relation between intensity and harmonic structure in voice. Psychol. Rec., 1939, 3, 59-67.
22. Boring, E. G. and Stevens, S. S. The nature of tonal brightness. Proc. Nat. Acad. Sci., 1936, 22, 514-521.

23. Bourguès, L. and Deneréaz, A. La Musique et la vie intérieure. Alcan, Paris, 1921.
24. Brennan, F. M. The relation between musical capacity and performance. Psychol. Monogr., 1926, 36, 190-248.
25. Briessen, M. v. Die Entwicklung der Musikalität in den Reifejahren. Langensalza, Beyer, 1929.
26. Brown, A. W. The reliability and validity of the Seashore Tests of musical talent. J. appl. Psychol., 1928, 12, 468-476.
27. Cameron, E. H. Tonal reactions. Psychol. Monogr., 1907, 8, 227-300.
28. Chapin, E. K. and Firestone, F. A. The influence of phase on tone quality and loudness. J. acous. Soc. Amer., 1934, 15, 173-180.
29. Chervais, M. Tests d'aptitude musicale. Bull. Soc. A. Binet., 1934, 34, 115-139.
30. Chomet, H. The influence of music on health and life. New York, Putnam, 1875.
31. Christianson, H. Bodily rhythmic movements of young children in relation to rhythm in music. Teach. Coll. Contrib. Educ., 1938, no. 736, x + 196.
32. Copp, E. F. Musical ability. J. of Heredity, 1916, 7, 297-304.
33. Dean, C. D. Predicting sight-singing ability in teacher education. J. educ. Psychol., 1937, 28, 601-608.
34. Densmore, F. What intervals do Indians sing? Amer. Anthro., 1929, 31, 271-276.
35. Diserens, C. Reactions to musical stimuli. Psychol. Bull., 1923, 20, 173-199.
36. Diserens, C. M. and Fine, H. A. A psychology of music. Cincinnati, Authors, 1939.
37. Drexler, E. N. A study of the development of the ability to carry a melody at the preschool level. Child Develpm., 1938, 9, 319-332.
38. Dunlap, K. Extensity and Pitch. Psychol. Rev., 1905, 12, 287-292.
39. Dunlap, K. The extensity theory of pitch. Psychol. Bull., 1909, 6, 58.
40. Dunlap, K. Tonal volume and pitch. J. exp. Psychol., 1916, 1, 183.
41. Dykema, P. W. An international study of music talent. Yearb. Mus. Educ. Nat. Conf., 1937, 94-96.
42. Emerson, L. E. The feeling-value of unmusical tone-intervals. Harvard Psychol. Stud., 1906, 2, 269-274.
43. Engel, G. Über den Stimmumfang sechsjähriger Kinder. Hamburg, 1889.
44. Engel, G. Ueber Vergleichungen von Tondistanzen. Ztsch. f. Psychol., 1891, 2, 361-378.
45. Erickson, C. L. The basic factors in the human voice. Psychol. Monogr., 1926, 36, 82-112.
46. Erpf, H. Der Begriff der musikalischen Form. Ztsch. f. Aesth., 1914, 9, 355-386.
47. Ewald, J. R. and Jäderholm, G. A. Die Herabsetzung der subjektiven Tonhöhe durch Steigerung der objektiven Intensität. Arch. ges. Physiol., 1908, 124, 29-36.
48. Farnsworth, P. R. An approach to the study of vocal resonance. J. acous. Soc. Amer., 1937, 9, 152-155.

49. Farnsworth, P. R. Auditory acuity and musical ability in the first four grades. J. Psychol., 1938, 6, 95-98.
50. Farnsworth, P. R. Changes in musical taste. J. of Musicol., 1939, 1, 1-4.
51. Farnsworth, P. R. Ending preferences in two musical situations. Amer. J. Psychol., 1926, 37, 237-240.
52. Farnsworth, P. R. Ending preferences among the three positions of the tonic chord. J. comp. Psychol., 1926, 6, 95-102.
53. Farnsworth, P. R. Further notes on the Seashore music tests. J. gen. Psychol., 1938, 18, 429-431.
54. Farnsworth, P. R. Further studies of the Seashore and Kwalwasser Batteries. Genet. Psychol. Monogr., 1934, 15, 45-49.
55. Farnsworth, P. R. Notes on the pitch of a combination of tones. Brit. J. Psychol., 1924-25, 15, 82-85.
56. Farnsworth, P. R. The effects of nature and nurture on musicality. Nat. Soc. for Study of Educ., Part 2, 1928, 233-245.
57. Farnsworth, P. R. The pitch of a combination of tones. Amer. J. Psychol., 1938, 51, 536-539.
58. Feis, O. Studien über die Genealogie und die Psychologie der Musiker. Grenzfrag. d. Nerven-u. Seelenlebens., 1910, 71.
59. Feldkeller, P. Der Anteil des Denkens am musikalischen Kunstgenuss. Ztsch. f. Aesth., 1925, 10, 161-190, 267-289.
60. Ferguson, D. N. The elements of expression in music. Bull. Amer. Musicol. Soc., 1939, 3, 24-26.
61. Fischer, A. Die Untersuchung des Gehörs und der musikalischen Fähigkeiten des Kindes und Jugendlicher. Päd. Reform., 1916.
62. Flatau, Th. S. und Gutzmann, H. A. R. Die Singstimme des Schulkindes. Arch. f. Lar., 1907, 20.
63. Fletcher, H. Newer concepts of the pitch, the loudness and the timbre of musical tones. J. Franklin Instit., 1935, 220, 405-429.
64. Fletcher, H. and Munson, W. A. Loudness, its definition, measurement and calculation. J. acous. Soc. Amer., 1933, 5, 82-108.
65. Fracker, G. C. and Howard, V. M. Correlation between intelligence and musical talent. Psychol. Monogr., 1928, 39, 157-161.
66. Gates, A. I. Musical interests of children. J. of Ped., 1898, 2.
67. Gaw, E. A. Five studies of the music tests. Psychol. Monogr., 1928, 39, 145-156.
68. Gehring, A. The basis of musical pleasure. New York, Putnam, 1910.
69. Gibling, S. P. Types of musical listening. Mus. Quart., 1917, 3.
70. Gilbert, J. A. Musical sensitiveness of school children. Stud. Yale Psychol. Lab., 1892-93, 1.
71. Gilliland, A. R. and Jensen, C. R. The reliability of the Seashore phonograph record for the measurement of pitch discrimination. J. exp. Psychol., 1922, 5, 214-222.
72. Gilliland, A. R. and Moore, H. T. The immediate and long time effects of classical and popular phonograph selections. J. appl. Psychol., 1924, 8, 309-323.
73. Gray, C. T. and Bingham, C. W. Musical ability of colored and white pupils. J. educ. Psychol., 1929, 20, 501-506.

74. Gundlach, R. Tonal attributes and frequency theories of hearing. J. exp. Psychol., 1929, 12, 187-196.
75. Guthrie, E. R. and Morrill, H. The fusion of non-musical intervals. Amer. J. Psychol., 1928, 40, 624-625.
76. Ham, L. B. and Parkinson, J. S. Loudness and intensity relations. J. acous. Soc. Amer., 1932, 3, 511-534.
77. Hancock, C. The effect of the intensity of sound upon the pitch of low tones. Psychol. Monogr., 1914, 17, 161-165.
78. Hattwick, M. S. The role of pitch level and pitch range in the singing of preschool children. Child Develpm., 1933, 4.
79. Hausegger, F. v. Die Musik als Ausdruck. Wien, 1885.
80. Heinlein, C. P. A brief discussion of the nature and function of melodic configuration in tonal memory, with critical reference to the Seashore tonal memory test. J. Genet. Psychol., 1925, 35, 45-61.
81. Heinlein, C. P. The affective character of music. Proc. Music Teach. Nat. Ass., 1939, 33, 218-226.
82. Heinrich, F. Die Tonkunst in ihrem Verhältnis zum Ausdruck und zum Symbol. Ztsch. fur Musik., 1925-26, 8.
83. Hentschel, M. Zwei experimentelle Untersuchungen an Kindern aus dem Gebiete der Tonpsychologie. Ztsch. f. ang. Psychol., 1913, 7.
84. Hevner, K. The aesthetic experience: a psychological description. Psychol. Rev., 1937, 44, 245-263.
85. Highsmith, J. A. Selecting musical talent. J. appl. Psychol., 1929, 13, 486-493.
86. Hirose, K. An experimental study of the principal pitch in the vibrato. Jap. J. Psychol., 1934, 9, 49-53.
87. Hohenmeser, R. Über Konkordanz und Diskordanz. Ztsch. f. Psychol., 1915, 72, 373-382.
88. Hollingworth, L. S. Musical sensitivity of children who test above 135 I. Q. J. educ. Psychol., 1926, 17, 95-109.
89. Hrabar-Passek, M. Verhältnis der Musikalität zu der Schulbegabung. Psychotech. Ztsch., 1928, 4, 115-116.
90. Hyde, I. H. and Scalapino, W. The influence of music upon electrocardiograms and blood pressure. Amer. J. Physiol., 1918, 46, 35-38.
91. Jacobi, H. Grundlagen einer schöpferischen Musikerziehung. Die Tat. Marzheft, 1922.
92. Jancke, H. Beiträge zur Psychologie der musikalischen Komposition. Arch. f. d. ges. Psychol., 1928, 66, 437-492.
93. Jancke, H. Das Spezifisch—Musikalische und die Frage nach dem Sinngehalt der Musik. Arch. f. d. ges. Psychol., 1931, 78, 103-184.
94. Jaquin, M. La mélodie, ses lois, son évolution. Nancy, Rigot, 1930.
95. Jaworsky, B. Die Struktur des melodischen Geschehens. Arch. f. d. ges. Psychol., 1934, 92, 315-344.
96. Jerome, E. K. Change of voice in male adolescents. Quart. J. Speech, 1937, 23, 648-653.
97. Jersild, A. T. and Bienstock, S. F. Development of rhythm in young children. Teach. Coll. Child Develpm. Monogr., 1935, no. 22.
98. Jode, F. Das schaffende Kind in der Musik. Wolfenbüttel, 1928.
99. Juhacz, A. Zur Analyse des musikalischen Wiedererkennens. Ztsch. f. Psychol., 1924, 95, 142-180.

100. Klaes, A. Studien zur Interpretation des musikalischen Erlebens. Langensalza, Beyer, 1933, 73.
101. Knudsen, V. O. Some cultural applications of modern acoustics. J. acous. Soc. Amer., 1938, 9, 175-184.
102. Knudsen, V. O. The sensibility of the ear to small differences of intensity and frequency. Phys. Rev., 1923, 21, 84-103.
103. Koch, H. and Mjøen, J. A. Die Erblichkeit der Musikalität. Ztsch. f. Psychol., 1926, 99, 16-73; 1931, 121, 104-136.
104. König, A. P. Die Entwicklung des musikalischen Sinnes bei Kindern. Die Kinderfehler. Ztsch. f. Kinderforsch., 1903, 8.
105. König, H. Über das musikalische Gedächtnis. Ztsch. f. Psychol., 1928, 108, 389-420.
106. König, H. Zur experimentellen Untersuchung der Musikalität. Wurzburg, 1925.
107. Kovacs, S. Über das Verhältnis des erkennenden und mitteilenden Gedächtnisses auf musikalischem Gebiet. Arch. f. d. ges. Psychol., 1917-18, 37, 283-299.
108. Kovacs, S. Untersuchungen über das musikalische Gedächtnis. Ztsch. f. ang., Psychol., 1916, 11, 113-135.
109. Kries, J. v. Wer ist musikalisch? Berlin, Springer, 1926.
110. Krueger, F. Consonance and dissonance. J. Phil. Psychol. Sci. Method., 1913, 10, 158-160.
111. Krueger, F. Die Theorie der Konsonanz. Psychol. Stud., 1906, 1, 305-387; 1907, 2, 205-255; 1909, 4, 201-282; 1910, 5, 294-409.
112. Kwalwasser, J. Tests and measurements in music. Birchards, 1927.
113. Kwalwasser, J. Tests and measurements in music. Psychol. Bull., 1928, 25, 284-301.
114. Lamp, C. J. and Keys, N. Can aptitude for specific musical instruments be predicted? J. educ. Psychol., 1935, 26, 587-596.
115. Larson, R. C. Studies on Seashore's "Measures of Musical Talent." Univ. Iowa Stud. Ser. Aims and Prog. Res. II (6), 1930.
116. Larson, W. S. Measurement of musical talent for the prediction of success in instrumental music. Psychol. Monogr., 1930, 40, 33-73.
117. Larson, W. S. Practical experience with music tests. Music Educators J., 1938, 2, 68-74.
118. Lee, V. Music and its lovers. New York, Dutton, 1933.
119. Lehman, H. C. and Ingerham, D. W. Man's creative years in music. Sci. Mon., 1939, 48, 431-443.
120. Leitner, H. Über Musikbegabung. Internat. Ztsch. f. Individual Psychol., 1927, 5, 379-383.
121. Lewis, D. Pitch: its definition and physical determinants. Univ. Iowa Stud. Psychol. Music, 1937, 4, 346-373.
122. Lewis, D. Psychological approaches to the analysis of timbre. Psychol. Bull., 1938, 35, 673.
123. Lewis, D. The construction of a timbre test. Psychol. Rec., 1939, 3, 115-136.
124. Lewis, D. Vocal resonance. J. acous. Soc. Amer., 1936, 8, 91-99.
125. Linder, F. E. Measurement of the pitch extent of the vibrato on attack, release, and transition of tone. Univ. Iowa Stud. Psychol. of Music, 1932, 1, 245-249.

126. Löffler-Herzog, A. Ein Beispiel von Vererbung musikalischer Begabung. Arch. Klaus-Stift. Vererb. Forsch., 1939, 14, 195-198.
127. Lorenz, C. Untersuchungen über die Auffassung von Tondistanzen. Philos. Stud., 1890, 6, 26-103.
128. Mainwaring, J. Experiments in the analysis of cognitive processes involved in musical ability. Brit. J. educ. Psychol., 1931, 1, 180-203.
129. Mainwaring, J. Tests of musical ability. Brit. J. educ. Psychol., 1931, 1, 313-321.
130. Mall, G. D. Wirkungen der Musik auf verschiedene Persönlichkeitstypen. Ber. Kongr. dtsch. Ges. Psychol., Tübingen, 1935.
131. Malmberg, C. F. The perception of consonance and dissonance. Psychol. Monogr., 1918, 25, 93-133.
132. Maltzew, C. v. Absolutes Tonbewusstsein und Musikalität. Psychotech. Ztsch., 1928, 3, 111-113.
133. Manzer, C. W. and Marowitz, S. The performance of a group of college students on the K. D. Tests. J. appl. Psychol., 1935, 19.
134. McCarthy, D. A study of the Seashore measures of musical talent. J. appl. Psychol., 1930, 14, 437-455.
135. McDougall, R. Musical imagery: A confession of experience. Psychol. Rev., 1898, 5, 463-476.
136. McGinnis, E. Seashore's measures of musical ability applied to children of the preschool age. Amer. J. Psychol., 1928, 40, 620-623.
137. Meinong, A. and Witasek, S. Zur experimentellen Bestimmung der Tonverschmelzungsgrade. Ztsch. Psychol., 1897, 15, 189-205.
138. Metfessel, M. Sonance as a form of tonal fusion. Psychol. Rev., 1926, 33, 459-466.
139. Metfessel, M. What is voice vibrato? Psychol. Monogr., 1928, 39, 126-134.
140. Meyer, M. Contributions to a psychological theory of music. Univ. Missouri Stud. Sci. Ser., 1901, 1, 80.
141. Meyer, M. Elements of a psychological theory of melody. Psychol. Rev., 1900, 7, 241-273.
142. Meyer, M. Experimental studies in the psychology of music. Amer. J. Psychol., 1903, 14, 192-214.
143. Meyer, M. On the attributes of sensations. Psychol. Rev., 1904, 11, 83-103.
144. Miles, W. R. Accuracy of the voice in simple pitch singing. Psychol. Monogr., 1914, 17, 13-66.
145. Miller, D. C. The Science of Musical Sounds. New York, Macmillan, 1926.
146. Miller, R. Über musikalische Begabung und ihre Beziehung zu sonstigen Anlagen. Ztsch. f. Psychol., 1925, 97, 191-214.
147. Miller, R. E. The pitch vibrato in artistic gliding intonation. Univ. Iowa Stud. Psychol. Music, 1932, 1, 250-268.
148. Mjøen, F. Die Bedeutung der Tonhöhenunterschiedsempfindlichkeit für die Musikalität und ihr Verhalten bei der Vererbung. Hereditas, 1925-26, 7, 161-188.
149. Mjøen, J. A. Zur Erbanalyse der musikalischen Begabung. Hereditas, 1925-26, 7, 109-128.

150. Moore, H. T. Feeling value of unmusical tone intervals. Harv. Psychol. Stud., 1906.
151. Moos, J. C. Some recent developments in music testing. Mus. Quart., 1933, 19, 318-330.
152. Moos, J. C. The yardstick applied to musical talent. Mus. Quart., 1930, 16, 228-262.
153. Mudge, E. L. The common synaesthesias of music. J. appl. Psychol., 1920, 4, 342-345.
154. Muhlmann, A. Vibrato and tremolo. Proc. Music Teach. Nat. Ass., 1937, 159-160.
155. Mull, H. K. The acquisition of absolute pitch. Amer. J. Psychol., 1925, 36, 469-493.
156. Müller-Freienfels, R. Das künstlerische Geniessen und seine Mannigfaltigeit. Ztsch. f. ang. Psychol., 1911, 6.
157. Müller-Freienfels, R. Psychologie der Musik. Berlin, Vieweg, 1936.
158. Mursell, J. L. Measuring musical ability and achievement. J. educ. Res., 1932, 26, 116-126.
159. Myers, C. S. Theories of consonance and dissonance. Brit. J. Psychol., 1904-5, 1, 315-316.
160. Myers, C. S. and Valentine, C. W. A study of individual differences in attitude toward tones. Brit. J. Psychol., 1914-15, 7, 68-111.
161. Nadel, S. Zur Psychologie des Konsonanzerlebens. Ztsch. f. Psychol., 1926, 101, 33-158.
162. Nesterle, A. Die musikalische Produktion im Kinderalter. Beiheft. Ztsch. f. ang. Psychol., 1930, 52.
163. Nielsen, J. T. A study on the Seashore motor-rhythm test. Psychol. Monogr., 1930, 40, 74-84.
164. Ogden, R. M. The attributes of sound. Psychol. Rev., 1918, 25.
165. Ogden, R. M. The tonal manifold. Psychol. Rev., 1920, 27, 136-146.
166. Ortmann, O. Notes on interval discrimination. Peabody Bull., 1932, 28, no. 2, 45-46.
167. Ortmann, O. The sensorial basis of music appreciation. J. comp. Psychol., 1922, 2, 227-256.
168. Ortmann, O. Theory of tone quality. Bull. Amer. Mus. Soc., 1937, no. 2, 3.
169. Ortmann, O. Span of vision in note reading. Yearb. Mus. Educ. Nat. Conf., 1937.
170. Ortmann, O. Visual, kinaesthetic, olfactory and gustatory effects of music. In Schoen, M. (ed.) The effects of music. New York, Harcourt, Brace, 1927, ch. 13.
171. Ortmann, O. Notes on the nature of harmony. Mus. Quart., 1924, 10, 369-383.
172. Pannenborg, H. J. and W. A. Die Psychologie des Musikers. Ztsch. f. Psychol., 1915, 73, 91-136.
173. Pear, T. H. The classification of observers as "musical" and "unmusical." Brit. J. Psychol., 1911, 4, 89-94.
174. Peterson, J. A functional view of consonance. Psychol. Rev., 1925, 32, 17-33.
175. Peterson, J. and Smith, F. W. The range and modifiability of consonance in certain musical intervals. Amer. J. Psychol., 1930, 42, 561-572.

176. Petran, L. A. An experimental study of pitch recognition. Psychol. Monogr., 1932, 42, whole no. 193.
177. Petran, L. A. Analysis of Ortmann tests. Bull. Amer. Mus. Soc., 1937, 2, 3.
178. Podolsky, G. The doctor prescribes music. New York, Stokes, 1939.
179. Pratt, C. C. Quarter-tone music. J. Genet. Psychol., 1928, 35, 286-293.
180. Pratt, C. C. The relation of emotions to musical value. Proc. Music Teach. Nat. Ass., 1939, 33, 227-229.
181. Pratt, C. C. Structural vs. expressive form in music. J. Psychol., 1938, 5, 149-156.
182. Preissler, W. Stimmumfänge und Gattungen der menschlichen Singstimme. Arch. gen. Phon., Abt. 2, 1939, 3, 65-85.
183. Reboud, R. La synthèse mentale et l'audition des accords musicaux. Rev. Phil., 1936, 36, 494-544.
184. Reuter, F. Das musikalische Hören auf psychologischer Grundlage. Leipzig, Kahnert, 1925.
185. Rich, G. J. A study of tonal attributes. Amer. J. Psychol., 1919, 30, 121-164.
186. Richards, I. A. The sense of musical delight. Psyche, 1934, 14.
187. Rigg, M. Musical expression: an investigation of the theories of Erich Sorantin. J. exp. Psychol., 1937, 21, 442-445.
188. Rigg, M. G. What features of a musical phrase have emotional suggestiveness? Bull. Oklahoma Agricultural and Mechanical Coll., 1939, 36, no. 13, 38.
189. Robertson, E. The emotional element in listening to music. Australian J. Psychol. and Phil., 1934, 12, 199-212.
190. Rogers, J. T. Music as medicine. Mus. Quart., 1918, 4, 365-375.
191. Ross, V. R. Intelligence, scholarship and talent. Calif. Bur. Jur. Res., 1937, ix+37.
192. Rothschild, D. A. The timbre vibrato. Univ. Iowa Stud. Psychol. Music, 1932, 1, 236-244.
193. Ruckmick, C. A. A new classification of tonal qualities. Psychol. Rev., 1929, 36, 172.
194. Ruckmick, C. A. Facts and theories of audition. Psychol. Bull., 1928, 25, 229-244.
195. Ruckmick, C. A. Recent research in the field of audition. Psychol. Bull., 1930, 27, 271-297.
196. Russell, G. O. Physiological cause of voice quality differences. Yearb. Carnegie Inst., Washington, 1935-36, 359-363.
197. Russell, G. O. Physiological cause of voice quality in singing. Yearb. Carnegie Inst., Washington, 1930-31, 463-471.
198. Sabanèev, L. The musical receptivity of the man in the street. Music and Letters, 1928, 9, 226-239.
199. Sabine, W. C. Melody and the origin of the musical scale. Science, 1928, 27, 841-847.
200. Sanderson, H. E. Differences in musical ability in children of different national and racial origin. J. genet. Psychol., 1933, 42, 100-120.
201. Scheinfeld, A. You and heredity. New York, Stokes, 1939, chs. 31, 32.
202. Schoen, M. Art and beauty. New York, Macmillan, 1932.

203. Schoen, M. Recent literature on the psychology of the musician. Psychol. Bull., 1921, 18, 484-489.

204. Schoen, M. (ed.) The Effects of Music. New York, Harcourt, Brace, 1927.

205. Seashore, C. E. A base for the approach to quantitative studies in the aesthetics of music. Amer. J. Psychol., 1927, 39, 141-144.

206. Seashore, C. E. Measurements on the expression of emotion in music. Proc. Nat. Acad. Sci., 1923, 9, 323-325.

207. Seashore, C. E. Music before five. Univ. Iowa Child Welfare Pamph., 1939, no. 72, 14.

208. Seashore, C. E. Musical inheritance. Sci. Mon., 1940, 50, 351-356.

209. Seashore, C. E. New approaches to the science of voice. Sci. Mon., 1939, 49, 340-350.

210. Seashore, C. E. (ed.) Objective analysis of musical performance. Univ. Iowa Stud. Psychol. Mus., 1936, 4.

211. Seashore, C. E. Psychology of the vibrato in voice and instrument. Univ. Iowa Stud. Psychol. Mus., 1936, 3, 1-156.

212. Seashore, C. E. The harmonic structure of a musical tone. Musical Quart., 1939, 25, 6-10.

213. Seashore, C. E. The inheritance of musical talent. Musical Quart., 1920, 6, 586-598.

214. Seashore, H. G. Variability of pitch in artistic singing. Proc. Music Teach. Nat. Ass., 1939, 33, 66-80.

215. Sherman, M. Emotional character of the singing voice. J. exp. Psychol., 1928, 11, 495-497.

216. Shower, E. G. and Biddulph, R. D. Differential pitch sensitivity of the ear. J. acous. Soc. Amer., 1931, 3, 257-287.

217. Silverstople, G. W. Zur Frage der Urmelodie. Ztsch. f. ang. Psychol., 1926, 27, 234-235.

218. Skinner, E. R. A calibrated recording and analysis of the pitch, force and quality of vocal tones expressing happiness and sadness; and a determination of the pitch and force of the subjective concepts of ordinary soft and loud tones. Speech Monogr., 1935, 2, 81-137.

219. Small, A. Present-day preferences for certain melodic intervals in the natural, equal-tempered and Pythagorean scales. J. acous. Soc. Amer., 1939, 10, 256.

220. Snow, W. B. Change of pitch with loudness at low frequencies. J. acous. Soc. Amer., 1936, 8, 14-19.

221. Sokolowsky, R. Ueber die Genauigkeit des Nachsingens von Tönen bei Berufssängern. Beit. z. Anat. d. Ohres, 1911, 5.

222. Sorantin, E. The problem of musical expression. Nashville, Marshall and Bruce, 1932, 122.

223. Starkow, K. Korrelation zwischen Musikalität, Musikleistung, und Begabung in einzelnen musikalischen Fächern. Psychotech. Ztsch., 1928, 3, 110-111.

224. Steinberg, J. C. The relation between loudness of a sound and its physical stimulus. Phys. Rev., 1925, 26.

225. Stevens, F. A. and Miles, W. R. The first vocal vibrations in the attack in singing. Psychol. Monogr., 1928, 39, 200-220.

226. Stevens, S. S. Are tones spatial? Amer. J. Psychol., 1934, 46, 145-147.

227. Stevens, S. S. The attributes of tones. Proc. Nat. Acad. Sci., 1934, 20, 457-459.

228. Stevens, S. S. The relation of pitch to intensity. J. acous. Soc. Amer., 1935, 6, 150-154.

229. Stevens, S. S. The volume and intensity of tones. Amer. J. Psychol., 1934, 46, 397-408.

230. Stevens, S. S. and Davis, H. Hearing: its psychology and physiology. New York, Wiley, 1938.

231. Stevens, S. S. and Davis, H. Psychophysiological acoustics: Pitch and loudness. J. acous. Soc. Amer., 1936, 8, 1-13.

232. Stewart, R. M. The effect of intensity and order on the apparent pitch of tones in the middle range. Psychol. Monogr., 1914, 16, 157-160.

233. Stout, B. The harmonic structure of vowels in singing in relation to pitch and intensity. J. acous. Soc. Amer., 1938, 10, 137-146.

234. Stumpf, C. Ueber die Vergleichung von Tondistanzen. Ztsch. Psychol., 1890, 1, 419-462.

235. Stumpf, C. Konsonanz and Dissonanz. Beiträge zur Akustik und Musikwissenschaft, 1898, 1, 1-108.

236. Tiffin, J. An approach to the analysis of the vibration of the vocal cords. Quart. J. Speech, 1938, 24, 1-11.

237. Updegraff, R., Heiliger, L., and Learned, J. The effect of training upon the singing ability and musical interest of three-, four-, and five-year-old children. Univ. Iowa Stud. Child Welf., 1938, 14, 83-131.

238. Valentine, C. W. The method of comparison in experiments with musical intervals and the effect of practice on the appreciation of discords. Brit. J. Psychol., 1914-15, 7, 118-135.

239. Vance, F. T. The lower limit of tonality. Psychol. Monogr., 1914, 17, 104-114.

240. Vance, F. T. Variation of pitch discrimination within the tonal range. Psychol. Monogr., 1914, 17, 115-149.

241. Vernon, P. E. A method of measuring musical taste. J. appl. Psychol., 1930, 14, 355-362.

242. Vernon, P. E. Synaesthesia in music. Psyche, 1930, 10, 22-40.

243. Vernon, P. E. The apprehension and cognition of music. Proc. of the Musical Assoc. Session, 1933, 59, 61-84.

244. Vernon, P. E. The phenomena of attention and visualization in the psychology of musical appreciation. Brit. J. Psychol., 1930, 21, 50-63.

245. Vidor, M. Was ist Musikalität? Munich, Beck, 1931.

246. Vivas, E. A definition of the esthetic experience. J. Phil., 1937, 34, 628-634.

247. Wagner, A. H. An experimental study in the control of the vocal vibrato. Psychol. Monogr., 1930, 40, 161-212.

248. Waiblinger, E. Dur und Moll. Arch. f. d. ges. Psychol., 1912, 24, 7-15.

249. Waiblinger, E. Zur psychologischen Begründung der Harmonielehre. Arch. f. d. ges. Psychol., 1913, 29, 258-270.

250. Washburn, M. F. Psychology of esthetic experience in music. Proc. Nat. Educ. Assoc., 1916, 600-606.

251. Weaver, H. E. Eye movements in reading music. Thesis, Stanford Univ., 1930 (unpublished).

252. Weaver, H. E. Syncopation: a study in musical rhythms. J. gen. Psychol., 1939, 20, 409-429.

253. Wedell, C. H. The nature of the absolute judgment of pitch. J. exp. Psychol., 1934, 17, 485-503.

254. Weinman, F. Zur Struktur der Melodie. Ztsch. f. Psychol., 1904, 35, 340-379, 401-453; 1905, 38, 234-239.

255. Wellek, A. Das absolute Gehör und seine Typen. Beih. Ztsch. f. ang. Psychol., 1938, no. 83, 368.

256. Werner, H. On musical "micro scales" and "micro intervals." Psychol. Bull., 1938, 35, 700.

257. Westerman, K. M. The physiology of the vibrato. Music Educators J., 1938, 24, 48-49.

258. Wever, E. G. Beats and related phenomena resulting from the simultaneous sounding of two tones. Psychol. Rev., 1929, 36, 402-418, 512-523.

259. Wever, E. G. and Bray, C. W. The perception of low tones and the resonance-volley theory. J. of Psychol., 1936, 3, 101-114.

260. Whitley, M. T. A comparison of the Seashore and the Kwalwasser-Dykema music tests. Teach. Coll. Rec., 1932, 33, 731-751.

261. Wilson, M. E. The psychology of music in relation to musical esthetics. Proc. Music Teach. Nat. Ass., 1938, 57-61.

262. Wright, F. A. The correlation between achievement and capacity in music. J. educ. Res., 1928, 17, 50-56.

263. Youtz, R. E. P. and Stevens, S. S. On the pitch of frequency modulated tones. Amer. J. Psychol., 1938, 51, 521-526.

264. Zoll, P. M. The relation of tonal volume, intensity and pitch. Amer. J. Psychol., 1934, 46, 99-106.

INDEX OF NAMES

INDEX OF SUBJECTS